Guitar Cultures

GW00383903

Guitar Cultures

Edited by
Andy Bennett and Kevin Dawe

Oxford • New York

First published in 2001 by
Berg
Editorial offices:
150 Cowley Road, Oxford, OX4 1JJ, UK
838 Broadway, Third Floor, New York, NY 10003-4812, USA

© Andy Bennett and Kevin Dawe 2001

All rights reserved.
No part of this publication may be reproduced in any form
or by any means without the written permission of Berg.

Berg is an imprint of Oxford International Publishers Ltd.

Library of Congress Cataloging-in-Publication Data
Guitar cultures / edited by Andy Bennett and Kevin Dawe.
     p. cm.
Includes bibliographical references and index.
     ISBN 1-85973-429-4 (cloth) -- ISBN 1-85973-434-0 (paper)
   1. Guitar--Social aspects.   I. Bennett, Andy, 1963-   II. Dawe, Kevin.
   ML1015.G9 G828 2001
   787.87'09--dc21

                                                         2001004388

British Library Cataloguing-in-Publication Data
A catalogue record for this book is available from the British Library.

ISBN 1 85973 429 4 (Cloth)
       1 85973 434 0 (Paper)

Typeset by JS Typesetting, Wellingborough, Northants.
Printed in the United Kingdom by Biddles Ltd, Guildford and King's Lynn.

Contents

Contents

Acknowledgements

The idea of a book on guitar cultures began to crystallize at the 1997 meeting of the International Association for the Study of Popular Music in Japan. Thanks must go to Toru Mitsui and all his team at Kanazawa University for organizing this conference. One evening during the conference we, the editors, found ourselves playing electric guitars onstage in a blues bar in central Kanazawa with guitarists and other musicians from Japan, Canada and the US. This unforgettable experience had a tremendous effect upon both of us – it made us reassess our relationship to the guitar and to its role in our lives – after all, we were 'talking' through and 'moving' with the instrument across cultures, time and space. Afterwards, in another bar, the talk naturally focussed upon the guitar, guitar players and guitar music. There was much to discuss. We found that, as a sociologist and ethnomusicologist respectively, we had skills and expertise that could perhaps be pooled to come up with quite a different study of the guitar. This would be a study that had, to our amazement, not been done before and one that was urgently needed given the ubiquity of the guitar in the musics of the world. It would be a study that looked at the role and meaning of the guitar in cultures and societies across the planet and one that looked at the cultures of the guitar as socially constructed and meaningful.

We were encouraged to pursue the idea by Dave Laing who suggested that we might consider procuring and editing a collection of papers on the subject. Indeed, over the next few days we mentioned the idea to fellow guitarists Peter Narváez and Denis Crowdy whose work on Canadian blues and stringbands in Papua New Guinea, respectively, seemed to compliment our own interests well. From this small nucleus of guitarists we built up a team of contributors over the next year or so. A book proposal was eventually sent to Berg and we received the go ahead. Thanks must go to Kathryn Earle and the team at Berg for their encouragement and foresight.

Andy Bennett would especially like to thank Moni for her support, the many musicians he has been privileged to meet and perform with over the years and his parents for their unerring interest in his musical and academic pursuits. Kevin Dawe would especially like to thank his wife Moira for all her hard work and support, especially during their field trips to Spain. He would also like to thank his parents for their love and support.

Notes on Contributors

Andy Bennett is Lecturer in Sociology at the University of Surrey and author of *Popular Music and Youth Culture: Music, identity and place*. He is Chair of the UK and Ireland branch of the International Association for the Study of Popular Music (IASPM). Andy has been playing guitar and mandolin for a number of years. Prior to studying for his PhD at the University of Durham he worked with the 'Frankfurt Rockmobil', a youth music-making project based in Frankfurt, Germany.

Martin Clayton has been Lecturer in Ethnomusicology at the Open University (OU) since 1995. He sold his first guitar in 1984, helping to finance a seven-month stay in India, which proved to be the start of a lifetime's interest in Indian music. On his return he studied at the School of Oriental and African Studies in London, where he obtained degrees in Music and Hindi (BA, 1988) and Ethnomusicology (PhD, 1993). Since then he has taught a wide range of ethnomusicological courses at numerous universities in the UK and US, and is currently co-editor of the *British Journal of Ethnomusicology*. He is author of *Time in Indian Music: Rhythm, metre and form in North Indian Raga performance*.

Denis Crowdy lectured at the University of Papua New Guinea from 1992–1999, carrying out various research projects on the stringband music of Papua New Guinea. He currently lectures at the Centre for Contemporary Music Studies at Macquarie University in Sydney, Australia.

Kevin Dawe is Lecturer in Ethnomusicology at Leeds University. A music and science graduate, he received a MSc in anthropology from the University of London and a PhD in social anthropology from Queen's University, Belfast. Kevin has worked as a professional guitarist, ethnomusicologist and organologist in a variety of cultural contexts. His research and publications are currently based on fieldwork in Greece and Spain, and on musical instrument research and collecting.

Moira Dawe received a Master of Education degree from Queen's University, Belfast. She is Head of Modern Languages at Belfast's first integrated school, Lagan College, where she teaches Spanish and French.

David Evans has been a blues researcher and guitarist since the early 1960s. He is the author of *Tommy Johnson* and *Big Road Blues: Tradition and creativity in* *the folk blues* both based in part in his fieldwork in Mississippi and other southern states. He is currently Professor of Music at the University of Memphis and editor of the 'American Made Music' book series for the University Press of Mississippi.

Peter Narváez is Professor of Folklore in the Department of Folklore, Memorial University of Newfoundland, St John's, Newfoundland, Canada, as well as a blues musician. He has published numerous articles on the music of Newfoundland as well as on African-American blues in major folklore journals. Recently his recordings of Skip James were released on a double CD for Document Records, Vienna, Austria (DOCD-5633, DOCD-5634). His other interests include custom and belief (he is the editor of *The Good People: New fairylore essays*) and the imbrication of folklore and popular culture (he edited with Martin Laba, *Media Sense: The folklore-popular culture continuum*). He is former president of the Folklore Studies Association of Canada.

Richard A. Peterson is Professor of Sociology at Vanderbilt University. Peterson was founding Chair of the Culture Section of the American Sociological Association. He has published research on various aspects of music from song writers and lyrics to the impact of changes in radio and digitalization within the 'production of culture' perspective. At various points the focus has been on rock, classical, jazz, or country music. His most recent major work is *Creating Country Music: Fabricating authenticity*.

Suzel Ana Reily is Senior Lecturer in Ethnomusicology and Social Anthropology at Queen's University Belfast. She has been conducting research on Brazilian music and culture since 1982, focussing upon popular Catholic ritual, popular musics and the historiography of Brazilian music. In recent years she has become interested in the use of hypermedia in Ethnomusicology, having produced a CD-Rom/website based on John Blacking's ethnography of Venda girls' initiation schools.

John Ryan is Professor and Chair of the Sociology Department at Virginia Polytechnic and State University where he teaches courses in organizational relations, culture, and the mass media. A graduate of Vanderbilt University, he specializes in mass media organizations and the production and consumption of symbolic culture. His latest book, *Media and Society: The production of culture in the mass media* was published in January 1999.

Steve Waksman is Visiting Assistant Professor of Ethnic Studies at Bowling Green State University. He is the author of *Instruments of Desire: The electric guitar and the shaping of musical experience* and has published several essays on music and popular culture. A guitarist for over twenty years, he prefers to rock out in the comfort of his living room.

Introduction: Guitars, Cultures, People and Places

Kevin Dawe and *Andy Bennett*

The guitar is in every respect a global phenomenon. The instrument has gained a central place in, and has helped to define, musical genres worldwide. Both electric and acoustic variations of the guitar are commonplace elements in the music of a variety of cultures around the world. As such, it is very difficult to provide satisfactory accounts of the guitar's cultural appeal using monocultural accounts. Rather, it is important to gain a sense of the guitar as a globally mobile instrument whose form, tonal textures and associated playing techniques are the product of its appropriation and use in a variety of locally specific musical contexts. Equally important in accounting for the cultural significance of the guitar is an understanding of the cultures to which the instrument itself has given rise. The term 'guitar culture', as it is used here, refers to the guitar makers, guitar players and audiences who imbue guitar music and the instrument itself with a range of values and meanings through which it assumes its place as a cultural icon. A key question addressed by this book is how, why and in what ways people use the guitar in the musical construction of self, others and communities. In other words, we are interested in the meanings that guitar makers, guitar collectors, guitar players and their audiences bring to guitars and guitar music. Similarly, we are also interested in examining the ways in which guitar makers, makes of guitar, and guitar players themselves become icons at national and global levels.

In order to examine the guitar phenomenon, we have assembled an international group of scholars working in a range of academic disciplines. As such, this book constitutes something of a first, bringing together for the first time in a single volume a collection of original studies of the guitar grounded in a wide range of disciplines including musicology, ethnomusicology, anthropology, ethnography, sociology, folklore, cultural studies and cultural history. Most of the contributors to this book have been directly involved with the guitar, for example, as performers, teachers and collectors, for a number of years. Combined with this experience, the contributors offer a wide range of theoretical perspectives on the role of the guitar in musical culture, the studies presented here arising out of varying degrees of direct and personal engagement with the instrument and with the societies and cultures that surround and create it.

The analytical and empirical approaches used in this book are intended to compliment, expand upon and reinforce a growing body of work on the study of musical instruments as social and cultural phenomena. It is, therefore, written from the point of view of researchers working on the social role and cultural significance of musical instruments and builds upon existing sociological, anthropological, ethnomusicological and cultural-historical approaches. We adopt crosscultural, comparative, ethnographic and social-historical methods of enquiry. It is also our intention to put a scholarly plough to a field that has already been tilled by a number of popular writers who have drawn attention to the richness of the guitar phenomenon.[1]

The Guitar in a Global Context

> Some instruments in the late twentieth century operate as indispensable ingredients of artistic expression simultaneously at the levels of culture, commerce and creativity. They are now part of a global cultural economy and circulate in transnational networks of practice, commodities and aesthetics. Instruments migrate along with musicians or are bought, sold and bartered in a multi-million dollar-a-year musical marketplace. (Neuenfeldt 1998: 5)

The guitar exists in cultural space nuanced by the convergence of both local and global forces. The guitar's material form and sound are relatively standardized in global circulation, yet at the same time it is the object of assimilation, appropriation and change in local settings by quite specific means and in quite specific ways. Indeed, the range of discourses that continue to emerge from the performance and reception of guitar music, guitar collecting and guitar construction show the instrument to be embedded, located and placed within communities that attach a similar but nevertheless distinct set of values to the guitar. Although the cultures of the guitar are in every respect both globally and locally constituted, the guitar's position in 'global music culture' is underscored by a seemingly infinite range of historical, cultural and musical contingencies.

In trying to illustrate the perpetual dialectic that exists between local and global forces and the bearing of the latter upon notions of cultural identity and difference, Robertson (1995) coined the term 'glocal'. According to Robertson, notions of cultural identity and difference are in a constant state of flux due to the dynamic interplay of the local and the global. The performance and reception of guitar music exemplifies the interplay between local and global cultures. Take, for example, the *blues*, one of the most established 'traditions' of guitar playing. The blues is a culturally mobile and constantly evolving form and, like other popular musics, has many interpreters around the world. It also provides an arena for intense debate between 'purists' and 'populists', indicative of the kind of debates that we aim to pick up on in this book. Based upon an appropriation of the acoustic parlour guitars by African Americans in the southern US, the blues subsequently evolved into an electrified version, known as *rhythm 'n' blues*, in northern US cities such as Chicago (Keil 1966, Chambers 1976). After this, it was appropriated by young white British guitarists, notably Eric Clapton, Jeff Beck and Jimmy Page, during the British 'blues boom' of the early 1960s (Gillett 1983). In this book, David Evans provides an insight into the involvement of the guitar with the early development of the blues, and Peter Narváez takes a critical and reflexive look at the subject of authenticity among blues guitarists in modern Newfoundland.

In 1966, African-American guitarist Jimi Hendrix arrived in Britain and took electric blues playing to an altogether different level, single-handedly pioneering a new style. Superlative manual dexterity was combined with a skilful manipulation of volume and electronic effects units such as the wah-wah pedal, the fuzz tone and the univibe. Commenting on the impact of Hendrix on the British music scene of the late-1960s, Palmer makes the following observations:

> [Hendrix's] music was an extraordinary blend of black culture as inspired by the Beatles and others and the original black music itself. Some British musicians, who emulated American blues artists, felt that they had discovered in Hendrix the real thing. (1976: 252)

During the period when Hendrix dominated the guitar scene, in the late 1960s, the electric blues sound was further modified by a number of guitarists. California-based Mexican guitarist Carlos Santana helped to pioneer a fusion of blues, rock, jazz, and Latin musics with Afro-Cuban rhythms that remains highly influential (we note the success of the Santana album *Supernatural*, released in 1999 and winning several Grammy awards). These types of localized reworkings, and to varying degrees, appropriations, translations, fusions and reconfigurations, can be seen in a number of guitar styles. As variously illustrated by the chapters in this book, there is an increasing tendency on the part of guitarists based in specific local settings to draw upon a range of styles and techniques borrowed from different musical cultures around the world. These are not just the vast range of styles glossed under blues, 'folk', country, rock, pop or metal but styles, techniques and sounds, for example, from Latin America, Indian 'classical' music and African guitar. Moreover, it is not just guitar players working in contemporary musical fields, such as rock and pop, who display such eclectic tastes. Classical guitarists play from a musical repertoire that spans the globe and which includes compositions by Joaquín Rodrigo (Spain), Leo Brouwer (Cuba), Manuel Ponce (Mexico), Heitor Villa-Lobos (Brazil), Michael Tippett (England) and Toru Takemitsu (Japan).

A vast range of styles and techniques make up guitar music. These include the aforementioned blues, rock and *avant-garde* virtuosity of Jimi Hendrix, the heavy metal playing of Eddie Van Halen, the anti-virtuosity of 'indie-guitar' and punk, the classically oriented music of John Williams and Julian Bream, the *flamenco*-based improvisations of Paco de Lucia, the jazz, jazz-rock and Indian music explorations of John McLaughlin, 'world music' productions by Ry Cooder, Ali Farka Toure and Pat Metheny, and performances by Vishwa Mohan Bhatt and Debashish Bhattacharya in the field of Indian classical music. This multifarious range of guitar styles and guitar players are but a few of those found within a vast and, certainly from an ethnographer's point of view, largely unexplored musical terrain traversed by the guitar. Suzel Ana Reily notes in this book how guitars and guitar-like instruments have been employed in countless localized musical styles in Brazil. Many of these styles of music have been adopted by the mainstream music industry, however many continue to be ignored by it. The same can be said for many other countries throughout the world. Thus, while a number of the guitar styles studied in this book will be familiar to many readers, other styles are far less well known being restricted to specific locales where their development remains largely unacknowledged by the global music industry.

Guitars and Places: Localizing Terms, Styles and Techniques

There can be no doubt that musical styles serve as important marketing devices for the global music industry, allowing for the categorization and packaging of music to appeal to certain audiences. At the same time, however, stylistic terms reflect back on and provide a crucial situating role for musicians and their audiences in a variety of ways. At one level this can be conceptualized as imagined connections between music and place; a series of powerful narratives of urban and rural spaces grounded in feelings, ideas and sensations drawn from the music itself. Frith has noted the intense power of this kind of relationship between sound and place: 'Accordions played in a certain way mean France, bamboo flutes China' (1987: 148). Missing from Frith's account, however, is an acknowledgement of the power of such narratives of sound and place to work increasingly both without and *within* those cultures with which they are associated. Chaney argues that 'all aspects of our lived experience are formulated, made manifest, through the constitutive activity of representational resources' (1994: 67). Music is a particularly potent representational resource in this sense, a means by which communities are able to identify themselves and present this identity to others. This is particularly significant in the case of guitar styles, which often simultaneously constitute geographic referents, for example, '*Flamenco*', 'Brazilian', 'Malagasy', 'Celtic', 'Hawaiian', 'Southern Blues'. Similarly, more indirect references to place are also to be found in terms such as 'surf', 'folk' and 'bluegrass'.

In this book we note the way in which various guitar styles perform a crucial situating role for performers and audiences. Moreover several chapters illustrate how the relationship between music and place is ingrained in the very language used in the description of particular local guitar styles. For instance, Denis Crowdy draws attention to the use of the terms *ovasis* and *lokal* (meaning 'overseas' and 'local' respectively in Tok Pisin) in Papua New Guinean stringband culture. Similarly, in his chapter on guitar culture in India, Martin Clayton notes that the Hindi word *desi* means 'local' where 'local culture' is seen as distinct although engaging with 'Pepsi culture' and 'the global' is represented by Anglo-American popular culture. As we hope to demonstrate, notions of cultural difference are fleshed out and tied up with concepts of musical style locally; styles whose local resonances carry through to a particular form of categorization or defining label. Such labels are particularly common in relation to descriptors of guitar-based musics, promoting particular images of those regions, cultures, peoples and places from which they originated. This in turn facilitates the use of such styles in the localized identity politics of both those individuals involved in the production of guitar music and those who come to listen. By nature of its differing locally acknowledged cultural resonances, the guitar is variously responded to as a symbol of protest, a medium of high art expression, an aspect of 'authentic' tradition, a means of asserting national identity, a resource in the articulation of 'underground', 'alternative' culture, and as a ritual medium.

Instances of the guitar's role in the articulation of such localized forms of discourse are provided throughout this book. For example, in his study of Papua New Guinean 'stringband' Crowdy illustrates how conflicts over the issue of authenticity in the genre are rooted in different generational experiences of stringband which range from its origins as a village-based music performed on self-made instruments to contemporary stringband which incorporates elements of rock and reggae and is performed largely for tourists. Similarly, in exploring notions of authenticity in relation to Spanish guitar, Dawe's chapter illustrates how a particular measure of authenticity is whether or not a guitar was handmade with the 'personal touch' of a master Spanish luthier. Nowadays, factory-made guitars as well as guitars made by hand outside of Spain continue to challenge the position of Spanish-made guitars in the market place, though the Spanish guitar is seen as fundamentally 'rooted' in Spain in the popular imagination.

Narváez in his chapter on the 'myth of acousticity' and its role in the performative practices of Newfoundland blues guitarists, shows how the 'cultural constructions of acoustic guitar and electric guitar as binary opposites' were shaped by the political ideologies that came to inform the 'folk' revival of the 1960s. Here, acoustic guitars were seen as 'authentic', 'real', 'true', 'democratic' and 'close to nature', and as 'sites of resistance' to a technocratic society as represented by the electric guitar. Although less concerned with these kind of statements about society, performing blues guitarists in Newfoundland today are still concerned with achieving an 'authentic sound' and an 'accurate presentation of acoustic guitar sound' from their instruments through a variety of individual set-ups that use pick-ups and contact microphones. Some guitarists are not willing to drill holes in or to spoil the look of their acoustic guitars for the purpose of installing 'on-board' technology, and others are more inclined to use the electric guitar so they can be heard. Blues guitarists like B.B. King and Muddy Waters preferred to use the electric guitar because, not only could they be heard but they also liked the sound.

Finally, in his chapter on UK 'indie-guitar', Bennett shows how the correct choice of guitars and amplification is deeply important for the construction of indie-guitar culture and the 'authentication' of its 'back-to-basics' sensibility. As Bennett illustrates, a carefully constructed aesthetic in indie-guitar culture maintains a relationship between the style's musical and material simplicity and its anti-mainstream, 'street-level' character.

The guitar, then, acts as a cultural signifier in a range of local and trans-local contexts. In recent years, however, the guitar's status as a cultural signifier has also assumed a rather different type of resonance in which the notion of culture aligns with Bourdieu's (1984) notion of cultural capital.

Consuming Guitars: Symbolic and Economic Exchanges

The critical 'first wave' dissemination of proto-guitars throughout the Americas (and the sharing of musico-cultural traits ever since across the 'Hispanic world') and elsewhere is the most pertinent historical example of what has now become a *worldwide* distribution of the guitar in its many forms. It is also important to note here that the 'early' guitar was taken around the world by Portuguese and Spanish sailors and, as Clayton's chapter illustrates, even reached India sometime in the sixteenth or seventeenth centuries. Today, it cannot be denied that, at a macro-economic and social level, the developing global flow of capitalism has also played a crucial role in facilitating the guitar's cultural mobility. The worldwide trade in guitars is driven by a large-scale manufacturing industry, with factories in places as far apart as Kalamazoo and Korea. The appearance of Fender and Gibson guitars must rival the production of Henry Ford's 'Model T' in scale with their firmly established 'Stratocaster' and 'Les Paul' models and variations on these themes (now echoed in the designs of a host of other large-scale guitar manufacturers). So musical instruments are part of what Bourdieu has called 'the field of cultural production' (Bourdieu 1993). Bourdieu describes what he calls fields of 'restricted' and 'large-scale' production, which affect the creation, dissemination and circula-tion of 'goods'. These systems are tied to systems of hegemony and cultural dominance and to the contestation, negotiation and working out of power relations. We might compare and contrast the large-scale manufacturing industry that is the

Fender factory with that of the low mechanization and often one-man operations of the guitar workshops in Spain, as described here in Dawe's chapter. Economies of scale must be noted along with the very different sales targets of Epiphone Gibsons in the US compared to Gibtone in India. In their chapter on vintage guitars, Ryan and Peterson review current data on guitar sales over the past fifty years and also discuss the current prices of collectable guitars. One cannot underestimate the role of merchants and catalogues for the dissemination of guitars. David Evans' chapter notes how guitars found their way into the Deep South through these means.

We might contrast the large-scale manufacture of guitars in North America with that of the scratch-built instruments once commonly found in Papua New Guinea (PNG) (see Crowdy's chapter) and other non-industrialized countries. For instance, ukuleles, predating guitars in that country, were made with wood from the bush and a round tinned meat can or with coconut shells and available timber. In PNG today imported, factory-made guitars are often amplified through rewired portable stereo cassette player/recorders. Guitarists around the world have a variety of needs that must be met by available guitar and amplification equipment. Indian guitar players, for instance, have their own set of terms that not only describe the technical features of their customized guitars but also relate to the musical performance practices of Indian classical music. Their usually acoustic guitars are played in a position that approaches the performance position of the Indian *vina* and their guitars have a variety of string arrays and configurations based on various Indian instruments. These string layouts enable them to play solo lines, accompaniment and sound sympathetic strings all at the same time. As noted in Clayton's chapter, this has led to a number of innovative guitar designs in India that are seen to have global appeal, including Debashish Bhattacharya's patented 'Hindustani Slide Guitar'.

Eddie Van Halen's name and reputation have assumed significant commodity value in conjunction not only with his band's music but also with the electric guitar and its accessories. As examined in Waksman's chapter, Eddie Van Halen's innovative playing and guitar designs have helped to redefine the instrument and its potential, a legacy of innovation handed down by Les Paul and taken up by many of Van Halen's peers including Joe Satriani and Steve Vai (parallel examples of innovative designs among Indian guitar players are discussed in Clayton's chapter). Whilst these professional guitarists have racks of guitars, amplification and effects, amateurs usually have one acoustic and one electric guitar. If they are serious amateur players they might augment their collection of instruments, particularly if they wish to play in a variety of styles where particular makes and models of guitar are seen as more desirable and appropriate (see Peterson and Ryan's chapter).

Equally important in the grounding of guitar culture, as we define it here, is the ability of certain instruments, particularly the range of *vintage* electric guitars, to absorb and thus speak for whole histories of guitar playing and innovation. Since they first began to emerge in the 1980s, a steadily expanding, globally linked network of vintage guitar shops have offered the serious buyer/collector or casual browser a selection of worn and battered guitars, many of which have been handed down through an indeterminate number of owners. The aura of authenticity that greets customers as they enter the shop is enhanced by sales-talk-centred rumour and speculation, for example, that 'the Telecaster in the corner belonged to Keith Richards' or a Hofner bass sold that morning had 'Paul McCartney's signature on the headstock'.

Of further significance in relation to the spectre of the 'vintage electric' and 'vintage acoustic' guitars is the way in which a product once deemed to be the result of an indiscriminate and belittling mass culture is now the obsessive focus for a worldwide form of musical elitism. For those who collect vintage guitars this is a very serious hobby, necessitating trips to fairs and conventions in different parts of the world. Similarly, such commitment to the art of collecting vintage guitars, and the money and time to invest in this pursuit is also suggestive of an expert knowledge of guitars and an ability to know and appreciate quality and 'collectability' in an instrument. This, in turn, gives rise to particular forms of discourse among guitar collectors, which is framed by particular conventions of knowledge, taste, passion and nostalgia for the guitar. As illustrated in Ryan and Peterson's chapter, guitar collectors are generally well-educated, high-income-bracket males in their forties. They play the guitar in a domestic setting and, like typical babyboomers, fit guitar playing in around marriage, family life and a career – if they can. Collectors form an interest group that is informed by a variety of media in print, including monthly magazines such as *Vintage Guitar* and *Acoustic Guitar*, and various buyers' guides and guitar equipment mart magazines.

Conclusion

The purpose of this book, then, is to examine the cultural significance of the guitar in some of its myriad everyday local contexts and, in doing so, begin to establish a picture of guitar performance, collecting and making – as well as the reception of guitar music – as both a global and a local phenomenon. We draw attention to the interaction of the guitar with local cultures, characterized by the instrument's appropriation and assimilation into a variety of socio-cultural contexts where it takes on new meanings fashioned by everyday experiences. In doing so we stress the way cultural difference is maintained by the guitar in the face of the challenge of globalizing media of which it is part. Above all, however, we emphasize the fact that an understanding of the cultural significance of the guitar can only be gained through a knowledge of the different everyday contexts in which the guitar is built, played, and listened to. It is through such everyday contexts that different forms of guitar and guitar style acquire their meanings, meanings that travel with the instrument as it becomes a global commodity and enters the global flow of musical performance and entertainment.

Notes

1. Readers just beginning to explore 'guitar cultures' might find the *small* selection of magazines and books listed below helpful alongside the wide range of references given in the chapters. Most large newsagents stock a range of guitar magazines, which, at the time of writing, may include: *Guitar Player, Guitarist, Guitar World, Total Guitar, Guitar Techniques, Guitar International,* and *Acoustic Guitar* among others. Richard Chapman's book *Guitar: Great players and their music* (2000), Dorling Kindersley, provides an up to date survey and includes reference to non-Western guitar cultures. The following books represent a sample of standard works on the guitar, including some first-rate scholarship: Ken Achard (1979) *The History and Development of the American Guitar*, London: New Musical Services; Tony Bacon and Paul Day (1991) *The Ultimate Guitar Book*, New York: Alfred A. Knopf; Stan Britt (1984) *The Jazz Guitarists*, Poole: Blandford Press; Donald Brosnac (1975) *The Steel String Guitar: Its construction, origin and design*, Los Angeles: Panjandrum Press; Bob Brozman with John Dopyera, Jr., Richard R. Smith and Gary Atkinson (1993*) The History and Artistry of National Resonator Instruments*, Fullerton CA: Centerstream Publishing; Manuel Cano (1986) *La Guitarra*, Universidad de Córdoba; Stephen Cherne (1998, 5th edition) *Blue Book of Electric Guitars* and *Blue Book of Acoustic Guitars*, Minneapolis: Blue Book Publications Inc.; Ralph Denyer (1994 revised and updated) *The Guitar Handbook*, London and Sydney: Pan Books; Tom and Mary-Anne Evans (1977) *Guitars: Music, history, construction and players from the Renaissance to rock*, New York: Paddington Press; Nick Freeth and Charles Alexander (1999) *The Acoustic Guitar*, Courage Books; Frederic V. Grunfeld (1969) *The Art and Times of the Guitar: An illustrated history of guitars and guitarists*, London: Macmillan; Norman Mongan (1983) *The History of the Guitar in Jazz*, New York: Oak Publications; Luis Leal Pinar (1988) *Antologia Iberoamericano de la Guitarra*, Ediciones Alpuerto; Richard Pinnell (1980) *Francesco Corbetta and the Baroque Guitar*, UMI Research Press; Richard Pinnell (1991) *Riplotense Guitar*, Westport, CT: The Bold Strummer; Eusebio Rioja (1993) *La Guitarra en la Historia*, Córdoba: Junta de Andalucía; Maurice J. Summerfield (1996, 4th edtition) *The Classical*

Guitar: Its evolution, players and personalities since 1800, Newcastle-upon-Tyne: Ashley Mark Publishing Company; Cynthia Schmidt (editor) 'The Guitar in Africa: The 1950s–1990s', Special Edition of *The World of Music*, available from the Department of Ethnomusicology at the University of Bamberg, Germany; Christian Seguiret (1997) *The World of Guitars*, Chartwell; Harvey Turnbull (1991 edition) *The Guitar from the Renaissance to the Present Day*, Westport, CT: The Bold Strummer. See also the entries on 'Guitar' in *The New Grove Dictionary of Music and Musical Instruments*, New York and London: Macmillan Ltd/Grove Dictionaries Inc. (1980, revised, updated and online). Too numerous to mention here are the sites on the Internet dedicated to the guitar, guitar makers, guitar players and guitar music.

References

Bourdieu, P. (1984), *Distinction: A social critique of the judgement of taste*, (trans. R. Nice). Cambridge, MA: Harvard University Press.

—— (1993), *The Field of Cultural Production*, Cambridge: Polity Press.

Chambers, I. (1976), 'A Strategy for Living: Black Music and White Subcultures', in S. Hall and T. Jefferson (eds) *Resistance Through Rituals: Youth subcultures in post-war Britain*, London: Hutchinson.

Chaney, D. (1994) *The Cultural Turn: Scene setting essays on contemporary cultural history*, London: Routledge.

Featherstone, M. (ed.) (1990), *Global Culture: Nationalism, globalisation and modernity*, London: Sage.

Frith, S. (1987) 'Towards an Aesthetic of Popular Music', in R. Leppert and S. McClary (eds) *Music and Society: The politics of composition, performance and reception*, Cambridge: Cambridge University Press.

Gillett, C. (1983), *The Sound of the City: The rise of rock and roll*, 2nd edn, London: Souvenir Press.

Keil, C. (1966), *Urban Blues*. Chicago: Chicago University Press.

Neuenfeldt, K. (1998), (ed.) 'Old Instruments in New Contexts', Special Edition of *The World of Music*, University of Bamberg.

Palmer, T. (1976), *All You Need is Love: The story of popular music*, London: Futura.

Robertson, R. (1995), 'Glocalization: Time-space and homogeneity-heterogeneity', in M. Featherstone, S. Lash and R. Robertson (eds) *Global Modernities*, London: Sage.

The Guitar in the Blues Music of the Deep South[1]

David Evans

The topic that I have chosen is a vast one, and I will merely outline its dimensions here, trying to set a framework for the further research that will be needed to fill in the details. My approach will be to note the socioeconomic, historical, and musical factors that surrounded, affected, and precipitated the introduction of the guitar to the folk music tradition of the Deep South. Following this, I will briefly discuss characteristics of the indigenous African-American folk music tradition that the guitar encountered. Finally, I will make some general observations on the resultant blues-centred folk guitar tradition that developed there.

I view the Deep South as a region with a large black population and an economy dominated by cotton, timber, and other extractive industries. White and black folk music traditions of the nineteenth century in this region relied on the fiddle and banjo as primary musical instruments. The guitar arrived as a new instrument at the end of the nineteenth century in association with the new musical genres of ragtime, jazz, and blues, with an emerging cash economy, and with new attitudes in the black community toward social and economic survival adopted in response to an increase of racial oppression. These attitudes incorporated a growing spirit of individualism and self-reliance. The guitar reached the rural Deep South through the American genteel parlour guitar tradition of the nineteenth century and through Italian, Spanish, Mexican, and Caribbean traditions introduced through immigration, America's military encounters, and travel by southern blacks in search of work. Ragtime, as the first of the new genres to become popularized, also influenced the more slowly emerging blues guitar tradition, as did the music of string bands and performance styles associated with the mandolin and piano. The blues tradition that absorbed the guitar and these outside musical and cultural influences was firmly based in a pre-existing African-American musical culture with many stylistic characteristics, structural elements, and musical instruments stemming ultimately from the African musical and cultural background of southern blacks. The encounter of the introduced elements and the indigenous tradition resulted in a musical and cultural clash, ultimately becoming a synthesis in the form of blues music and blues culture, which grew and developed over the twentieth century. The early finger-picked guitar style was largely superseded around mid-century by the modern lead guitar style, which arose with the introduction of the electronically amplified instrument. The older style exists today largely within a revival movement of musicians that is international in scope.

My treatment of this topic draws from a number of academic disciplines and from direct involvement with the southern blues guitar tradition as a fieldworker, collector, and musician. My main training was in the fields of folklore and mythology, and I view the blues as a folksong and music tradition that drew significantly on older traditions and that developed within a folk community. My professional career has involved me in the fields of anthropology and ethnomusicology, and from these I view blues guitar in the context of broader cultural movements and interactions and as a strictly musical phenomenon. Even before I began to study folklore in the mid-1960s, I became interested in blues guitar as a musician and as a record collector. I have continued to collect and study records and to learn about blues guitar, mainly through fieldwork in southern blues traditions. I have also accompanied and toured with a number of southern blues guitarists since 1980.

The territory that I am calling the Deep South is a vast region of lowlands and gentle hills stretching from central Georgia westward to east Texas and up the Mississippi River to approximately where it joins the Ohio River. During the period under consideration here, the 1890s to roughly the middle of the twentieth century, this was primarily cotton country. In sections that were prone to flooding or where the soil was poor, a timber industry typically flourished. This area excludes the Atlantic Coast and the Gulf Coast, the French-speaking parts of Louisiana, the tobacco-growing regions of Virginia and the Carolinas, and the upland South. These excluded territories were generally settled in the seventeenth and eighteenth centuries by English, French, or Spanish-speaking whites and their black slaves. In contrast, the Deep South was not extensively settled until the early decades of the nineteenth century, much of it not until the forcible removal of the indigenous Indian population in the 1830s and the wresting of Texas from Mexico in the same decade. Even early in the twentieth century, parts of the Deep South retained something of a frontier character. With the exception of the mining and industrial area centred in Birmingham, Alabama, cities of the region mainly functioned as trading, distributional, and administrative centres, and later as places of settlement for those who had made their fortunes in the region's extractive activities or as places of refuge for both blacks and whites fleeing rural poverty. Few of the cities supported major manufacturing industries, and few had large ethnic immigrant communities.

Through the nineteenth century and the first half of the twentieth, the Deep South was an area of heavy black population. In many parts they constituted the majority. This black population was in the lead when it came to adopting and developing the guitar in its folk music, and in general, it appears to have been in the lead in developing new instrumental folk and popular music traditions in this region, often even supplying music for the white population. The main instrument in older white folk music of the region was the fiddle. In adopting the guitar, whites initially did not take it much beyond the role of bassing and chording behind the fiddle, within string bands, or behind the human voice. The exceptional cases where more distinctive guitar styles were developed can almost always be explained as influences from black-originated styles such as ragtime and blues guitar around the beginning of the twentieth century, Hawaiian guitar in the 1910s and 1920s, and jazz guitar in the 1930s and 1940s.

If we examine nineteenth-century accounts of folk music in the rural South, we do not encounter the guitar very much until the end of that century. If it occurs in folk music at all, either during the slavery period (up to 1865) or in the quarter-century following emancipation, it almost always exemplifies penetration of the folk music tradition by the genteel, cultivated, urban guitar tradition. Then suddenly, during the period 1890 to 1910, the guitar is everywhere in the rural South, especially in black music and especially in the Deep South, in string bands and in the newly emerging genres of ragtime, jazz, and blues.[2] The guitar soon became the quintessential blues instrument, and it still remains the dominant instrument in both the sound and imagery of the blues some one hundred years later.

Around the 1890s the guitar came to the rural South as essentially a new instrument, beginning gradually to replace older folk music instruments such as the fiddle and banjo. The guitar's previous role in American music had largely been that of a polite parlour instrument found in middle and upper-class homes, associated with a kind of semi-classical music. The 1890s and turn-of-the-century period were an age of industrialism, manufacturing, invention, and growing consumerism in American life. Home and cottage manufacturing declined, while shops and factories greatly increased. The guitar was something that was made in a factory and normally purchased from a merchant or a catalogue. It was not home made by the musician or bartered from a community craftsman. It came into the rural South as part of a wave of consumer goods that included other musical instruments, such as the piano, the pump organ, the harmonica, horns, and drums. These instruments held prestige for their players and their listeners because they were new, because they were paid for with cash, and because they carried an aura of urbanity, gentility, social status, and upward mobility, precisely because they were not rural and traditional. For blacks in particular the guitar also lacked any residual associations with slavery, minstrel music and its demeaning stereotypes, or even with the South. It was something novel with very little cultural baggage other than symbolic associations that appeared to conform to notions of progress and success. It cost money, but it did not have to be terribly expensive. Cheap but serviceable guitars were available through Sears Roebuck and Montgomery Ward mail order catalogues, and ones at similar prices could be purchased at stores in the larger towns and cities of the South, even at some plantation commissaries. Although many black farmers as well as white ones had lost their land in the quarter-century after the Civil War and had been reduced to sharecropping, there were still opportunities for them to make cash money. There was a growing demand for low-skilled wage labourers in lumber camps, turpentine camps, sawmills, railroad jobs of all kinds, levee camps, and seasonal farm work, such as picking cotton, fruit, or nuts. In Texas and here and there throughout the rest of the Deep South there was wage work herding cattle. Gambling, moonshining, and preaching might be other ways to supplement one's income, as was performing music itself. A sharecropper in the Mississippi Delta in the 1890s, for example, might not only clear some money from a successful crop: he could make additional cash helping with the cotton harvest in the fall on the large plantations, cutting or hauling timber in the uncleared parts of the Delta, laying railroad tracks, building levees, and making moonshine liquor, all without going far from home or moving to a city. Such a farmer with a little extra money could purchase a guitar and symbolically enter a new world of musical, cultural, and social life.[3]

The growth of a cash economy and incipient consumerism in the 1890s coincided with a new secularism, worldliness, realism, and pragmatism in black life and culture. The previous era from the end of the Civil War (1865) to about 1890 had been dominated by religiosity, sentimentality, and moralism, often viewed as necessary attributes for entry into the mainstream of American life, which seemed to have been promised by emancipation. This promise, however, was dashed by the rise of Jim Crowism, disenfranchisement, lynching, and terrorism, which reached their peak in the 1890s. Blacks who had come to maturity in this decade realized that they were not slaves, as most of their parents and grandparents had been, but were not altogether free either. Their reassessment of their status had a far-reaching sociocultural impact, which included the creation of new musical forms. Rugged individualism, as exemplified best by war hero – and later president – Theodore Roosevelt, could lead to fame and fortune in mainstream society, but for most blacks it was simply a key to survival. With all of their collective institutions under threat, young black men and women realized that ultimately they had to rely on their individual efforts if they were going to live with any degree of success or security. In the musical realm this attitude led to new forms that emphasized soloing, improvisation, and display. The lone ragtime pianist, the jazz soloist, and the barrelhouse blues pianist and itinerant guitarist became familiar figures in both urban and rural communities. Musical instruments, which had been dismissed as frivolous by their sober and devout elders or even viewed as playthings of the devil, were now reassessed for the usefulness they might have in providing some solace or pleasure in life, some outlet for self-expression in the midst of repression, or even some means of making a living. Indeed, instruments were even being incorporated into the new Pentecostal and Holiness Churches that were beginning to spring up at this time and attract southern worshippers.

The impact of the guitar in Southern black music at this time can be gauged by examining some contemporary accounts of observers and later recollections of musicians and their associates and family members. W.C. Handy, born in Florence, Alabama, in 1873 to an upwardly mobile family of Methodist ministers, fell under the lure of a guitar by the age of twelve, when this instrument was still associated primarily with polite parlour music. Handy began working odd jobs and wrote:

> Out of my earnings I bought clothing, books and school supplies, and began saving enough small sums in the hope of buying a guitar . . . Work meant nothing now. It was a means to an end . . . Setting my mind on a musical instrument was like falling in love. All the world seemed bright and changed . . . With a guitar I would be able to express the things I felt in sounds. I grew impatient as my small savings grew. I selected the instrument I wanted and went often to gaze at it lovingly through the shop window.

When Handy finally was able to purchase the instrument, he wrote: 'I could scarcely wait till I reached home to break the news to my father and mother. I knew how the other youngsters would gather around, bug-eyed with curiosity and admiration, and I had no doubt that soon I would be able to entertain the girls royally.' The reaction of his parents was not what he expected. His father gasped: 'A guitar! One of the devil's playthings. Take it away. Take it away, I tell you. Get it out of your hands. Whatever possessed you to bring a sinful thing like that into our Christian home? Take it back where it came from. You hear? Get!' His father forced him to exchange the guitar for a dictionary but later supported his son's musical ambitions to the extent of paying for lessons in church organ music (Handy 1970: 8–11). W.C. Handy later learned guitar anyway and used it to accompany his own singing and that of quartets. He found greater musical opportunities, however, playing the cornet. In 1892 he left Florence and spent most of the next ten years playing cornet in community bands and touring minstrel bands. Around 1903, however, while based in Clarksdale in the Mississippi Delta and leading a community band, he encountered the newly emerging blues music of the region. Of an itinerant guitarist who serenaded him at a railroad station and played by pressing a knife on the strings, Handy wrote: 'The effect was unforgettable.' He described it as 'the weirdest music I had ever heard' and said 'the tune stayed in my mind'. Soon after this Handy was impressed when a string trio of guitar, mandolin, and string bass playing during his band's intermission performed 'one of those over-and-over strains that seem to have no very clear beginning and certainly no ending at all'. Handy wrote: 'A rain of silver dollars began to fall around the outlandish, stomping feet. The dancers went wild . . . There before the boys lay more money than my nine musicians were being paid for the entire engagement. Then I saw the beauty of primitive music' (Handy 1970: 78–81). These encounters would change Handy's musical direction and lead to his becoming the most important early composer of blues and eventually to the honoured status of 'Father of the Blues'. Even in the 1910s as he was establishing his reputation as a composer and leader of a large band that featured blues tunes, Handy took occasional performing jobs as a guitarist in a string trio, and as late as 1938 he recorded a session for the Library of Congress recalling some early blues and folksongs and accompanying his singing with the guitar.

At the same time that Handy was encountering the blues guitar tradition in the Delta, other observers were also taking note of black guitar music there and elsewhere in the Deep South. Archaeologist Charles Peabody, excavating a site near Clarksdale in 1901 and 1902, observed the musical performances of his black workers. He wrote: 'Their singing at quarters and on the march with the guitar accompaniment was naturally mostly "ragtime" with the instrument seldom venturing beyond the inversions of the three chords of a few major and minor keys.' The term 'blues' had not yet become associated with a genre of music, but Peabody's description of songs with three chords in major and minor keys suggests strongly that some of the 'ragtime' music he encountered was actually blues. His transcriptions of lyric and melodic fragments reinforce this impression. (Peaboy 1903). Working only a few years later in nearby Lafayette County, Mississippi, and Newton County, Georgia, sociologist and folklorist Howard W. Odum collected a large harvest of folksongs from black informants, many of which were quite clearly blues, although Odum was not yet familiar with that term for a musical genre when he published his findings in 1911. He wrote:

> In general, the majority of the songs of the evening are accompanied by the 'box' [the guitar] or fiddle when large or small groups are gathered together for gayety; when a lonely negro sits on his doorstep or by the fireside, playing and singing; when couples stay late at night with their love-songs and jollity; when groups gather after church to sing the lighter melodies; when the 'musicianers', 'music physicians', and 'songsters' gather to render music for special occasions, such as church and private 'socials', dances, and other forms of social gatherings. Special instances in which a few negroes play and sing for the whites serve to bring out the combined features of restrained song and the music of the instrument. The old-time negro with his 'box' (a fiddle or guitar), ever ready to entertain the 'white folks' and thus be entertained himself, is less often observed than formerly. The majority of younger negroes must be well paid for their music. (Odum 1911: 258)

Odum described the new phenomenon of itinerant 'music physicians', stating:

> With a prized 'box', perhaps his only property, such a negro may wander from town to town, from section to section, loafing in general, and working only when compelled to do so, gathering new songs and singing the old ones. Negroes of this type may be called professionals, since their life of wandering is facilitated by the practice of singing. Through their influence, songs are easily carried from place to place. There are other 'music physicians' whose fields of activity are only local. (Odum 1911: 259)

Odum described harmonies made up mostly of minor keys, repetition of words and music, changes of mood and theme within a song, and the setting of different songs to the same tune, all common characteristics of what would soon become known as the blues. He noted 'knife-songs', 'devil-songs', and 'train-songs' among the types that were played with guitar accompaniment and described how the wandering musicians would appeal to white and black audiences, and especially to women friends, for pity and assistance, securing shelter, food, money, and attention with their 'box' (Odum 1911: 260–1, 269).

The lives of many of the oldest blues singers and guitarists whom we know by name reflect similar patterns to those described by Handy, Peabody, and Odum. Huddie Ledbetter ('Leadbelly'), born in 1888 near Mooringsport in north-western Louisiana, was attracted to the guitar as well as the accordion, mandolin, harmonica, Jew's harp, piano, and organ. His father, a sober farmer, somewhat reluctantly acceded to his pleading for a guitar and purchased him an instrument around 1903. Learning from relatives and neighbours, young Huddie was soon playing for country frolics. From there he would go on to play at storefronts in town on Saturday afternoons and at saloons at night. By the following year he was performing in the nearby city of Shreveport in barrelhouses and brothels, encountering other musicians who were living primarily from their music. It was in this environment that he first heard the blues. (Wolfe and Lornell 1992: 14–36). Charley Patton was born in 1891 between Bolton and Edwards, Mississippi, and showed an interest in the guitar around the age of fourteen. He would sneak away from home and play a borrowed guitar behind other singers. When his father, a Baptist deacon, learned of this, he beat Charley with a bullwhip, but eventually he relented and bought his son a guitar. Charley soon became a professional musician, roaming over much of the Mississippi Delta until his death in 1934, doing little other work except to help his father in farming and hauling timber. He played mainly at cafes and juke houses,[4] stores, house parties, and outdoor picnics, and recorded over fifty songs between 1929 and 1934, most of them blues. He typically made between fifty and a hundred dollars a week from music, while the average wage worker on a farm earned about ten. His nephew described him as wearing fine clothes, driving a car, having a different woman every year, and having gold coins plastered around the rim of one of his guitars (Evans 1987a). Tommy Johnson, born near Terry, Mississippi, in 1896, was a sometime partner of Charley Patton. Johnson learned guitar from relatives around 1911 or 1912 and soon ran off to the Delta with an older woman. When he returned home about two years later, he was a much better musician. His older brother recalled that a white man for whom the family worked gave Tommy a horse, which he promptly sold for enough money to buy a new guitar and a rifle, much to their father's dismay. His younger brother Mager Johnson, also a guitarist, stated that Tommy mainly played music for a living:

Mostly a bunch would follow him every which a way he go, playing around here. And probably when he was playing in Jackson. He was grown then and married, but he didn't act as a married man. He'd still go and play music. You could hear him about half a mile before he'd get to the house, way late in the night sometimes coming down the road with that guitar, playing and singing. He came through Freetown up here, and a bunch would get out behind him sometimes following. He'd just go, and wherever he found a place to stop, if it was at somebody's house, it wouldn't make no difference. You know, as he played a piece or so, somebody would probably ask him to come over. They was going to put on a party for him. And he'd go play for parties and things like that, you know. After he played a piece or two, maybe he'd play a piece or two in town up there, somebody'd want to put on a party for him. And he'd go right there. He mostly played his music by hisself. And then me and him and my other brother Clarence, we'd get together, play plenty of parties and things . . . We'd go up to the Delta and pick cotton. Sometimes we'd be in Rolling Fork, and Hollandale, Anguilla, and Belonzi, Greenville and Greenwood. We'd be all up around them places. And it be not raining, that's all we'd do, go from town to town, playing old guitars. (Evans 1971: 29)

Tommy Johnson went on to make seventeen blues recordings in 1928 and 1929 and continued performing music right up to the night of his death in 1956. Later generations of blues guitarists from the Deep South described the lure of the guitar to folklorist Barry Lee Pearson, who recounted their tales of learning and performing in chapters titled 'I'm Gonna Get Me a Guitar If It's the Last Thing I Do', 'They Used to Say It Was the Devil's Music', and 'Sounds So Good to Me' (Pearson 1984: 46–88). There can be little doubt that the guitar was creating a stir in black music of the Deep South in the late nineteenth and early twentieth centuries and that it was rapidly becoming associated especially with the developing blues music tradition and the culture and community that was building around this music. Yet, as we have noted already, the guitar came to this region and this music as something new from outside the tradition. We should, therefore, examine other musical traditions with which the guitar had been associated to see what effect they may have had on the emerging sounds of the blues.

Although we tend to think of the demographics of the Deep South strictly in terms of African-American and Anglo-American populations, there were a number of factors and events during this period that opened the region up to a variety of ethnic cultural influences that might have included guitar music. The Deep South, particularly the rural areas, generally had little experience of the massive waves of immigrants who flocked to America's shores in the years between the Civil War and World War One. Nevertheless, in parts of the plantation South, especially the Mississippi Delta, there were various schemes at this time to import Chinese, Mexicans, and Italians as sharecroppers under the belief that they were more reliable and had stronger work ethics than the uncertain black labour force. In general, these schemes were miserable failures, as most of the immigrants left the plantations after a few years. Often, however, they remained in the area as merchants. Further numbers of Italians came to the South as carpenters and masons, and many stayed in the towns and cities as grocers and merchants, saloon keepers, and theatre owners. Although specific cases of musical influence on the developing blues tradition are almost impossible to trace, we do know that both the Mexicans and Italians had indigenous traditions of guitar music and may at least have helped to introduce this instrument in many areas of the South. Additional contact with Texas-Mexicans and the Spanish culture of the Southwest was gained by many blacks who went to Texas to work as cowboys in the growing cattle industry or who served as soldiers in the forts of west Texas, New Mexico, and Arizona in this period, guarding against Indian uprisings and Mexican incursions. Undoubtedly the popularity of the twelve-string guitar among blacks throughout the South in the early twentieth century was due at least in part to contact with the Texas-Mexican culture, where that variety of the instrument plays an important role in the indigenous folk and popular music.[5] Further contact with the guitar traditions of Spanish-speaking lands was gained by the many black soldiers who served in Cuba and Puerto Rico during the Spanish-American war in 1898 and its aftermath. Other southern blacks served as merchant seamen and in the US Navy in the Pacific, reaching the Philippines, the South Seas, and Hawaii, where Spaniards, Portuguese, and Puerto Ricans had introduced the guitar. The Hawaiian guitar tradition would later have a significant interaction with both black and white southern guitar styles, with influences passing in all directions.

Coming from within black musical tradition, like blues at this time, ragtime began to achieve mass popularity in the latter half of the 1890s. Its rapid ascent to popularity was probably aided by its association with the piano, print, and a degree of harmonic complexity that made it accessible and attractive to some formally trained musicians.

Many early ragtime exponents were reading musicians, but the music certainly drew from folk sources for some of its melodies and rhythms. Folk musicians in the Deep South accompanied ragtime songs and performed instrumental rags on the guitar at this time, and ragtime material can still be heard in the recordings of many 'blues' guitarists in the 1920s and later (Oliver 1984: 18–139). Ragtime music, among other things, provided an opportunity for a major new exploration of the complexities of Western harmony by black American musicians. This exploration certainly penetrated to the level of folk guitarists without formal training, including many in the Deep South, as our previous sources have noted. W.C. Handy's bands performed ragtime tunes in the 1890s, and he later composed rags himself, even viewing some of his first blues efforts as a type of ragtime music. Leadbelly, Charley Patton, and Tommy Johnson all display ragtime influences in their recordings, as do many other blues guitarists of their generation. Particularly prominent is the common VI-II-V-I 'circle of fifths' chord sequence as a structural pattern for many songs by early Southern black guitarists or as a harmonic element inserted into their blues structures. While the guitar would become the emblematic instrument of the blues, its harmonic versatility and the ease of making many chords on it must have given it special appeal for musicians with a bent for the new ragtime music. It was far more versatile than the older five-string banjo in this respect. The guitar had a melodic range of two octaves in its open strings, twice the range of the melody strings of the banjo, meaning that more complex tunes as well as richer chords could be played on it. Its fullness of sound and the mellow sustaining quality of its notes must have made the guitar preferable to the plunking banjo for many players.

As for the genteel parlour guitar tradition, most of its tunes probably had decreasing appeal for Southern black folk musicians as the blues gained ascendancy. The songs associated with the genteel tradition were mostly sentimental, romantic, or moralistic, in contrast to the much franker and more realistic expression of the blues. Nevertheless, the image of the guitar as a parlour instrument suitable for both men and women in accompanying sentimental songs and serenading undoubtedly did have appeal, and some sentimental and romantic songs turn up in the repertoires of early blues songsters such as Leadbelly and Mississippi John Hurt. These songs especially appealed to women. While most blues guitarists have always been men, it is remarkable how many first and second generation bluesmen of the Deep South, like Tommy Johnson, Blind Willie McTell, and Curley Weaver, had mothers and sisters who played the guitar and had some influence on their early musical development in a family setting. Few black women guitarists recorded in the 1920s, and most of those who did performed strictly blues material and a few ragtime pieces. One of the rare exceptions who recorded sentimental material was Lulu Jackson, whose handful of recordings in 1928 included *You're Going to Leave the Old Home, Jim, Careless Love, After You've Had Your Way, Little by Little You're Breaking My Heart*, and *Little Rosewood Casket*, along with a few blues and gospel titles.[6] Of these sentimental songs, only *Careless Love* continued to have much currency among other blues guitarists.

The genteel guitar tradition probably helped to introduce basic chord positions to aspiring blues guitarists as well as the idea of the guitar as an accompanying instrument for songs that one listened to seriously. It also contributed two very important novelty tunings that blues guitarists would eagerly embrace. One of these was Spanish tuning (open G – high to low: D-B-G-D-G-D), which very likely was introduced through the instrumental Spanish Fandango, which employs this tuning. It was reinforced by a similar tuning widely used on the banjo that corresponds in its four melody strings to the first four strings of the guitar in 'Spanish' tuning. Versions of Spanish Fandango have been encountered in the repertoires of Deep South black guitarists such as Mississippi John Hurt. The other novelty tuning from the genteel tradition was 'Sebastopol' (open D – high to low:

D-A-F#-D-A-D), which became even more widespread than 'Spanish' tuning, although the piece from which it was derived, *The Siege of Sebastopol*, does not seem to have survived as well in southern folk guitar tradition. The name, however, has stuck in variant forms such as 'Vastapol', 'Vestibule', and 'Faster Feel', and the tuning is still used today by some gospel electric guitarists. Many early blues were recorded in 'Spanish' and 'Sebastopol' tunings, some of them in the 'knife' or 'slide' style.

String bands had become popular in American music by the 1890s, probably influenced by Italian, Spanish, and Latin American music, and black musicians eagerly embraced this type of ensemble. The typical instrumentation, sometimes only partially achieved, was violin and/or mandolin playing lead, guitar playing bass notes and runs and chordal rhythm, and a string bass providing the bottom. Sometimes the older sound of fiddle, banjo, and percussion was grafted in whole or in part to these groups, or the guitar simply replaced the banjo as accompaniment to the fiddle. In almost all cases the guitar's role was limited to rhythmic and harmonic background and bass notes and runs.

Nevertheless, its role in string bands undoubtedly helped to introduce certain basic chord positions into blues guitar tradition and to popularise certain keys, such as C and G, that were favourites of string band players. Black string bands such as Nap Hayes and Matthew Prater, Chatman and McCoy, the Mississippi Sheiks, the Dallas String Band, and Peg Leg Howell and His Gang recorded rather extensively in the 1920s, but by then their repertoires were predominantly blues. Some black string bands, such as the Son Sims Four, Sid Hemphill's Band, and the Mobile Strugglers were documented on recordings as late as the 1940s. In the 1970s the group of Martin, Bogan, and Armstrong revived this style for the last time.

Other new instruments that were gaining popularity among black musicians at the same time as the guitar also influenced the emerging blues guitar styles. Particularly important in this regard were the mandolin and the piano. The mandolin would be especially significant for introducing the tremolo technique to blues guitar. This would normally have been done with a plectrum, as on the mandolin, but some players have been known to achieve it on the guitar with rapid movement of a finger or the thumb. Among early guitarists who used the technique were Blind Lemon Jefferson, Charlie McCoy, and James 'Yank' Rachell. The latter two also made recordings playing mandolin. Chicago guitarist and mandolinist Johnny Young continued to use the technique into the 1960s. The piano, via ragtime music, was probably one of the chief sources of alternating bass patterns played on the guitar. Alternation between a bass note and chord is a fundamental left-hand technique in ragtime piano, and a comparable technique can be heard in the work of many early blues guitarists like Mississippi John Hurt, Furry Lewis, and Frank Stokes. The piano continued to influence developing blues guitar styles. By the

1920s and 1930s guitarists such as Blind Lemon Jefferson, Blind Roosevelt Graves, Leadbelly, and Robert Johnson were incorporating boogie woogie and walking bass patterns into their guitar work. Robert Johnson also pioneered in adapting the piano's lush chordal complexity to the guitar.

As all of these socio-economic, historical, and musical factors were affecting the Deep South around the beginning of the twentieth century, they encountered a pre-existing African-American musical culture with certain established characteristics. Black folk music was a thriving tradition throughout the nineteenth century, with a rich legacy of African musical style and aesthetics. (Evans 1978a, 1987b; Oliver 1970; Merwe 1989; Kubik 1999). This tradition featured the strident vocal quality characteristic of the field holler; the use of 'blue notes' or flexible pitch areas at certain points on the scale; a tendency toward pentatonism and tunes that don't suggest any 'chord changes' in the Western sense; the use of instruments as voices, often responding to and punctuating the singing voice rather than merely providing rhythmic and harmonic background; the use of 'riffs' or repeated short melodic/rhythmic phrases; a forceful, percussive approach to sound production and an enjoyment of a full range of sound qualities, including growling, buzzing, whining, and screaming sounds. All of these qualities are antithetical to those of the guitar traditions that were introduced to the Deep South from outside around the end of the nineteenth century, so that the uses to which the guitar was put in the developing blues tradition of this region often suggest a musical and cultural clash. This is illustrated by many of the early recordings of Deep South folk blues in the 1920s by artists such as Charley Patton, Ishman Bracey, Barbecue Bob, and Blind Lemon Jefferson, as well as by recordings of artists in more recent decades, such as Muddy Waters, John Lee Hooker, Fred McDowell, and Robert Pete Williams. Mississippi bluesman Ishman Bracey's *Woman Woman Blues* (Paramount 12970), recorded near the end of 1929, provides a concise example of this sort of clash. Its first two measures strongly suggest the use of a Western diatonic major scale with full tonic and dominant chords outlined in the vocal melody and guitar part, including the prominent appearance of the major third and major seventh. Then, suddenly and dramatically Bracey leaps into a falsetto register, and blue notes begin to sound throughout the vocal and guitar lines, strings are bent violently on the guitar, and the end of the melody is followed by a series of guitar riffs. Other blues in the Deep South tradition seem to dispense altogether with any overt acknowledgement of Western musical conventions.

The reasons why Deep South folk blues guitar did not simply assume wholesale the characteristics of Latin American, Italian, parlour, string band, and ragtime guitar styles have much to do with this pre-existing, largely African-based musical tradition and folk aesthetic. This tradition even contained some specific instruments that contributed to folk guitar styles in the region.[7] One of these is the familiar five-string banjo, which can be traced to west African instrumental prototypes

(Conway 1995). This instrument probably contributed to or reinforced three characteristics that often appear in Deep South folk blues guitar. One is the use of open-chord or modal tunings that heavily exploit the sounding of open (unfretted) strings; another is the use of only one or two fingers of the left hand for fretting strings or making chord positions; and the third is the use of the right-hand thumb to play off-beats. The other important folk musical instrument is one consisting of a single strand of broom wire or baling wire mounted on a board or on the wall of a house. It is usually found as a children's instrument and has a geographical distribution stretching from western Georgia over to the lower Mississippi River Valley. The player strikes the string with a finger of the right hand or an object held in that hand and slides a bottle or knife or some other hard smooth object along the string to vary the pitch and produce whining and percussive sounds. This instrument has prototypes in central and west Africa, where it also serves largely as a children's instrument. The African varieties are usually played by two children, one striking the string and the other sliding an object along it. This African and African-American instrument type is undoubtedly the main source of the slide (or 'bottleneck' or 'knife') guitar style that is so common in the early blues of the Deep South, particularly the percussive riff-based style heard in recordings by artists such as Charley Patton, Son House, Robert Johnson, Bukka White, and Fred McDowell (Evans 1970, 1978b). Over the course of the development of blues slide guitar in the twentieth century, this percussive riff-based style has undergone various blendings with the more melodic and harmonic Hawaiian guitar style, which also uses a slide technique. Hawaiian guitar began to make a major impact on mainland American popular music around 1914, when blues was still in an early stage of development. The slide technique in blues guitar, however, is documented in the Deep South as early as 1903 by W.C. Handy and Howard W. Odum.

The result of the encounter of the guitar and its associated new styles with the indigenous black folk music tradition of the Deep South was a new folk guitar tradition that juxtaposed and blended elements of the recently introduced and non-native guitar styles with elements from the older indigenous music. This new tradition was largely centred on blues and bluesy versions of ragtime and popular songs. The elements drawn from ragtime guitar, the genteel parlour style, ethnic traditions, and string bands included a certain degree of harmonic complexity and development, the basic chord positions of standard tuning, the use of the twelve-string guitar, and patterned picking techniques, particularly the use an of alternating right-hand thumb. The indigenous black folk music tradition and its aesthetic contributed ways of achieving blue notes, such as string bending and the use of a slider, the use of repeated riffs, tune structures that avoid or downplay standard Western chords and chord changes, the use of only one or two fingers of the left hand for fretting or making chords, non-patterned picking, and a generally percussive approach to playing. The open-chord tunings of 'Spanish' and 'Sebastopol' appear to represent elements from the genteel tradition reinforced by an indigenous preference for open and modal tunings.

Early blues guitarists varied in the degree to which they absorbed elements introduced from guitar traditions outside of African-American folk music or adapted elements from within this indigenous tradition to the new instrument. Some, for example, could play in four or five keys of standard tuning and one or two open tunings. Among such artists were great bluesmen like Mississippi John Hurt, Leadbelly, Tommy Johnson, Robert Wilkins, Bo Carter, and Blind Willie McTell. Others, equally outstanding in an artistic sense, played mainly or exclusively in the key of E in standard tuning and/or one or two open tunings. Among these artists are Charley Patton, Son House, Big Joe Williams, Arthur 'Big Boy' Crudup, Skip James and Fred McDowell. By the late 1940s, as the electric guitar made its entrance into the blues tradition, this latter approach intensified to the point where younger blues guitarists were not learning to play in the keys of G, C, and D in standard tuning at all. Some had been using the key of A in standard tuning as a transition into modern electric lead guitar style, usually played with a plectrum. Those who continued to play guitar in a finger-picking style, whether electric or acoustic, almost always used only the key of E in standard tuning and/ or one or two open tunings. (The key of E in standard tuning, more than any other key, enables the player to exploit the use of open strings. In this key all six open strings provide notes found in a pentatonic blues scale.) Among the artists in this category are such well-known figures as John Lee Hooker, Muddy Waters, and Jimmy Reed, as well as more recent discoveries such as R.L. Burnside, Jessie Mae Hemphill, and Robert Belfour. There are now hardly any African-American musicians in the Deep South under the age of sixty, who learned blues guitar in a traditional community setting and who perform in a finger-picking style, as nearly all of the early blues guitarists did. There are some who perform electric lead guitar with the thumb and fingers rather than a plectrum, but this is about the closest one can get to it among artists who have learned guitar in a traditional setting. Much of the finger-picking tradition is barely a living tradition at all, and what is left of it is being carried on by perhaps a couple of dozen active performers, some of them now in their eighties. There is, however, an active and growing revival movement, predominantly white but with some black participation, whose age range generally leaves off where the older tradition's begins. This movement is international in scope, eclectic in style, and lacking in the kinds of localism and community context found in the older tradition. Nevertheless, it is inspired by the older tradition, and most of its participants have had the opportunity to learn directly from some of the older traditionalists or at least from their many recordings. This revival movement probably represents the best hope that Deep South finger-picking blues guitar will remain viable for the future. If it becomes popular enough, it may eventually take on its own character of localism, community context, and tradition.

Notes

1. An earlier version of this paper was first presented at a seminar entitled 'Fingerstyle Guitar: 150 years of Musical Tradition and Innovation' at Middle Tennessee State University, Murfreesboro, 17 February, 1995.
2. On the rarity of the guitar in American folk music before the 1890s, the emergence of guitar-based blues in the Deep South at the turn of the century, and its somewhat later prevalence in the East Coast States, see Epstein (1977); Evans (1982); Bastin (1986); Cohen (1996).
3. For views of the Delta and its music during this period see Cobb (1992) and Lomax (1993).
4. A juke house is a structure designed for music, dancing, drinking, and some-times other activities such as gambling and prostitution. It can be either a place used exclusively for these purposes or an actual house converted temporarily for them.
5. For more on possible black-Mexican musical interaction see Narváez (1978).
6. Discographies of this and other recording artists mentioned here are printed in Dixon, Godrich, and Rye (1997).
7. For a survey of African musical instruments in the United States see Evans (1999).

References

Bastin, B. (1986), *Red River Blues: The blues tradition in the southeast*, Urbana: University of Illinois Press.

Cobb, J.C. (1992), *The Most Southern Place on Earth: The Mississippi delta and the roots of regional identity*, New York: Oxford University Press.

Cohen, A.M. (1996), 'The Hands of Blues Guitarists', *American Music*, 14: 455–79.

Conway, C. (1995), *African Banjo Echoes in Appalachia: A study of folk traditions*, Knoxville: University of Tennessee Press.

Dixon, R.M.W., Godrich, J., and Rye, H.W. (1997), *Blues and Gospel Records: 1890–1943*, 4th ed., Oxford: Clarendon.

Epstein, D. (1977), *Sinful Tunes and Spirituals: Black folk music to the Civil War*, Urbana: University of Illinois Press.

Evans, D. (1970), 'Afro-American One-Stringed Instruments', *Western Folklore*, 29: 229–45.

—— (1971), *Tommy Johnson*, London: Studio Vista.

—— (1978a), 'African Elements in Twentieth-Century United States Black Folk Music', *Jazzforschung*, 10: 85–110.

—— (1978b), booklet notes to *Afro-American Folk Music from Tate and Panola Counties, Mississippi,* Archive of Folk Song AFS L67, 12" LP, Washington: The Library of Congress.

—— (1982), *Big Road Blues: Tradition and creativity in the folk blues*, Berkeley: University of California Press.

—— (1987a), 'Charley Patton: The Conscience of the Delta', in R. Sacré (ed), *The Voice of the Delta-Charley Patton and the Mississippi Blues Traditions – Influences and Comparisions, An International Symposium*, Liège: Presses universitaires de Liège.

—— (1987b), 'The Origins of Blues and its Relationship to African Music', in D. Droixhe and K.H. Kiefer (eds), *Imáges de l'africain de l'antiquité au Xxe siècle*, Bayreuther Beiträge zur Literaturwissenschaft, Band 10, Frankfurt: Peter Lang: 129–41.

—— (1999), 'The Reinterpretation of African Musical Instruments in the United States', in I. Okpewho, C.B. Davies, and A.A. Mazrui (eds), *The African Diaspora: African origins and New World identities*, Bloomington: Indiana University Press: 379–90.

Handy, W.C. (1970), *Father of the Blues*, New York: Collier.

Kubik, G. (1999), *Africa and the Blues*, Jackson: University Press of Mississippi.

Lomax, A. (1993), *The Land Where the Blues Began*, New York: Pantheon.

Merwe, P. van der (1989), *Origins of the Popular Style: The antecedents of twentieth-century popular music*, Oxford: Clarendon.

Narváez, P. (1978), 'Afro-American and Mexican Street Singers: An ethnohistorical hypothesis', *Southern Folklore Quarterly*, 42: 73–84.

Odum, H.W. (1911), 'Folk-Song and Folk-Poetry As Found in the Secular Songs of the Southern Negroes', *Journal of American Folk-Lore*, 24: 255–94, 351–96.

Oliver, P. (1970), *Savannah Syncopators*, London: Studio Vista.

—— (1984), *Songsters and Saints: Vocal traditions on race records*, Cambridge: Cambridge University Press.

Peabody, C. (1903), 'Notes on Negro Music', *Journal of American Folk-Lore*, 16: 148–52.

Pearson, B.L. (1984), *'Sounds So Good to Me': The bluesman's story*, Philadelphia: University of Pennsylvania Press.

Wolfe, C., and Lornell, K. (1992), *The Life and Legend of Leadbelly*, New York: HarperCollins.

–3–

Unplugged: Blues Guitarists and the Myth of Acousticity[1]

Peter Narváez

On a summer's day in 1992, a blues musician friend of mine, who had been playing at clubs in and around St John's, Newfoundland for twenty years, was eating lunch in his kitchen when his teenage daughter excitedly raced in with a friend and exclaimed, 'Dad you've got to hear this – it's cool!' She thrust Eric Clapton's new CD *Unplugged* into his hand. Examining it with some interest, my friend immediately realized that the hot item thrilling his daughter and her friends was an album of acoustic blues, many of which were old chestnuts (*Nobody Knows You When You're Down and Out, Alberta, Walking Blues*) from the blues canon.

'It looks good', he replied jadedly, 'I've been playing several of those songs at my solo acoustic gigs for years.' 'You have?!' she exclaimed with disbelief and no small degree of dismay.

A major point arises from the foregoing anecdote – while acoustic blues in North America has experienced noticeable surges of popularity from time to time (for example, the fad for W.C. Handy's published piano blues arrangements 1912–15; the recording of vaudeville and downhome African-American blues artists from the 1920s into the 1940s; the 'rediscovery' of early African-American blues recording artists and the jugband craze in the 1960s; commencing in 1971, Bonnie Raitt's acoustic blues recordings; the hit two-CD set re-issue of *Robert Johnson: The Complete Recordings* [Sony Music] in 1990; Eric Clapton's *Unplugged* [WEA/ Warner Brothers] 1992; and the growing popularity of African-American acoustic blues artists Guy Davis, Keb Mo', and Corey Harris in the 1990s), it has been continually played by local and regional artists for most of the twentieth century.

Different groups have exhibited diverse reasons for supporting this music, however, and many of these varying attitudes and ideas have focused on the guitar as the primary medium of the form. This chapter will compare views of the guitar from the standpoints of: African-American acoustic blues performers from the southern US; blues revivalists of the late 1950s and 1960s; and a sample of Canadian blues performers today. It will be shown that the first stance was pragmatic, the second embraced 'country blues' and the cultural 'myth of acousticity', an idea cluster that mixed authenticity with ideology, and the third position has returned to practical considerations but retains a strong sense of 'acoustic authenticity'. Finally, some reasons will be offered for the decline of the 'myth of acousticity'.

African-American Blues Artists and the Guitar

African-American blues artists have usually played acoustic and electric guitars for utilitarian as well as aesthetic reasons; they have not entertained the 'acoustics-versus-electrics' dichotomy that has surfaced amongst blues revivalists from time to time, a dichotomy that will be discussed in detail below. For traditional blues performers the essence of the guitar has been its integral voice rather than its particular form. As Alabama sharecropper and blues artist Horace Sprott related to Frederic Ramsey, 'I used to follow guitars all the time. That's where I learned a heap of different songs, on the guitar . . . I'd rather beat down the dust than eat, to hear 'em' (Ramsey 1960: 49). Mississippi-born Chicago street singer Blind Jim Brewer was attracted to electric guitars because of their sound.

> When I was down in Mississippi there I didn't have one of these electric guitars, just one ole plain guitar . . . So when I came to Chicago some fellers was sittin' on the street there . . . playin' these electric guitars and I thought that was the best music ever was played on a guitar . . . So anyway, I bought a guitar and when I found out I put a pick-up on the outside of it and run it through one of those cheap amplifiers . . . I thought I had somethin' and I went around blowin' my top . . . (Oliver 1965: 143–4)

In 1944 Muddy Waters (McKinley Morganfield) purchased his first electric for playing in Chicago clubs simply because 'couldn't nobody hear you with an acoustic' (Palmer 1981: 15; Rooney 1971: 112). Similarly, in 1945, while living in Memphis with his older blues artist cousin, Bukka White, Riley (later 'Blues Boy' or 'B.B.') King purchased a Gibson electric guitar and amplifier primarily to have more volume in clubs. Later, through the inspiration of recordings by Charlie Christian and T-Bone Walker, he developed an amplified single string style that has wielded international influence (Sawyer 1982: 159). Yet the guitar per se has retained his primary allegiance. Consider his reaction to hearing records of Belgian jazz acoustic guitar pioneer Django Reinhardt:

> His music fortified an idea I held close to my heart – that the guitar is a voice like no other. The guitar is a miracle. Out of the strings and the frets comes this personality – whether a blind man from Texas [Blind Lemon Jefferson] or a Gypsy from Belgium – of a unique human being. (King 1996: 105)

The Myth of Acousticity

In contrast to the pragmatic and aesthetic views of African-American blues musicians toward guitars, the cultural constructions of acoustic guitar and electric guitar as sonic binary opposites, which emerged in the 1950s and early 1960s amongst European and North American blues revival audiences and performers, arrived with considerable ideological baggage. It was during that period, of what Neil Rosenberg has called the 'great folk boom' (1993: 27–33), that a commitment to what will be referred to here as the 'myth of acousticity' developed. This myth pits the supposedly superior, authentic, 'natural' sound of the traditional wooden guitar, as perceived by sensory media (ears and eyes), against the inferior amplified sounds of guitars employing electronic magnetic pick-ups, sound processors, and amplifiers. In part, the 'tonal-purity-of-the-acoustic-guitar' argument may be understood as a legacy of cultural hierarchy, a well-worn High Culture aesthetic for instruments used in the performance of cultivated art music, the guitar now being 'firmly established as a respectable classical instrument' (Evans 1977: 167).[2] In addition, however, the myth of acousticity, which was embraced during the folk boom, attaches ideological signifieds to the acoustic guitar, making it a democratic vehicle vis-à-vis the sonic authoritarianism of electric instruments. During the latter 1930s and early 1940s the groundwork for viewing the acoustic guitar as an active medium for democracy was well developed by the folk music sectors of the Popular Front, a left-wing coalition centred in New York City (Reuss 1971), which involved African-American blues artists such as Huddie Ledbetter ('Leadbelly'), Josh White, Brownie McGhee and Sonny Terry (Denisoff 1971; Lieberman 1989; Wolfe and Kornell 1992). There was perhaps no better dramatization of this than when, in 1944, folksinger-songwriter Woodrow ('Woody') Wilson Guthrie (1912–67) toured with a sign on his guitar that read 'This Machine Kills Fascists' (Klein 1982; Hampton 1986: 93–148).

As an ubiquitous element of folk clubs and festivals during the folk boom, the acoustic guitar became an integral part of a 'site of resistance to the centralization of power' (Kirschenblatt-Gimblett 1992). Folk Festivals, the best-known being the Newport Folk Festival and the Mariposa Folk Festival (Brauner 1983; Usher 1977), which included blues artists, became cultural scenes where acoustic guitars and performance were pervasive, places in which participants believed that music was democratized, situations where participants experienced what Jacques Attali has described as the 'jongleurs' return'.

> ... there is a resurgence in the production of popular music using traditional instruments, which often are handmade by the musicians themselves – a resurgence of music for immediate enjoyment, for daily communication, rather than for confined spectacle. No study is required to play this kind of music, which is orally transmitted and largely

improvisational. It is thus accessible to everyone, breaking the barrier raised by an apprenticeship in the code and the instrument. It has developed among all social classes but in particular among those most oppressed . . . (Attali 1985: 140)

For white middle-class proponents of blues, the billing of African-American, guitar-playing 'country' or 'folk' blues artists from the southern US, such as Mississippi John Hurt, Skip James, and Revd. Robert Wilkins for concerts and workshops at folk fests, provided participation by oppressed performers of 'source' music. Although the lyrics these blues performers sang were usually not socially conscious, the placement of these artists in politically charged musical contexts metonymically sent ideological messages. Such scenes bolstered bonds of acousticity and social democracy.

Dave Van Ronk, Fred Neil, Maria Muldaur, Geoff Muldaur, Dave Ray, Spider John Koerner, Eric Von Schmidt, Paul Geremia, and John Hammond Jr were a few of the better known North American folk revival blues players of the late 1950s and 1960s. Of these, perhaps New York City's Dave Van Ronk best personified the merger of folk revival ideological imperatives and the performance of acoustic blues. John Hammond Jr has described him as a 'great guitar player', and a 'politically aware' 'big guy', who 'nobody messed with' (Woliver 37). Tom Pasle has observed,

David was enchanted with the idea that you could be a one-man band by using a six-string guitar and most of the fingers on the right hand when you play. It was astounding that a non-black, political intellectual was interested in something as obscure as an acoustic guitar and mostly twelve and nine bar blues. (Woliver 1986: 38–9)

An activist in many civil rights and peace causes of the era, blues artist Van Ronk has portrayed the 1960s as a time when folk music performers in Greenwich Village possessed a collective consciousness: 'We were very conscious that something important was going on . . . Essentially, everybody was performing for everybody else. The community was the audience that counted' (Pollock 1984: 27).

Coincidentally with the beginnings of the folk boom in North America, well publicized controversial appearances by Muddy Waters in Britain contributed to the myth of acousticity in Europe. To provide the historical setting, beginning in 1949 with concert performances by Huddie Ledbetter ('Leadbelly') in Paris, a succession of African-American blues singer-guitarists toured Europe and Britain through the 1950s, notably Josh White, Lonnie Johnson, Big Bill Broonzy, and Brownie McGhee (accompanied by harmonicist extraordinaire Sonny Terry) (Groom 1971: 7–16). All these artists played acoustic guitars and at one time or another had encountered folk revival scenes in the US. Then, in the fall of 1958, Muddy Waters, a Mississippi blues artist having acoustic blues roots but most prominently known as one of the fathers of Chicago electric guitar blues, made several appearances in England. The reception to his electric guitar playing was, to say the least, less than enthusiastic. Palmer explains:

> Muddy, innocent of this audience's expectations, cranked up his amplifier, hit a crashing bottleneck run, and began hollering his blues. SCREAMING GUITAR AND HOWLING PIANO is the way Muddy remembers the next morning's newspaper headlines. 'I had opened that amplifier up, boy, and there was these headlines in all the papers. Chris Barber, he say, "You play good, but don't play your amplifier so loud. Play it lower". 'Cause, see, I'd been playin' here in Chicago with these people who turned theirs up'. Paul Oliver noted wryly in *Jazz Monthly*, 'When Muddy Waters came to England, his rocking blues and electric guitar was meat that proved too strong for many stomachs', but the tour turned out well after Muddy toned down a bit. He was more than willing to be accommodating. 'Now I know that the people in England like soft guitar and the old blues', he told *Melody Maker's* Max Jones shortly before he left to return to Chicago. (Palmer 1981: 257–8)

Country Blues and Folk Blues

The intellectual groundwork for blues revivalists' acceptance of the myth of acousticity was further developed by popular music author Samuel B. Charters. As indicated by its title, his influential book, *The Country Blues*, first published simultaneously in the US and in Britain in 1959, generically defined African-American blues played on acoustic instruments through historical associations with rural environs. Despite attempts since that time, to supersede the generic label 'country blues', most notably Jeff Todd Titon's suggestion of 'downhome blues' (Titon 1977: 3), the phrase is still tenaciously maintained in many blues accounts. According to Charters, the greater artistry of country blues performers was supplanted in the post-war period by electric guitar styles. He lamented:

> Within two or three years after the war, the recordings of Big Bill, Tampa Red, Washboard Sam and others from the old lists were selling very poorly. There was a restlessness and aggressiveness in the young coloured audiences that was much more excited by the fierce shouting of newer singers – Lightnin' Hopkins, B.B. King, John Lee Hooker, Smokey Hogg and Bo Diddley – than it was in the more sophisticated styles of Big Bill or Brownie McGhee . . . The young blues singers who crowded Big Bill and the others out of the picture were loud, mean and sometimes magnificent. The beat had slowed down and the guitars were turned up; so that there was almost an unbearable tension to their singing. The piano was used less and less and the accompaniments used shrill electrified harmonicas and guitars, with an undertone of monotonous drumming. The records were overpowering in their crude immensity . . . After the war, there were more and more young blues artists who used their new electric guitars at an increasingly high

volume. The poorer musicians turned it up to hide their weaknesses and the others were forced to go along. The ringing electric guitars became the standard blues sound of the post-war years. (1959: 159–60)

'Folk blues', a phrase like country blues, also signifying blues played on acoustic instruments, was advanced by record companies and festival promoters as a direct result of the folk boom; it was largely a tactic for enlarging markets. As with Gottfried von Herder's original romantic concept of *Volkslied*, folk blues was put forward as a kind of folksong with roots in rural tradition. Authentic, real, true blues was close to nature. When Riverside Record Producer Bill Grauer produced *The Folk Blues of John Lee Hooker* (RLP 12-838) in 1959, therefore, he stripped Hooker of the usual electronic gear he used as a major Vee-Jay recording artist and put him in the studio with only a Goya acoustic guitar. According to notes writer Orrin Keepnews, the solo performances on this album in which Hooker sang 'in a rough timbred voice that [was] deeper' than on his usual rhythm and blues numbers, demonstrated that Hooker was 'a most authentic singer of the way-back, close-to-the-soil kind of blues.' Interestingly, the producer at first wanted Hooker to sing a group of songs associated with Leadbelly, 'but it turned out that Hooker didn't know Leadbelly's songs as such . . . [E]ach blues-singer (like, presumably each medieval troubadour) is essentially his own man, . . . creating an ultimate product that is stamped with his own mark' (Keepnews 1959).

Canadian 'Acoustic Blues' Today

In Canada today, four decades and several blues revivals later (Narváez 1993: 241–57; Titon 1993: 220–40), perceptions of working guitarist-singer performers of downhome-style blues vary considerably from their counterparts of the late 1950s and 1960s. In general, they do not uphold the myth of acousticity – no mention is made of the democratic qualities of acoustic instruments or music. On the other hand, they retain strong views regarding the relation of acousticity and authenticity. Most play professionally in a variety of venues, including blues festivals (the Fredericton Blues Festival; the Harbourfront Blues Festival [Toronto]), folk festivals (Winnipeg, Vancouver), workshops sponsored by blues societies (Toronto Blues Society), folk clubs (Yellow Door [Montreal], the Ship Inn [St. John's]), as well as clubs which feature 'acoustic blues' nights and acts (The Silver Dollar Room [Toronto]; The Fat Cat [St. John's]). Musicians such as Denis Parker, Rick Zolkower, Ken Hamm, Ken Whiteley, Carlo Spinazzola, Colin James, and Colin Linden play acoustic or 'semi' acoustic guitars (using a piezo pick-up [contact microphone] and/or an on-board microphone) when playing solo or small group versions of downhome blues. A minority, specifically Montreal's Ray Bonneville and Toronto's Morgan Davis, play solid body (Davis) or hollow body (Bonneville) electric guitars having only magnetic pickups, employing finger-picking styles derived from the techniques of African-American blues musicians who recorded with acoustic guitars. These two artists see no contradiction or loss of authenticity in doing this. As Davis has explained:

> I tour with my little tiny 12-watt amplifier and I play electric guitar in 30 to 60 seat clubs and coffee houses. Some people ask me why I'm not playing acoustic, since that's what they expect from solo blues players. But I tell them that this is what a lot of the guys that I love did. Lightnin' Hopkins, John Lee Hooker, lots of guys. If Robert Johnson had lived just a few more years, you can bet your bottom dollar that he would've been playing electric guitar, too. I just know it. (Morgan Davis quoted in Scoles 1999)

Davis's symbolic associations of the electric guitar with contemporaneity and acousticity with the past echo blues debates of the 1960s. In *Urban Blues* Charles Keil described those who adhered to 'country blues' as being old-fashioned 'moldy figs' (1966: 34). Keith Negus's recent discussion of 'technophobia' contextualizes such controversies as being episodes 'in a long running argument which has claimed that the use of technology in popular music has been steadily devolving musicianship and alienating musicians from both their artistic creations and from audiences' (1992: 28).

But the majority of my contemporary, professional, Canadian blues musician informants do not dismiss the authentic aesthetics of acousticity so simply.[3] Tellingly, they are not conversant with the phrase 'country blues' or 'folk blues', but instead refer to 'acoustic blues'. Like so many working blues musicians today, most possess a collection (from three to twenty-six) of, and play, both acoustic and electric guitars (see figure 3.6 of the guitar collection of St John's blues guitarist Steve Hussey). They do not simply entertain the acoustic-electric dichotomy as a value judgement. The guitar(s) they perform with depend(s) on the venue and the nature of the performance. The reason that they continue to play acoustic guitars, often in finger-picking styles, is that the resulting, percussive sounds do not qualitatively translate when executed on electric guitars with magnetic pick-ups. Generally, when playing in styles originated by artists like Blind Lemon Jefferson, Charley Patton, Reverend Gary Davis, Big Bill Broonzy, and Lonnie Johnson they want 'unplugged' sound or, if amplification is necessary, the sound provided by piezo pick-ups (contact microphones), and/or microphones. When they play the sustained-note, single-string styles of T-Bone Walker, Albert King, or B.B. King they use their electrics. For them, blues is a wedding of sound and style that proceeds from what they have heard on recordings as well as from what they have heard in person from performers connected to those recorded traditions. As Colin Linden indicated to me, 'I've collected tons of blues reissues; that's how I've learned to play' (Linden 1999).

Likewise, the guitar priorities of Canadian blues artists questioned appear to be more dependent on past blues associations than with conventional purchasing trends and market values. The sounds of acoustic guitars on early, pre-war recordings, whatever the fidelity of those records, provide a rationale and a sense of authenticity in the choices of guitars purchased by contemporary performers. Acoustic guitars are prioritized over electrics. When asked the question, 'if you could only have one guitar, of the ones you own, which one would you choose?' over 80 per cent of respondents indicated an acoustic model. Cape Breton (Nova Scotia) blues artist Carlo Spinazzola explained: 'Everything about an acoustic [guitar] – the sound, the feel – is natural to me' (Spinazzola 1999).

Some guitars, to be sure, may also serve as status objects of conspicuous consumption. Over half of the informant pool cited Martin or Gibson guitars, the two oldest, most prestigious and expensive commercial guitar makes in the US, as their 'dream' guitar. The primary reasons offered for this choice, however, were based on sonic considerations, not price and prestige. Smaller to mid-sized models (Gibson 'L'; Martin 'OM', 'O', 'OO', and 'OOO') were preferred, it was argued, because of their 'balanced tone' for finger-picking, a tone not achievable on larger jumbo models (Gibson J-200, Martin D-18) which exhibit excessive bass tonality.

Photographs of African-American blues artists with their instruments have also influenced contemporary Canadian blues musicians' taste in guitars. Since many depictions of blues personalities of the 1920s and 1930s portray those artists with small-bodied parlour guitars, it is not surprising that instruments of that size would be coveted or possessed by today's blues players.[4] Blues illustrations on record jackets and in well-known publications have also affected the symbolic value of guitars, regardless of trademark or market value. Canadian acoustic blues singer-guitarist Ken Hamm obtained and restored an original L model Gibson because he saw a photo of the legendary Robert Johnson, one of his favourite blues artists, playing one (see cover picture and figure 3.1). Photos of blues great Memphis Minnie Douglas holding a National archtop guitar inspired Canadian blues performer Sue Foley to obtain a similar, 1940s Hofner archtop (see figure 3.2). When asked about guitars in their possession, most informants responded with 'good' and 'cheap' guitar categories. Interestingly, some appeared more excited when describing cheap models linked to specific artists than when relating the details of their more expensive instruments. Association of a Harmony Sovereign with the playing of Texas songster Mance Lipscomb increased its blues value for Newfoundland's Denis Parker when he purchased that model in the 1960s (see figures 3.3 and 3.4). Another Newfoundland blues musician, Scott Goudie, treasures an old, originally budget-priced, Stella guitar that he has refurbished, associating the make with Leadbelly and Johnny Shines. Similarly, left-handed blues guitarist Steve Hussey of St. John's was inspired to purchase a particular model of Stella guitar because of Paul Oliver's photograph of Sleepy John Estes playing one in

The Story of the Blues (1969; see figures 3.5 and 3.6). Like many contemporary Canadian blues artists, Hussey has assembled a guitar collection of various values and types based on his African-American blues influences (see figure 3.7). Thus sonic and visual clues (recordings, photographs) have influenced the desires of Canadian blues guitarists in attaining their goal – to master and develop what they consider to be the authentic sounds of acoustic blues, when playing in that idiom.

But beyond attempting to achieve authentic sounds on particular acoustic guitars, blues guitarists today are primarily interested in using technology to amplify these sounds as realistically as possible in the working conditions of concerts and clubs. Far from being technophobic, the occupational folklife of these musicians reveals their technophilia in their appreciation of technologies that provide excellent, loud but listenable acoustic sounds. Of the various amplification methods for achieving realistic sounds through PA systems without unwanted 'feedback' noise, the advent of the piezoelectric pickups or 'piezos', contact microphonic materials that are

Photographs of African-American and Canadian Blues artists with their instruments

Figure 3.1 Ken Hamm with his restored L model Gibson (Photo: Victor Dezso)

Figure 3.2 Sue Foley with her 1940s Hofner archtop guitar, which she calls her 'Memphis Minnie' guitar (Photo: © 2001 Steve Rogers)

Figure 3.3 Mance Lipscomb playing a Harmony Sovereign (Photo: Chris Strachwitz, Arhoolie Records)

Figure 3.4 Denis Parker and his Harmony Sovereign (Photo: Narváez)

Figure 3.5 Sleepy John Estes playing a Stella flattop guitar (Photo: Paul Oliver)

Figure 3.6 Steve Hussey with his Stella guitar (Photo: Narváez)

Figure 3.7 Blues guitarist Steve Hussey's 'guitar wall'. TOP ROW, left to right: 1970s Mosrite replica of Silvertone electric, a model played by Hound Dog Taylor and Honeyboy Edwards; 1970s Pan replica of Fender Stratocaster electric, a model played by Homesick James, R.L. Burnside, Jimi Hendrix, and many others; 1990s Danelectro replica of 1956 U2 Danelectro electric, a model played by Houston Stackhouse; 1952 Supro archtop acoustic with Fishman piezo pickup; early 1960s Silvertone archtop acoustic, a model played by Fred Mcdowell; early 1940s Bronson square neck lap guitar, a model played by Kokomo Arnold. BOTTOM ROW, left to right: circa 1926 Gibson L1, a model played by Robert Johnson; 1920s Maurer parlour guitar; 1950s Stella, a model played by Sleepy John Estes (see photo); late 1930s Harmony Monterey; 1990s Epiphone Casino (Photo: Narváez)

usually either attached to a guitar top or permanently installed under the saddle (notched device which the strings pass over) of the bridge (block of wood near the soundhole), has altered the public uses of acoustic guitars more than any other device. One musician explained his 'conversion' to piezos.

> I used to gig at a noisy club every Thursday night and I'd mike the Gibson. Anyway, I remember the first night I tried out a Barcus Berry [piezo brand]. It felt a lot different than the mike but at least you could hear the fingerpicking! I remember all these people coming up to me during my breaks saying, 'Wow, your playing is amazing tonight!' and stuff like that you know. Anyway, I was playing the very same way I'd been playing there for months. The difference was now you could hear it! That sold me on transducers [piezo pick-ups] (Anonymous 1999).

It is important to stress, however, that despite the popularity of piezo pickups, as technophiles, acoustic blues guitarists are very creative in developing their own setups for live performance. Colin Linden, for example, does not use a piezo pickup, preferring a magnetic pickup-microphone combination. This arrangement takes into account both sonic and visual aesthetics, the latter reflecting a reluctance to modify the appearance of a guitar.

> When I'm on stage what I do is use a Sunrise magnetic pick-up in the soundhole. It's not the best thing in the world but it sounds good. I don't want to carve up my guitars at all. I don't even want to put an endpin hole in the back. What I generally do is use the magnetic pick-up to monitor with. Then I'll take a condenser mike – if I can access one, an AKG C-3000 – or something like that. You know a decent condenser, one that works okay live but also works okay in the studio, and I'll use that for the house mike and I'll use the pick-up for my monitor (1999).

Conclusion: Why 'Country Blues' to 'Acoustic Blues'?

Since the blues revival that accompanied the great folk boom of the late 1950s and 1960s, thinking about blues has shifted from a perspective of 'country' or 'folk blues', which reflected the myth of acousticity, to 'acoustic blues', which today is more concerned with the accurate presentation of acoustic guitar sounds than with reflecting ideology. Why this shift? A pivotal event that fostered this switch for many was Bob Dylan's experience at the Newport Folk Festival in 1965. Dylan, a folk hero of the time, who had always been heavily influenced by African-American blues (see Gray 1999: 268–379), appeared with an electric guitar, backed up by the Paul Butterfield Blues Band, a revival, Chicago style, electric blues ensemble. Jim Miller has succinctly described the ensuing events.

[Dylan] launched into a loud new blues called 'Maggie's Farm' . . . the crowd jeered: 'Play folk music! Sell-out!' . . . After singing two more songs, he abruptly left the stage, as did his band. He returned alone for an abbreviated encore, performing acoustic versions of two more songs, 'Mr. Tambourine Man', and 'It's All Over Now, Baby Blue'. Superficially, both were gentle ballads. But their lyrics were filled with obscure and delirious images as remote from the conventions of folk music as the amplified roar of his band. (1990: 18)

Backstage, while the band had been playing, the 'folk music mafia' had been rioting. Bob Spitz's portrayal is revealing:

[Alan] Lomax charged the soundboard, this time with Pete Seeger nipping at his heels. Both were determined to stop the desecration once and for all. Pete tried several times to yank [Paul] Rothchild's hands off of the board, while the engineer struggled to maintain the levels. Stagehands had come to Rothchild's aid . . . (1991: 306).

Although Richard Middleton has interpreted this event as dramatizing 'the equations of "acoustic" [with] "folk authenticity", [and] "electric" [with] "commercial sell-out"' (1990: 90), its significance for blues guitarists transcended that dichotomy. It signalled the end of the myth of acousticity; it emancipated blues from ideological confines. As blues revival artist of the period Eric von Schmidt and Jim Rooney have observed:

[Dylan] was no longer writing songs about 'causes', about peace and civil rights. He was no longer traveling the same highway as those who had bummed around during the Depression . . . Many of the younger performers at the Festival agreed with Dylan. The politics of the folk movement weren't necessarily their politics. They were really in it for the music, which they dearly loved. (1979: 264)

Overtly political events also accelerated the move toward disassociating blues from the politics of the folk music movement. For Dave Van Ronk, 'the election of Nixon in 1968 was the turning point . . . Everyone who was involved in folk music certainly felt it. The whole left-wing wave had passed. Thermidor had arrived' (Pollock 1984: 30).

The development of the acoustic steel-stringed guitar as a legitimate form on its own has furthered an appreciation of blues as acoustic art form without ideological attachments. In the late 1960s John Fahey's elaborate instrumental creations, which inspired many other serious guitarists, most prominently Leo Kottke, were based on the techniques and sounds of blues stylists. Such pieces have been viewed by some as constituting a new 'classical' tradition for the steel-string guitar. The use of acoustic guitars in folk-rock (Dylan; Crosby, Stills, Nash, and Young; the Byrds), combined with the ever bigger acoustic sounds enabled by improving technology, has ensured the acoustic guitar a permanent place in popular music today, the music of the Dave Matthews Band being a sterling example. These developments are part of the African-American acoustic blues heritage. Tom and Mary Anne Evans have discerned: 'The increased exposure of young players to blues guitar, on record and in performance from the early 1960s onwards, has helped the development of the steel-string guitar as a major solo concert and recording instrument' (Evans 1977: 329).

In closing, it is worthy of note that in dismissing the political messages of the myth of acousticity, blues revival artists were also coming to terms with the sexuality of traditional African-American blues, a characteristic exhibited in the dance contexts of blues (Hazzard-Gordon), blues song lyrics (see Garon), and in the tendency of blues artists to personify their guitars as lovers. The latter point is well elaborated in B.B. King's comment about his guitar, 'Lucille':

> I liked seeing my guitar as a lady. I liked seeing her as someone worth fighting or even dying for. I liked giving her a name and attitude all her own. Truth is, from the time I put a wire string on a broom handle till today, I've turned to Lucille – and there have been seventeen different Lucilles – for comfort and relief. Just to pick her up and stroke her settles me down. (King 1996: 130)

Although Middleton has privileged the electric guitar in this regard, maintaining that it 'inescapably' 'signifies "passion" and "sexuality"' (1990: 90), most blues musicians I have queried believe that acoustic guitars convey the same erotic signifieds. Colin Linden remarked that an acoustic guitar is a 'personality instrument', and that 'when you hold it in your arms it's so incredibly intimate and personal'. The lyrics of an original blues, *Aaron's Song*, by Carlo Spinazzola (1999) will end this discussion. They poetically express the sensual personification of a guitar by a young Canadian acoustic blues artist, who like many other players, thinks of the guitar as a lifelong companion with a character and voice of its own:

> When he'd lost her he'd sworn he'd lost it all,
> From a darkened corner he heard the guitar call,
> So he picked her and he held her, as if he were holding you,
> All that she would sing was twelve solid bars in blue.

Notes

1. A version of this article was read at the Tenth International Association for the Study of Popular Music (IASPM) International Conference, University of Technology, Sydney, Australia, 9–13 July 1999. I wish to thank all the musicians

I consulted and interviewed for this project as well as the editors and Holly Everett for their helpful comments.

2. Just as Andrés Segovia, the Spaniard most responsible for bringing the classical guitar to international prominence, refused to even use a microphone in concert, so too folk music devotees in Britain continue to resist the use of PA systems in folk clubs (MacKinnon 1993: 119–26).

3. I have discussed these issues informally with over twenty Canadian blues musicians. Of these I have conducted formal interviews with fourteen. Informants hail from five provinces; one is from the UK and two are from the US. They range in age from 23 to 57, the majority being in their thirties. Three of the informants are women.

4. Indeed, when recognized by a guitar manufacturer's brand name, the symbolic and market value of a guitar played by a blues giant of the past can soar. Steve LaVere's publication of two photos of Robert Johnson in the 1980s revealed one to be a Gibson L1 (see cover picture). The L1 was one of Gibson's most inexpensive and least resonant models when it was first marketed in the 1920s. With knowledge that Johnson played this model, Gibson produced a new L1, Robert Johnson model, a replica of its predecessor, with a substantial price tag.

References

Anonymous, 'Personal communication', 16 March 1999.

Attali, J. (1985), *Noise: The political economy of music*, trans. B. Massumi, Minneapolis: University of Minnesota Press.

Brauner, C.A. (1983), 'A Study of the Newport Folk Festival and the Newport Folk Foundation', MA Thesis, Memorial University of Newfoundland.

Cantwell, R. (1996), *When We Were Good: The folk revival*, Cambridge: Harvard University Press.

Charters, S.B. (1959), *The Country Blues*, London: Michael Joseph.

Denisoff, R.S. (1971), *Great Day Coming: Folk music and the American Left*, Urbana: University of Illinois Press.

Evans, T. and Evans, M.A. (1977), *Guitars: Music, history, construction and players from the Renaissance to rock*, New York: Facts on File.

Garon, P. (1996), *Blues and the Poetic Spirit*, San Francisco: City Lights.

Gray, M. (1999), 'Even Post-Structuralists Oughta Have the Pre-War Blues', in *Song and Dance Man III: The art of Bob Dylan*, London: Cassell.

Groom, B. (1971), *The Blues Revival*, London: Studio Vista.

Grunfeld, F.V. (1974), *The Art and Times of the Guitar*, 1969, New York: Da Capo Press.

Hampton, W. (1986), *Guerrilla Minstrels: John Lennon, Joe Hill, Woody Guthrie, and Bob Dylan*, Knoxville: University of Tennessee Press.

Hazzard-Gordon, K. (1990), *Jookin': The rise of social dance formations in African-American culture*, Philadelphia: Temple University Press.

Keepnews, O. (1959), 'Notes', *The Folk Blues of John Lee Hooker*, New York: Riverside Records LP 12-838.

Keil, C. (1966), *Urban Blues*, Chicago: University of Chicago Press.

King, B.B. (1996), *Blues All Around Me: The autobiography of B.B. King*, New York: Avon.

Kirshenblatt-Gimblett, B. (1992), 'Mistaken Dichotomies', in R. Baron and N.R. Spitzer (eds) *Public Folklore*, Washington DC: Smithsonian Institution Press.

Klein, J. (1982), *Woody Guthrie: A life*. New York: Ballantine.

Lieberman, R. (1989), *'My Song is My Weapon': People's songs, American communism, and the politics of culture, 1930–1950*, Urbana: University of Illinois Press.

Linden, C. (1999), 'Personal communication', July 4.

MacKinnon, N. (1993), *The British Folk Scene: Musical performance and social identity*, Buckingham, UK: Open University Press.

Middleton, R. (1990), *Studying Popular Music*, Milton Keynes: Open University Press.

Miller, J. (1990), 'Bob Dylan', in E. Thomson and D. Gutman (eds) *The Dylan Companion: A collection of essential writing about Bob Dylan*, New York: Delta.

Narváez, P. (1993), *'Living Blues Journal*: The Paradoxical Aesthetics of the Blues Revival', in N.V. Rosenberg (ed.) *Transforming Tradition: Folk music revivals examined*, Urbana: University of Illinois Press.

Negus, K. (1992), *Producing Pop: Culture and conflict in the popular music industry*, London: Edward Arnold.

Oliver, P. (1965), *Conversation With the Blues*, New York: Horizon.

Palmer, R. (1981), *Deep Blues*, New York: Viking..

Pollock, B. (1984), *When the Music Mattered: Rock in the 1960s*, New York: Holt, Rinehart & Winston.

Ramsey, F. Jr. (1960), *Been Here and Gone*, New Brunswick: Rutgers University Press.

Reuss, R.A. (1979), 'The Roots of American Left-Wing Interest in Folksong', *Labor History* 12 (2): 259–79.

Rooney, J. (1971), *Bossmen: Bill Monroe and Muddy Waters*, New York: Dial Press.

Rosenberg, N.V. (ed.) (1993), *Transforming Tradition: Folk music revivals examined*, Urbana: University of Illinois Press.

Sawyer, C. (1982), *B.B. King: The authorized biography,* London: Quartet.

Scoles, J. (1999), 'Morgan Davis: A True Independent', *Blues Scene Quarterly* 2 (4): 4–7.

Spinazzola, C. (1999), 'Personal communication', September 12.

Spitz, B. (1991), *Dylan: A biography*, New York: Norton.

Titon, J.T. (1977), *Early Downhome Blues: A musical and cultural analysis*, Urbana: University of Illinois Press.

—— (1993), 'Reconstructing the Blues: Reflections on the 1960s Blues Revival', in N. Rosenberg (ed.), *Transforming Tradition: Folk music revivals examined,* Urbana: University of Illinois Press.

Turnbull, H. (1978), *The Guitar from the Renaissance to the Present Day*, 1974, New York: Charles Scribner's Sons.

Usher, B. and Page-Harpa, L. (eds) (1977), *'For What Time in This World': stories from Mariposa.* Toronto: Peter Martin.

von Schmidt, E. and Rooney, J. (1979), *Baby Let Me Follow You Down: The illustrated story of the Cambridge folk years*, New York: Anchor.

Wolfe, C. and Lornell, K. (1992), *The Life and Legend of Leadbelly*, New York: HarperCollins.

Woliver, R. (1986), *Bringing it All Back Home: Twenty-five years of American music at Folk City*, New York: Pantheon.

–4–

'Plug in and Play!' UK 'Indie-Guitar' Culture

Andy Bennett

In the context of the UK, 'indie-guitar' has become an essentially generic term in popular music vocabulary to describe a loosely defined, guitar-based sound and its attendant performance/consumption aesthetic.[1] Despite the claim of British popular music journalists at various points during the last twenty years that guitar-based bands are 'a thing of the past', a claim most recently made with the rise of dance music in the late 1980s, guitar music, and particularly 'indie-guitar', has shown considerable resilience. In relation to indie-guitar, such resilience is undoubtedly due in part to the perception among indie-guitar bands and their fans of indie-guitar as a more 'authentic' musical style than, for example, 'boy' or 'girl' band music, or the various forms of 'commercial' dance music that currently dominate the UK charts. Central to the ethos of indie-guitar is a 'back to basics' sensibility grounded in the notion that *good* and *meaningful* music can be made without the showbusiness trappings of the mainstream music industry, relying instead on minimal stage set-ups, 'small-club/pub' venues (Street 1993) and a sense of 'community' between bands and their audiences (Fonarow 1995). Similarly, the originally 'shoestring' production of indie-guitar music by small-scale independent record companies with 'localized networks of production and distribution' has also done much to enhance indie-guitar's self-styled 'alternative' ethic (Burnett 1996: 59). Although such definitions of indie-guitar are, as Negus (1992) points out, problematized due to its increasing incorporation into the mainstream music industry, indie-guitar bands and their fans continue to buy into the notion of indie-guitar as an 'independent' and alternative music, the resulting 'sense of "otherness" [being] crucial to the development of a sense of group identity' (Street 1993: 50). Indeed, this self-styled indie belief is by no means unique to the UK, the 'myth' of independence just described also being central to the construction of 'otherness' in other indie scenes, for example in New Zealand (Bannister 1999) and the US (Santiago-Lucerna 1998).

While several studies have analysed indie-guitar using a subcultural type of analysis, in which song titles, lyrics, visual style (see, for example, Mohan and Malone 1994) or the emphasis on regionalism and roots culture as a means of 'resist[ing] the . . . dominant rock/pop aesthetics' (Strinyer 1992: 19), have been a central focus, little attention has been directed towards the role of the guitar itself within the array of 'alternative' cultural sensibilities that inform the indie-guitar scene. Yet it is clear that the guitar styles employed in indie-guitar music, as well as the 'choice' of instrument, amplification and range of effects used by indie-guitarists, are of deep importance in the construction of the culture of indie-guitar music, from the point of view of both musicians and consumers. During the course of this chapter I want to consider the role of the guitar in the culture of indie-guitar music. I will begin by charting the roots of indie-guitar, both in the localized 'garage' scene of the US and UK 'pub rock' and in the trans-Atlantic genres of punk and new wave. I will then go on to consider how the guitar styles, sounds and range of instruments used by indie-guitar bands contribute to the rhetoric of otherness underpinning the culture that has grown up around indie-guitar. Finally, I will examine how the construction and representation of gender, so central to issues of production and performance across a range of popular music styles (see, for example, Frith and McRobbie 1978, Bayton 1987 and Negus 1992), manifests itself in relation to indie-guitar culture.

My analysis of indie-guitar culture is framed around a sociological method of enquiry that, in addition to using secondary empirical data sources, also reflects time spent in the field as a participant observer. The sections of this chapter dealing with aspects of indie-guitar style, sound and on-stage performance draw on my own experience of playing with college and university-based indie-guitar bands during the 1980s and early 1990s. In addition to performing in a number of well-known UK venues for 'indie-guitar' music, such as the Riverside in Newcastle and the Adelphi Club in Hull, several of the groups I played with filled support slots for college and university dates headlined by more established indie-guitar groups of the time such as the Red Guitars, the Brilliant Corners and Cable.

The Roots of Indie-Guitar

While the term 'indie-guitar' came into common usage in the UK around twenty years ago, to denote a new style of 'alternative' music that grew up in, and effectively filled, the void left by punk, its roots can be traced back to musical developments on both sides of the Atlantic between the mid 1960s and the early 1970s. Perhaps one of the earliest formative influences on indie-guitar was the US garage band scene of 1965 to 1968, described by Logan and Woffinden as 'a transitional period in the development of American Rock 'n' Roll . . . between [the] Beatles/Stones-led British invasion and [the] San Francisco-based rock renaissance' (1976: 405). Possessing very little in the way of conventional musical skill and performing experience, garage bands applied their rudimentary knowledge of guitar, bass, drums and, occasionally, electronic organ in copying the style of British bands of the time such as the Beatles, the Rolling Stones, the Kinks and the Who. Garage bands played at high-school dances and 'Battle of the Bands' competitions, recording at most one or two singles before disbanding. Some of the more well known examples of garage bands include the Kingsmen (who had a hit with 'Louie Louie'), the Standells, Swingin' Medallions and the Electric Prunes.

If the roots of indie-guitar's non-mainstream, alternative sensibility began to take form with the low-key, localized garage scene of the mid-1960s, then it was further developed by the New York punk scene of the mid-1970s. Initiated by groups and artists such as Richard Hell and the Voidoids, the Talking Heads and Patti Smith, the New York punk scene took its inspiration both from the garage bands and the Velvet Underground who, with help of leading avant-garde artist Andy Warhol, had become an established part of New York's underground scene, regularly 'stunn[ing] audiences with harsh vocals and droning electronic music' (Cagle 1995: 81). The New York punk bands drew on the musical aesthetic of the Velvet Underground, combining this with the 'hands on' approach of the 1960s garage scene, believing that anyone who wished to form a band could and should do so. This was in stark contrast to the general trend in popular music at the time. During the early 1970s increasing emphasis was being placed upon the technical ability of musicians, this being matched by a new direction in popular music, 'progressive rock', which, as its name suggests, centred around increasingly ambitious stage sets, state-of-the-art amplification systems and large-scale venues (see, for example, Lull 1992, Macan 1997 and Martin 1998). The New York punk scene represented a rejection of the progressive rock ethos. It was small-club music, played in a straightforward, musically uncomplex fashion. Thus, as Lenny Kaye, guitarist with the Patti Smith group explains:

> . . . in the early 70s . . . rock 'n' roll had gotten very complicated. Progressive rock, a sense that rock was an 'adult' medium . . . a sense that complexity and song cycles and . . . instrumental prowess and musicianship were the driving force. The fact that you could play three chords and get up on stage within a week was being lost.[2]

Similarly, David Bryne, vocalist, lead guitarist and principle songwriter with the Talking Heads, whose early live performances were at CBGBs, the now legendary New York punk venue, makes the following observation:

> Punk wasn't a musical style, or at least it shouldn't have been . . . It was more a kind of 'do it yourself – anyone can do it' attitude. If you can only play two notes on the guitar you can figure out a way to make a song out of that.[3]

A parallel development in the UK at this time also inspired the small-club, back to basics sensibility that would later become a central focus for indie-guitar.

Similarly opposed to progressive rock, whose primary early 1970s exponents Yes, Genesis, Emerson Lake and Palmer and Pink Floyd were all UK based, a number of London-based groups, including the Stranglers, Dr Feelgood and Kilburn and the Highroads (who later became Ian Dury and the Blockheads) created a new music scene around the London pub venue circuit, motivated by the belief that live music meant 'small' venues in which band and audience could share equally in the event. In the same way that the New York punk scene drew its inspiration in part from the US garage band scene of the mid-1960s, the London pub bands' emphasis on the importance of small venues was inspired by the live music scene in Britain as this had existed prior to the arrival of progressive rock. Thus as Laing explains

> . . . the virtue of smallness was taken by pub bands from their memory of the Merseybeat and British R&B era. The size of the bar-room allowed for, even insisted upon, the intimacy between musicians and audience they believed was somehow essential for meaningful music. Pub rock's stance implied that things went wrong for bands when they became superstars and 'lost touch' with their original audiences. (1985: 8)

In December, 1998 I interviewed Wilko Johnson, former guitarist with Dr Feelgood, and asked about his experience of performing on the London pub circuit. Johnson's comments, and those of his bass player Norman Watt Roy (formerly a member of Ian Dury's backing band the 'Blockheads'), support Laing's observation:

> *Norman*: There was all this really technical music around at the time, big production stuff, and the pub rock bands were against that. I mean that's why people liked Dr Feelgood so much, it was just straightforward.
> *Wilko*: Yeah that's right. With Feelgood there wasn't any bullshit, it was just about getting up there and doing it.

In an interview with music journalist Charles Shaar Murray, Johnson expands on this last point:

> . . . we were reacting against the notion of what a rock star was supposed to be, with costumes and technology. We were just bashing away at guitars and drums, wearing clothes you could walk down the street in, with a look you could get together for a fiver. (1987: 17)

The performance ethic of the London pub rock bands was inherited by the UK punk scene. Indeed, as Friedlander points out: 'Some band members, such as Joe Strummer of the 101ers, simply stepped over the line from pub to punk' (1996: 251). In many respects, punk was even more critical of progressive rock's musical elitism than pub rock, articulating its opposition through a rejection of even the most rudimentary musical skills and the creation of a sound bordering on white noise. Thus, as Chambers explains the possibility of discussing 'artistic' qualities and 'musicianship' was brutally mauled. In punk's almost anonymous simplicity a previous musical sense was rudely transformed into "nonsense"' (1985: 177). In keeping with much of the writing which has focused on the UK punk scene (see, for example, Hebdige 1979 and Savage 1992), Chambers' description of punk rock is suggestive of an anarchic quality in the music based on what Hebdige has deemed to be an 'appropriation of 'the rhetoric of crisis which had filled the airwaves throughout . . . the late 1970s' as the UK entered a protracted period of economic decline (1979: 87).

However, it is important not to overstate this aspect of UK punk. If at one level punk's significance could be interpreted in terms of a radical commentary on the UK's depressed state during the late 1970s, at the same time punk opened the door for a number of other groups and artists who, despite embracing the back-to-basics sensibility of the punk rock style, adopted a musical ethic that went beyond punk's 'frantic guitar rhythms [and] resolutely untutored vocals', reinstating an emphasis on melody and harmonic content but confining these qualities to three minute pop songs (Chambers 1985: 177). Although musically diverse, such groups, which included Elvis Costello and the Attractions, Squeeze, the Motors and Ian Dury and Blockheads, were collectively labelled 'new wave' by the UK music press. It is within the nexus of the DIY alternativism forged by pub rock and, latterly, punk and 'new wave', that the current UK indie-guitar scene must be located and understood. During the rest of the chapter I will examine this scene with a particular focus upon the role of the guitar in the construction of indie-guitar's anti-mainstream, alternative sensibilities. In doing so I will consider the way in which particular conventions of guitar style, sound and even choice of guitar, amplification and effects units all contribute to the authentication of indie-guitar culture's perceived sense of 'otherness'.

'Small Amps are Best!': Indie-guitar's 'Plug in and Play' Aesthetic

When it was put to Shirley Manson that Garbage, the band that she fronts as lead singer, performs a style of music that is reliant upon state-of-the-art technology, Manson replied: 'People are so determined to be Luddites that they don't realise that technology is so sophisticated now that it allows you unbeatable spontaneity' (Simmons 1999: 56).[4] Manson's claim, although intended as a commentary on contemporary popular music production and performance arrangements, can be placed in a historical context which, as I have previously demonstrated, dates back to the US punk and UK pub rock scenes of the early 1970s. Indeed, the rejection of technology with UK punk and UK pub rock was such that it was regarded as a distraction from 'real' music-making. Such a viewpoint was inherited by UK punk and has, in turn, been appropriated by UK indie-guitar bands, technological embellishments such as light shows and guitar effects units often being quite self-consciously rejected as *getting in the way* of the music. Speaking about electric guitarists' increasing reliance on electronic effects pedals such as chorusing and digital echo, Kevin Shields, one of the guitarists with early 1990s cult indie-guitar band My Bloody Valentine stated in an interview for Q magazine:

> . . . we don't use any of those effects on our guitars. The effect comes from the way we play them, or from doing other things, like messing around with four amps facing each other. It's got nothing to do with plugging into a GP-16.[5] (Gill 1992: 41)

In addition to such an insistence on musical 'purity', there is also an accepted maxim in indie-guitar circles that on-stage equipment should be kept to a minimum, that it should not detract from the band or, more importantly, the music the band performs. This applies especially to the guitar, which is the focal point for indie-guitar music. The notion of the guitar as a 'plank of wood with six strings and a volume control' is ingrained into the discourse of indie-guitar playing. Playing down the obviously more complex structure of the electric guitar – for example, the fact that it is actually *several* highly crafted pieces of wood skilfully joined together, and that the sound is produced through one or several magnetic pickups connected to the amplifier by intricate wiring systems (see, for example, Bacon 1991) – reduces both the guitar and its player to an essentially workmanlike and 'street level' status. Any discussion of the more technical features of the guitar is equated with the interview speak of rock guitarists and those involved in specialist fields such as jazz and jazz rock and is, therefore, quite self-consciously avoided. Thus, even ways of *talking* about the guitar confer important 'indie' credentials on guitarists, which are as central to the preservation of an authentic indie-guitar identity as the sound and image of indie-guitar bands.

It is also important to create the right on-stage look with guitars and amplification systems. Given the vast choice of guitars and amplification now available, it is vital that both complement the indie-guitar image by avoiding obviously high-tech features such as locking tremolo units or amplifiers with digital displays. The author's own experience of playing with an indie-guitar group while at university illustrates the extent to which the 'look' of on-stage equipment plays a central role in the preservation of the indie-guitar aesthetic. Thus, the slightly battered look of my Fender Stratocaster, a type of guitar widely endorsed in indie-guitar circles because of its 'simple' design and status as one of the 'original', and thus 'authentic', electric guitar models, and the compactness of my valve-driven Marshall 50 watt combo amplifier were thought by other members of the band to be 'cool' because of their worn-in, non-technical and 'old' appearance. In effect, my guitar and amplifier ceased to be merely musical instruments, ways in which to convey a particular sound to an audience, and became extra-musical links between the image of the band and the music it created.[6] Through their ability to express a dual simplicity, that of the band's on-stage image and also the musically uncomplex nature of the songs performed, the guitar and amplifier became cultural signifiers – articulations of an indie-guitar sensibility shared by the band and its audience.

A useful theoretical model for understanding this process is Chaney's concept of lifestyle 'sites and strategies' (Chaney 1996: 91). According to Chaney, lifestyle *sites* refer to the 'physical metaphors for the spaces that actors can appropriate and control', while *strategies* denote the 'characteristic modes of social engagement, or narratives of identity, in which the actors concerned can embed the metaphors at hand' (Chaney 1996: 92). In proposing such a model for the understanding of how contemporary lifestyles are constructed and subsequently lived out by individuals, Chaney effectively re-maps the cultural terrain of late modern social life, rejecting the crude determinism of mass cultural theory (see, for example, MacDonald 1953) and considering anew the role of mass cultural products in the everyday lives of social actors. Through an application of Chaney's model to 'indie-guitar' culture, it is possible to see how material objects such as guitars and amplifiers become as central to the marking out of an indie-guitar lifestyle as the clubs in which indie-guitar music is performed and listened to (see Fornarow 1995) and the record shops where indie-guitar music is bought and discussed, both over the counter and between customers (see Frith 1988 and Shank 1994). The notion of lifestyle politics implicit in Chaney's work allows for the interpretation of indie-guitar as a scene that is both highly reflexive, in terms of the system of beliefs which underpins it, and overtly selective in terms of those things which are deemed 'authentic' in indie-guitar terms. The question thus becomes not one of the 'commercial versus non-commercial', a debate that in any case quickly founders, but rather how things are *accepted* or *rejected* as components of indie-guitar culture.

Such reflexive selectivity is exemplified by indie-guitar's wholesale embracing of 'lo-fi' recording as a more 'natural' means of music making. Facilitated by the recent availability of cheap but high-quality home recording equipment (see Smith and Maughan 1997), lo-fi has proved a valuable resource for indie-guitar in its claims to 'cottage industry' status as groups and singer-songwriters, equipped in many cases with little more than a tape recorder, microphone, electric guitar and bass, simple drum kit and/or drum machine, have recorded complete CD or cassette albums, the latter being available only through specialist shops or via mail order direct from the artist. An example of this approach to recording and distribution is the album *A Plea For Tenderness* released on Brinkman records by Dump (the name assumed for solo projects by James McNew, guitarist and vocalist with US alternative band Yo La Tengo). The sleeve notes for the album, presented in a reproduced hand-written style read:

recorded mostly while wearing pajamas [sic], on a Tascam Porta - 5 cassette machine between 8/95 and 4/97, in Brooklyn and Hoboken. Mixed by Peter Walsh in his living room . . .

For much of the album, the electric guitar is the central instrument, several of the tracks being guitar instrumentals with one or, at most, two overdubs. Apart from light echo and occasional chorusing, the guitar is played 'clean', that is, without electronic effects, and is plugged directly into the Tascam home recording unit. The essentially 'unproduced' sound of the guitar performs a crucial soundscaping role, setting the tone for the intended 'lo-fi' feel of the album.

Through their collective interpretation of lo-fi music as an 'authentic', grassroots cultural statement, indie-guitar groups and their audiences articulate a shared disinterest in mainstream music and what are deemed to be the routinized show-business conventions that surround it. In an article on Olivia Tremor Control, an alternative rock group based in Athens, Georgia, who rely largely on lo-fi recording techniques, music journalist Barney Hoskyns describes how one member of the group had expressed his surprise 'when kindred spirits Gorky's Zygotic Mynci asked the Olivias why they weren't on a major label' (Hoskyns 1999: 27). Similarly, another member of the group suggested that, as a result of the wider access to recording created by 'lo-fi': 'People are starting to realise that they can take the power into their own hands, that they can take care of themselves and put out their records themselves'(Hoskyns 1999: 27).

'No Solos'! Indie-guitar's Deconstruction of the Guitar 'Hero'

If the choice of guitar, amplifier and even recording technique represents one of the ways in which indie-guitar marks itself out from other guitar-based musics, then similarly important are the techniques of style employed by indie-guitar players. One of the most distinctive features of indie-guitar, and a product of its punk roots, is an overtly self-conscious deconstruction of many conventions central to other styles of electric guitar playing, especially those employed in rock and heavy metal. Indeed, indie-guitar's unerring emphasis on simplicity and directness in style and delivery has stood in increasing contrast to the approach of rock guitarists. The rise of indie-guitar in the early 1980s was matched by significant developments in rock guitar, the flagging progressive rock style being replaced by a new brand of rock and heavy metal music influenced by the 'new virtuosity' of guitarist Eddie Van Halen whose bi-manual finger tapping (a technique whereby the fingers of both hands are used to finger frets on the neck of the guitar) pushed back the musical limits of rock guitar playing, allowing guitarists to move beyond the blues-based structure of conventional rock styles and to incorporate harmonic intervals and scales associated with classical music (Walser 1993; see also Steve Waksman's chapter in this book).

While exponents of this new rock guitar style claimed that their musical experiments marked a healthy and long-overdue deconstruction of the divisions between rock and classical music (a position effectively satirised in Rob Reiner's film *This is Spinal Tap*, see Denisoff and Romanowski 1991), indie-guitar players saw it as a sign of rock's increasingly high-brow and detached nature. Thus, just as Pete Shelley, lead vocalist and rhythm guitarist with Manchester-based post-punk band The Buzzcocks has claimed that 'punk was a response to the boredom of [the] twenty minute guitar solos'[7] that often characterized 1970s rock and progressive rock music, so indie-guitar players criticized the new breed of heavy metal guitarists for their blatant exhibitionism. By the mid-1980s, not only was the guitar solo a virtually 'forbidden' entity in indie-guitar music, but many exponents of indie-guitar openly championed what they considered to be the sheer emotive quality of the non-technical. Thus as Marc E. Smith, singer with UK indie-guitar group The Fall, said of Fall guitarist Craig Scanlon:

> . . . he plays cheap guitars, he plays very weird chord sequences nobody's ever heard of, a lot of his chords are out of tune and stuff – he's very *artistic* with it in a way [but] he doesn't know it . . . That's why he's good. (Cooper 1987: 10)

Such simplicity in indie-guitar is also highlighted by music journalists who often regard the 'direct' and unfettered approach of the indie-guitar style as an indication of the music's 'street credibility'. Indeed, when featured in the discursive prose of journalistic articles on indie-guitar bands or other artists who, while not strictly 'indie', are seen to embrace the indie aesthetic, the guitar is often used as a literary device – as a personification of the artist's 'indie-guitar' credentials. This is clearly illustrated in the following extract from an article by Paul Du Noyer on Billy Bragg, the Essex-born singer-songwriter who, performing solo with an electric guitar plugged into a small and very basic amplifier, has represented a number of socio-political causes and was also involved in Red Wedge, an organization formed by left-wing musicians and the Labour Party during the mid-1980s in an attempt to revive young people's interest in politics (see Frith and Street 1992). Du Noyer (1987: 27) describes Bragg thus:

> A solo performer, his voice is not technically perfect, being a gruff sort of thing that aspires to tenderness but has to wade through thick puddles of East-London to get there. He knocks out rudimentary riffs on the electric guitar with more spirit than finesse.

In Du Noyer's account, the images of Bragg's untutored voice and his working-class East London identity resonate perfectly with the description of the singer's guitar playing as 'rudimentary'. The implication here is that the guitar serves simply as a mediator for the conversion of a series of observations on the everyday life of ordinary people into a musicalized dialogue, rather than being an end in itself – an object of spectacle or artistry. Such a commentary neatly reveals how indie-guitar's technical simplicity feeds into and is, in turn, fed by a deep-seated aesthetic whereby indie-guitar bands forge a link between their musical statements and their outlook on life. Often focusing lyrically on the struggles and personal or inter-personal dramas that characterize everyday life, indie-guitar bands reinforce such a focus through the unfettered, 'unpretentious' guitar style employed in their music.

There is, however, a further reason why indie-guitar's systematic deconstruction of the guitar-hero image is centrally important to indie-guitar culture. Elsewhere in this book David Evans notes how in acoustic blues guitar culture technical ability became a measure of the African-American bluesman's physical toughness and resilience to oppression. In indie-guitar culture a broadly opposite set of values can be observed. I have previously noted how, from the point of view of indie-guitar bands, one of the main measures of authenticity is an ability to be 'in touch' with the audience. From a musical point of view, a vital part of such 'in-touchness' is the ability of an indie-guitar band to present itself as a *band*, as a group of people working together, and perhaps more importantly, with the audience, to create an 'atmosphere' – and with it a sense of 'community'. Within this shared aesthetic of the indie-guitar gig the guitar plays a major anchoring role. Rather than breaking up the performance with a series of long, intricate guitar solos or 'breaks', and the opportunities for demonstrations of individual musical expertise and exhibitionism that the latter facilitate, the indie-guitarist's task is to remain firmly within the parameters of the song, providing layers of chording or riffing that add to, rather than distract from, the rhythm and vocal melody lines provided by the other members of the band. This is a convention that is rigidly adhered to even by more technically accomplished indie-guitarist's such as Johnny Marr, formerly of The Smiths, and subsequently The The. While Marr's work with The Smiths was critic-ally acclaimed, such acclaim stemmed the guitarist's distinctive chording style and ability to embellish singer Morrisey's lyrics with a series of signature hooks and riffs that accentuated the tone of the lyric, a typical example of this being the song *How Soon is Now* with its disturbing backwards slide guitar effect, dubbed over a Bo Diddley-style shuffle rhythm, which is reduced to an irregular stutter due to the use of an electronic vibrato effect.

'Okay for the Boys but What About the Girls?' Indie-guitar Culture and Gender

Thus far, I have been concerned to evaluate the role of the electric guitar in indie-guitar's culture of 'otherness'. Through a consideration of issues such as choice of instrumentation and equipment, sound and techniques of style, I have argued that the guitar becomes a crucial resource in indie-guitar's rejection of dominant rock aesthetics and the construction of an alternative cultural space. However, while indie-guitar is characterized by such forms of resistance to all things deemed to be mainstream, there also remain significant points of convergence between indie-guitar culture and more 'mainstream' cultures of music-making, particularly in relation to the imbalance of gender.

In all genres of popular music, the electric guitar is still a predominantly male instrument. Indeed, in some cases particular conventions of guitar style actively function to exclude female players. Thus, for example, studies of rock and heavy metal music have emphasized the acutely 'gendered' nature of these genres, arguing that conventions of stage performance in which the electric guitar becomes a phallic symbol result in male bonding and female exclusion (see, for example, Frith and McRobbie 1978 and Walser 1993). This view of the guitar's central place in rock's macho ethic is summed up by Frith and McRobbie's term *cock rock*. Thus, they argue: 'Cock rockers' musical skills become synonymous with their sexual skills . . . Cock rockers are not bound by the conventions of the song form, but use their instruments to show "what they've got", to give vent to their macho imagination' (Frith and McRobbie 1978: 374).

This use of the guitar in rock and heavy metal is in stark contrast to its role in indie-guitar music where the guitar is viewed as a centrally defining aspect of indie-guitar's 'back to basics', alternative image rather than as a symbol of male dominance and power. Such placing of the guitar within indie-guitar ideology is complemented by the on-stage posturing of indie-guitar players – movement being rather more limited than in rock and heavy metal. Indeed indie-guitar players often assume a rather static on-stage posture, looking down at their fret boards or the floor, a tendency that has resulted in the coining of the term 'shoe-gazing' by music journalists (see, for example, Gill 1992). The use of the guitar in any form of on-stage posturing that even remotely resembles the thrusting movements of heavy metal players appears to be an unwritten taboo within indie-guitar circles. In many ways the rejection of such machoistic and overtly sexist performance traits represents a further facet of indie-guitar's self-conscious manoeuvring into an anti-rock position. A similar point is made by Santiago-Lucerna who suggests that the image of grunge artists such as Kurt Cobain served as 'a strong statement against the glam aesthetic of eighties heavy metal and the slick elegance of techno-pop' (Santiago-Lucerna 1998: 190).

However, if approaches to guitar playing itself attempt to negate some of the more restrictive machoistic and exclusionary aspects associated with rock guitar playing, the fact remains that, like rock and heavy metal, indie-guitar is primarily a male concern.[8] This has much to do with the fact that, despite its alternative claims, indie-guitar is inextricably tied to a wider system of norms and values that, whether expressed at the corporate or grassroots level, permeate the production and performance of popular music and systematically discriminate against women.

The career path of female indie-guitar bands inevitably involves the negotiation of the 'stereotypes' imposed on women singers and musicians by the male-dominated music industry. This observation is supported by Gottlieb and Wald's study of Riot Grrrl, the term used to a describe a wave of all-female, or predominantly female, guitar-based alternative bands from the US such as Hole and Burning Bush. Gottlieb and Wald illustrate the problems that such groups encounter in gaining respect not only from male musicians but from male members of their audiences whose feelings of camaraderie with male indie-guitar bands are replaced by a sexism-infused refusal to take female bands seriously. Conversely, argue Gottlieb and Wald, the efforts of the US music press to take Riot Grrrl music seriously has also ultimately had the effect of essentializing the music through a subconscious use of gender-coded discourse:

> . . . rock journalism has had a significant role in molding and disseminating the belief that all-women bands and particular women artists represent a new and noteworthy presence in the rock music scene . . . [However,] although these journalistic treatments may have reflected, and continue to reflect an important reality, they serve an ambivalent function in both defining a new trend and limiting it, and in diminishing the diversity of women's performance and musical styles under a single label . . . [thus] marginalizing it as 'women's music' (Gottlieb and Wald 1994: 253–4).

Such socio-cultural barriers to the progress of female indie-guitar groups exist not only in the commercial and professional spheres of music-making but also manifest themselves at local, grass-roots levels. This is clearly illustrated in a recent UK TV documentary series entitled *The Sound of the Suburbs* in which celebrated indie DJ John Peel embarked on a tour of Britain's 'tower blocks, housing estates, suburbs and small towns . . . in an attempt to unearth [the] social, cultural and economic influences'[9] of locally based musicians in cities and towns as far apart as Oxford, Hull and Glasgow. Peel's interest in and support for indie-guitar and more widely 'alternative' styles of music was clearly reflected in the music featured and local musicians interviewed during the series. While the series provided an important insight into the variety of local indie and alternative scenes around Britain, many of them being located in the worse hit areas of Britain's economic and industrial decline, the fact that the majority of Peel's interviewees were male points to a parallel lack of opportunity for female musicians at the grassroots level. Writing about the general absence of female musicians in local, grassroots music scenes, music researchers have attributed such absence to the structural inequalities that shape gender roles and place particular expectations on men and women. Thus, for example, Bayton (1988) illustrates how aspirant female musicians must often balance their musical ambitions with their roles as child carers and housewives, expectations that are not generally placed upon male musicians. Similarly, in her research on music-making in Liverpool, Cohen (1991) argues that women were systematically excluded from music-making activities by male musicians who were wary of the 'threat' they felt women pose to the unity of a group should they be or become emotionally involved with one of the members.

Thus, as the above examples illustrate, despite indie-guitar's overtly articulated rejection of rock aesthetics, a series of gender-encoded norms galvanized by rock, heavy metal and other commercial mainstream musics, together with structurally imposed restrictions to female involvement in music-making at the grass roots level, contrive to ensure that indie-guitar culture, as with many other rock and pop-based music cultures, remains a primarily male concern. Indeed, there is a sense in which the relative absence of women from indie-guitar culture has resulted in a form of male-centred 'scene-writing' on the part of journalists and other music writers, which inevitably leads to a cycle of exclusion, even as more female indie-guitar or alternative groups are now beginning to emerge. Thus, if indie-guitar is founded upon a series of musical, stylistic and performance sensibilities that have sought to redefine the cultural significance of the guitar through a conscious deconstruction of the norms of expertise, technical sophistication and sexualized posturing that pre-figures rock and heavy metal styles, then such reworking and reconstruction of guitar culture have already been defined in countless magazine articles, music press reports, fanzines and so on as a *male* undertaking.

A similar form of scene-writing can be seen in relation to punk's earlier attack against rock during the mid-1970s. Thus despite the presence of female punk musicians such as The Slits and Siouxsie Sioux (see, for example, McRobbie 1980), punk's musical deconstruction of the rock aesthetic is accredited by most writers and observers to male punk bands, notably the Sex Pistols, who are documented as placing themselves in opposition to male rock acts, such as Led Zeppelin and Queen (see, for example, Savage 1992). Clearly then, despite the expressed philosophy of indie-guitar culture that anybody who wants to should be able to 'get up on stage' and that the essence of indie-guitar is to 'plug in and play' without the frills and trappings that accompany 'mainstream' genres of music, such a discourse is built upon a spurious double standard. The expressed 'openness' of indie-guitar culture is in fact grounded in a series of hardened discourses that have been established by male indie-guitar bands, their predominantly male audiences and the male journalists and writers who have effectively 'written' the indie-guitar scene into existence, and constructed its 'history', on male terms.

Conclusion

During the course of this chapter I have examined the role of the electric guitar in shaping and defining the sensibilities of UK indie-guitar culture. I have illustrated how the roots of indie-guitar in the DIY ethic of punk and the back to basics approach of the UK pub rock scene served as a cultural blueprint for indie-guitar's anti-rock ethos, an aspect of the indie-guitar style that has remained ingrained in its cultural discourse even as the production and marketing of indie-guitar music has been largely incorporated into the mainstream music industry. Turning to issues of instrument and equipment choice among indie-guitar players, I have suggested that such consumption choices are transformed by indie-guitar players into cultural statements regarding the virtue of indie-guitar's musical and visual simplicity, the latter being re-articulated through the techniques of style employed in indie-guitar that reflexively deconstruct the more technically accomplished and exhibitionist guitar styles featured in other genres of pop and rock. The anti-rock sensibilities of indie-guitar, I have argued, also inform the on-stage posturing of indie-guitar players who self-consciously reject the blatantly machoistic guitar posing common in rock and heavy metal. However, while this form of rock rejectionism may function at the level of the symbolic, the point remains that masculinized discourses of maverick individualism, innovation and 'in your face' creative defiance continue to circumscribe the culture of indie-guitar, thus excluding women musicians. Such discourses combine with structured gender inequalities encountered at the local, grassroots level, which act as further barriers to the entry of women into the indie-guitar scene.

Notes

1. In the US the term 'alternative' is used in a broadly similar fashion to indie-guitar as a means of describing guitar-based music deemed by musicians and fans to be non-mainstream (see Santiago-Lucerna 1998).
2. Quoted from the BBC TV series *Dancing in the Street*, broadcast in July 1995.
3. Quoted from the BBC TV series *Dancing in the Street*, broadcast in July 1995.
4. A similar emphasis upon the authenticity of the non-technical can be seen during the folk revival movement of the early 1960s (see Narváez's chapter in this book).
5. A GP-16 was a signal processing device used by many electric guitarists during the 1980s.
6. For a similar analysis of the significance of guitar and related equipment in rock and heavy metal, see Waksman's chapter in this book.
7. Quoted from the BBC Arena special *Punk and the Pistols*, broadcast in October 1994.
8. If indie-guitar is male centred it is also a predominantly white genre. This has also led to criticism, not least because of the stylistic overlap between elements

of indie-guitar with the Britpop movement of the mid-1990s. The latter's use of Union Jack imagery in a discourse of 'Englishness' from which ethnic minorities were seemingly excluded, led a number of observers to equate the musical and stylistic aesthetics of Britpop guitar bands with an inherently racist 'little Englandism' (see, for example, Cloonan 1995; Sutherland and Batey 1997).

9. Quoted from the Channel 4 TV series *The Sound of the Suburbs*, presented by John Peel. Broadcast in August 1999.

References

Bacon, T. (1991), *The Ultimate Guitar Book*, London: Dorling Kindersley.

Bannister, M. (1999), *Positively George Street: A personal history of Sneaky Feelings and the Dunedin Sound*, Auckland: Reed Publishing.

Bayton, M. (1988), 'How Women Become Rock Musicians', in S. Frith and A. Goodwin (eds) (1990), *On Record: Rock, pop and the written word*, London: Routledge.

Burnett, R. (1995), *The Global Jukebox: The international music industry*, London: Routledge.

Cagle, V.M. (1995), *Reconstructing Pop/Subculture: Art, rock and Andy Warhol*, London: Sage.

Chambers, I. (1985), *Urban Rhythms: Pop music and popular culture*, London: Macmillan.

Chaney, D. (1996), *Lifestyles*, London: Routledge.

Cloonan, Martin (1995), '"What Do *They* Know of England?": Englishness and popular music in the mid-1990s', conference paper presented at Music on Show: Issues of Performance – International Conference of the International Association for the Study of Popular Music (IASPM), University of Strathclyde, Glasgow, UK.

Cohen, S. (1991), *Rock Culture in Liverpool: Popular music in the making*, Oxford: Clarendon Press.

Cooper, M. (1987), 'Petulent', in *Q Magazine*, February: 9–10.

Denisoff, R.S. and Romanowski, W.D. (1991), *Risky Business: Rock in film*, New Jersey: Transaction.

Du Noyer, P. (1987), 'Bound for Glory', in *Q Magazine*, March: 26–31.

Fonarow, W. (1995), 'The Spatial Organization of the Indie-guitar Music Gig' in K. Gelder and S. Thornton (eds) (1997), *The Subcultures Reader*, London: Routledge.

Friedlander, P. (1996), *Rock and Roll: A social history*, Boulder CO: Westview.

Frith, S. (1988), *Music for Pleasure: Essays in the sociology of pop*, Oxford: Polity Press.

Frith, S. and McRobbie, A. (1978), 'Rock and Sexuality', in S. Frith and A. Goodwin (eds) (1990), *On Record: Rock, pop and the written word*, Routledge, London.

Frith, S. and Street, J. (1992), 'Rock Against Racism and Red Wedge: From music to politics, from politics to music', in R. Garofalo (ed.), *Rockin' the Boat: Mass music and mass movements*, Boston MA: Southend Press.

Gill, A. (1992), 'About Bloody Time', in *Q Magazine*, January: 40–1.

Gottlieb, J. and Wald, G. (1994), 'Smells Like Teen Spirit: Riot Grrrls, revolution and women in independent rock', in A. Ross and T. Rose (eds), *Microphone Fiends: Youth music and youth culture*, London: Routledge.

Hebdige, D. (1979), *Subculture: The meaning of style*, London: Routledge.

Hoskyns, B. (1999), 'Olivia Tremour Control', in *Mojo*, April: 26–7.

Laing, D. (1985), *One Chord Wonders: Power and meaning in punk rock*, Milton Keynes: Open University Press.

Logan, N. and Woffinden, B. (eds) (1976), *The NME Book of Rock 2*, London: Wyndham.

Lull, J. (1992), 'Popular Music and Communication: An introduction' in J. Lull (ed.), *Popular Music and Communication*, 2nd edn, London: Sage.

McRobbie, A. (1980), 'Settling Accounts with Subcultures: A feminist critique', in S. Frith and A. Goodwin (eds) (1990), *On Record: Rock, pop and the written word*, London: Routledge.

MacDonald, D. (1953), 'A Theory of Mass Culture', in B. Rosenberg and D. White (eds) (1957), *Mass Culture: The popular arts in America*, Glencoe, Illinois: The Free Press.

Macan, E. (1997), *Rocking the Classics: English progressive rock and the Counterculture*, Oxford: Oxford University Press.

Martin, B. (1998), *Listening to the Future: The time of progressive rock*, Chicago: Open Court.

Mohan, A.B. and Malone, J. (1994), 'Popular Music as a Social Cement: A content analysis of social criticism and alienation in alternative-music song titles', in J. Epstein (ed.), *Adolescents and their Music: If it's too loud, you're too old*, New York: Garland.

Murray, C.S. (1987), 'Pure Essex Voodoo', in *Q Magazine*, August: 16–18.

Negus, K. (1992) *Producing Pop: Culture and conflict in the popular music industry*, Edward Arnold, London.

Palmer, T. (1976), *All You Need is Love: The story of popular music*, London: Futura.

Santiago-Lucerna, J. (1998), '"Frances Farmer Will Have Her Revenge on Seattle:" Pan-capitalism and alternative rock' in J. Epstein (ed.), *Youth Culture: Identity in a postmodern world*, Oxford: Blackwell.

Savage, J. (1992), *England's Dreaming: Sex Pistols and punk rock*, London: Faber & Faber.

Shank, B. (1994), *Dissonant Identities: The rock 'n' roll scene in Austin, Texas*, London: Wesleyan University Press.

Simmons, S. (1999), '"Ugly and Defiant?" Meet "Sweet and Innocent"', in *Mojo*, July: 50–6.

Smith, R. and Maughan, T. (1997), *Youth Culture and the Making of the Post-Fordist Economy: Dance music in contemporary Britain*, Occasional Paper, Department of Social Policy and Social Science, Royal Holloway, University of London.

Street, J. (1993), 'Local Differences?: Popular music and the local state', in *Popular Music*, 12 (1): 43–54.

Strinyer, J. (1992), 'The Smiths: repressed (but remarkably dressed)', in *Popular Music*, 11 (1): 15–26.

Sutherland, S. and Batey, A. (1997), 'Discredit to the Nation?', in *Vox*, June: 60–1.

Walser, R. (1993), *Running With the Devil: Power, gender and madness in heavy metal music*, London: Wesleyan University Press.

Discography

Dump, *A Plea for Tenderness*, Brinkman Records, 1997.

The Smiths, *How Soon is Now* from the album *Meat is Murder*, WEA: 1985; see also *Hatful of Hollow* (compilation album of songs from two BBC Radio 1 sessions), WEA: 1984.

5

Handmade in Spain: The Culture of Guitar Making

Kevin Dawe with *Moira Dawe*

In this chapter we aim to reveal some of the forces converging upon and mechanisms operating within the world of guitar making in Spain. Local discourses of identity and authenticity emerge in the distinctly 'between-worlds' setting of the guitar workshop, this local world made all the more distinctive though a poetics of place and a politics of craftsmanship. In these discourses 'here', rather than 'there', is 'better'; whilst 'better' is 'made by hand' rather than 'made by machine'. This quite specific case of 'the global' being apprehended by 'the local' shows that workshops are not places where guitar makers exist in splendid isolation; rather, their lives and works must be seen as having a dynamic relationship with the outside world and viewed within particular social and cultural settings.

Clearly, within the dimensions of Arjun Appadurai's 'global cultural economy' a set of fluid and overlapping landscapes – ethnoscapes, mediascapes, technoscapes, finanscapes and ideoscapes – converge upon and interact with the guitarscape of the workshop in quite specific and subtle ways.[1] This merging of -scapes comes in many forms, from the rising prices of timber to the fluctuating interest in the classical guitar, from the ways in which global tourism enters into the workshop to the dialogue between small workshop owners and internationally acclaimed guitarists. However, guitar makers also inhabit a world formed out of a unique intersection of material, social and cultural worlds. In this musical *habitus* (this nexus of practices, structures and structuring forces, Bourdieu 1977), these musical artisans function not merely as makers of cultural artifacts, but as agents setting a variety of social practices in motion. Lives and livelihoods are literally built around the guitar and the guitar workshop.

Guitar makers are in a position of power and authority, and are custodians of the knowledge that brings the guitar to life. So we consider guitar making as the basis for the construction of cultural difference in Spain in the manner that we consider other aspects of Spanish guitar culture. We use this material to emphasize the importance of the guitar in Spanish culture as a whole, especially as a site for a range of social and cultural exchanges. For instance, the Córdoba International Guitar Festival epitomizes a convergence of 'the local' and 'the global', the meeting of cultures that this book tries to illustrate and understand. The organizers and participants of the festival present a showcase of world guitar, yet preserve a sense of the intensely local world of the guitar in Andalusia and in their 'guitar city'.

The inclusion of an article on the Spanish guitar, especially guitar makers (*guitarreros*) in Spain, is arguably fundamental to a book such as this. However, we merely provide an introduction to a huge and important subject. Whilst we refer readers to a fairly extensive literature on the history of the Spanish guitar, its players and its composers, as well as the anthropology of *flamenco*, we have yet to find substantial studies of the culture and sociology of the guitar let alone guitar making in Spain.[2] We begin our survey by discussing the multifaceted role of the guitar in Spanish culture.[3]

Guitars and the Nation: the Tarantula's Web

The guitar is entangled in a web of culture that brings the instrument to life. In turn, the guitar becomes socially active, weaving 'like the tarantula' (Lorca 1954 [1922]) an intricate web of its own out of the fabric of Spanish culture. It helps to knit various social worlds together. Clearly, musical instruments are empowered, not only by their sound but also by the written word, verbalizations, visual imagery, gestures and movements imbued with values and ideals that are created and maintained within specific social, cultural, political and economic settings. In Spain, this model of expressive culture could be applied, for example, to *flamenco* shows as much as to the workshops of guitar makers. In these contexts, meaning is, so to speak, embodied, ingrained and absorbed into the woodwork of the guitar and in turn reflected and played out from it. Moreover, like the tarantula, guitar players, makers and enthusiasts are sensitive to the slightest tremor upon the intricate material, social and cultural webs that they weave and within which they are entangled. Strings are pulled and monitored for slack, and web sites (including Internet sites) are maintained.

The guitar is a powerful symbol of Spanish culture internationally. If one is asked to think of something Spanish, does not an impression of the guitar eventually form in one's mind? That is alongside such things as bullfighting and *flamenco* dancing, or other sensationalized images of Spain propagated by tourism, advertising and the media. However, as we have seen elsewhere in this book, images of the guitar, guitarists, and guitar practices are apprehended and intercepted by local cultures, whenever there is a convergence of both local and global forces. In Spain, this local intervention is apparent in the works of great poets and artists like Federico García Lorca (1898–1936) (see, for example, *La Guitarra*)[4] and Pablo Picasso (1881–1973) (see, for example, *Guitar*)[5] as much as it is in the workshops of the great guitar makers or the life of the itinerant guitarist.

Figure 5.1 Paco de Lucia meets All Saints in a record shop window display in Madrid

The modern forms of both the classical and *flamenco* guitar evolved from the mid-nineteenth century in the Spanish workshop of Antonio Torres Jurado (c.1817–92). Don Pohren notes that 'Torres was not only the creator of the modern Spanish guitar, but was also the first constructor to begin successfully differentiating between *flamenco* and classical guitar construction techniques' (Pohren 1990: 201; see also Romanillos 1987). These forms have their origins in a long and dynamic interplay between Spanish musical culture and a confluence of Mediterranean cultures from the Medieval period to the mid-1500s. This interplay between cultures later shifted to a solely European context where, for example, in Italy, France and England, guitar making also became established (see Chase 1959; Grunfeld 1969; Turnbull 1991). However, from around the 1500s 'the Spanish' are said to have 'never wavered in their fidelity to the guitar, which they revered as the king of instruments' (Chase 1959: 53). One naturally considers the possibility that, in comparison with all the other guitar cultures featured in this book, the guitar in Spain is more caught up with 'the soul' of that country than anywhere else in the world. There is a legacy of waxed lyrical writing about the guitar, its music and its players in Spain. These powerful lyrical statements about the guitar pluck the heartstrings of 'the nation' and provide for the potency of the guitar as a symbol in Spanish cultural politics.[6]

Throughout this chapter, we continue to emphasize the fact that the guitar is as much played by artists, writers and politicians in Spain as musicians and luthiers. This is more than a spin-off from the web of guitar culture, as the guitar influences many aspects of the Arts. The guitar is influential across the entire realm of expressive culture in Spain, as a multimedia phenomenon. Examples of this include the interdependency and dynamic interplay of the guitar, voice, dance and percussion within a *flamenco* performance or Lorca's ability to capture the guitar in words 'with a poetry at once musical and painterly in its effects' (Ward 1978: 232). Indeed, Lorca, poet, playwright, artist, and musician, belonged to a long line of polymaths whose work was often centred around, or greatly influenced by, the culture of the guitar and who, in turn, made a significant contribution to the construction of guitar culture. Similarly, Vincente Espinel (1550–1624) was a poet, novelist, composer, guitarist, soldier and priest. He was either responsible for adding a fifth string to the guitar or, at least, for the popularization of this idea. This freed the guitar from the restrictions of a limited strummed repertoire, encouraging greater physical dexterity and notably the refinement of plucking techniques (see Chase 1959: 61–2; Ramirez III 1993: 11–13).[7] According to some authors, this is when the 'Spanish guitar' was born:

> The Italians, French and other nations added 'Spanish' to the name of the guitar. Formerly it had only four strings, but in Madrid Maestro Espinel, a Spaniard, added the *quinta* [fifth string] and from this it derived its perfection. The French, Italians and other nations, imitating ours, also added the *quinta* to the guitar and for this reason called it the Spanish guitar. (Sanz 1674 in Chase 1959: 62)

Many people worldwide have been caught in the web of the Spanish guitar since the time of Espinel. In Spain, besides Lorca, there is the poet Antonio Machado who wrote poems such as *Dice la guitarra* (Says the guitar), poets, critics and *aficionados* of *flamenco* like Felix Grande, and guitar makers such as José Ramirez III, perhaps the most important acoustic guitar maker of the twentieth century. One cannot underestimate the contribution that guitarist Andrés Segovia (1893–1987) made to the establishment of the Spanish classical guitar and its repertoire, or the impact that guitarist Paco de Lucía (b.1947) has made upon the world of *flamenco*. Both these artists have changed the face of the Spanish guitar world, opening up their music to international audiences.[8]

The names of many Spanish art music composers are synonymous with guitar music. These composers have written pieces especially for the guitar or have had their work arranged for it. This group of Spanish composers whose work now forms a large part of the classical guitar repertoire includes Fernando Sor (1780–1839), Francisco Tarrega (1852–1909), Isaac Albeñíz (1860–1909), Enrique Granados (1867–1916), Manuel de Falla (1876–1946), Joaquín Turina (1882–1949) and Joaquín Rodrigo (1901–98). The Second Movement (Adagio) of Rodrigo's Guitar Concerto, the *Concierto de Aranjuez* is one of the most popular art music compositions to come out of the twentieth century. One of the greatest foreign interpreters of Spanish music, Julian Bream, says that the *Concierto* 'is a lasting tribute to Spain, yet it is also an inspired incantation for the instrument that has personified and illuminated so beautifully her musical heritage' (Bream 1985).[9] However, the idea that the guitar is *the* national instrument of Spain is a subject of intense debate, as is the role and work of a great many of its champions (for example, Andrés Segovia[10] and Paco de Lucía).

The cultural politics of *flamenco* has been written about elsewhere (Manuel 1989; Pohren 1993; Mitchell 1994; Washabaugh 1994, 1995, 1996, 1998). These studies have shown how *flamenco* is tied up with the identity politics of 'the nation' and what it is to be 'Andalusian' and 'gypsy' in relation to what it is to be 'Spanish'.[11] Peter Manuel also notes how notions of class are reconfigured in the 'contemporary *flamenco* complex' in relation to Andalusian and gypsy identity (Manuel 1989). The politics of authenticity are played out in the *flamenco* club or *peña* circuit where guitarists, as well as dancers and singers, are seen as 'true to the tradition' or 'purer' than others if they are of gypsy origin (see deWaal Malefyt 1998).

However, the ubiquity of the acoustic guitar in Spain cannot be explained by the *flamenco* phenomenon alone, nor does *flamenco* have the monopoly on debates about authenticity. The Spanish classical guitar has a significant and increasing role in regional musics, including the *laudes españoles* ensemble.[12] The Spanish guitar features little in the regional musical traditions of northern Spain, particularly Galicia, where *gaita* or 'bagpipe' ensembles form the major musical instrumentation. Nevertheless, *flamenco* and *flamenco* guitar are found throughout Spain, even if they are seen as something *quintessentially* Andalusian. Similarly, for some ethnic communities in Spain, particularly the Basques, the guitar is not symbolic of national identity. The guitar has a problematic role in the construction of centre-periphery relations in Spain, adding to the tensions that arise in the construction of 'the nation' from a set of autonomous regions. Figures ideally 'central' to a construction of Spanish musical identity, such as 'national composers', sometimes do not quite fit in with the master plans of the spin doctors and image makers. For example, both Francisco Tarrega and Joaquín Rodrigo were born in peripheral and coastal Valencia and factory-made guitars from Valencia pose something of a threat to the established *centres* of guitar making in Andalusia and 'central' Madrid. Many *flamenco* guitarists in Andulusia play, for example, Conde Hermanos guitars that are made in Madrid rather than Andalusia (and played by high profile non-Spanish guitarists like Al Di Meola), so there are also tensions between these *centres*. However, all 'top' guitars are generally 'handmade' *wherever* they are made. Fernando Sor, perhaps the greatest exponent of the classical guitar during the late eighteenth and early nineteenth century, was from Catalonia – a native of

Barcelona. Ripples such as these merge to create waves in the stream of national consciousness.

Cities, towns and villages actively encourage and incorporate guitar events as part of their national and 'cultural heritage' agendas. They organize *festivals* that seek to reaffirm the position of the guitar, firstly, as a part of that city's cultural and artistic heritage and secondly, Spain's national heritage. Marcos notes that 'the 1991 Guitar Festival of Córdoba has gone a long way to ensuring that the city achieves its goal of becoming the guitar capital of the world' (Marcos 1991: 13). The Córdoba International Guitar Festival (begun by Paco Peña in 1981) is an attempt to bring together professional performers, teachers, composers, students and constructors of the guitar from around the world.[13] The festival is good news for guitar buffs and students, as well as providing yet another opportunity for administrators, politicians and sponsors to make a statement about the role and position of their 'guitar city' in both regional, national, and international settings. The 1998 International Guitar Festival in Córdoba included the internationally acclaimed performer Pepe Romero and the Cuban, Córdoba-based composer-guitarist Leo Brouwer. Whilst at the 1998 festival, we met artist and museum curator Eugenio Chicano from Málaga. Chicano's Picasso-inspired guitar pictures constituted a major exhibition at the festival and attracted the attention of the Romero brothers (Pepe and Celi) and Manolo Sanlucár (the flamenco guitarist and Paco de Lucía's one-time musical sparring partner) among others.

The organizers and participants of the festival present a showcase of guitar playing from around the world, yet preserve a sense of the intensely local guitar world that is Andalusia and the guitar as featured in a variety of media (from stage performance to painting exhibition). Indeed, the striking iconography of the Córdoba guitar festival leaflet cover (see overleaf) reminded us of the power the guitar has to evoke numerous associations in the minds of all those who come across it, if not 'fatally seduce' them (after José Ramirez III). Promoters and advertisers are well aware of this potential, as indeed are guitar makers who not only create the *form* of the guitar but must also survive in an intensely local but internationally driven music market.

Constructing Culture: Guitar Makers and the Global Market

> Everything I do in my shop I do by the old system. I am really old-fashioned. I do it all myself, in the traditional way: the sanding, the varnishing, all by hand. I know a *guitarrero*, a very famous one, who sprays his guitars with commercial varnish, just like you spray a car. I think it is sacrilege to do that to a guitar. (Manuel Reyes, in George 1969: 57)

> At the beginning, my grandfather did not place any labels on these industrial guitars. How was he to put his name on those 'things'? (José Ramirez III 1993: 37)

Figure 5.2 Córdoba guitar festival leaflet cover (1998)

There are also those who affirm that my guitars are machine-made, as if it were possible to do high-quality work other than by hand. Wood is a heterogeneous, unstable and quite rebellious material, and however perfect a machine is, it cannot adapt to the infinite number of variables involved in building a high-quality instrument. Therefore, no mass-produced, machined guitar can achieve the volume and quality of sound achieved by a handmade one. That is like expecting a battalion of the Prussian army to gracefully perform 'Swan Lake'. (José Ramirez III 1993: 8)

The response of guitar makers in Spain to an internationally and technologically driven music market has been mixed. We note here the dramatic and significant level of debate and tension that exists about changes from traditional hand-crafting to modern mass production. Although famous guitar makers such as Manuel Contreras embarked on a quest for 'the perfect guitar' and spent years working to precise formulae in their designs, they preferred to balance the steady demand for *handmade* instruments with low cost and relatively simple mechanisation. They had also to make a living and make the most of a demand for their instruments. Guitars made *by hand*, that is, crafted by a master luthier from start to finish (and not shaped and finished by computer) are still favoured by professional performers and luthiers alike though.

The ebb and flow of demand, and the increased commodification and mass consumption of musical instruments are, of course, not new phenomena. Guitar makers are able to confront these challenges with a honed set of strategies built up over generations. They keep amateur and student models – those that can be made quickly by apprentices and with some machine work – at the front of their shops; the 'better' and more expensive models are kept out the back. As a consequence it can be difficult for amateur guitarists to buy a 'good' guitar (where 'better' and 'good' mean *handmade to the highest standards by master luthiers with significant experience and reputation*). Even professional guitarists find themselves on waiting lists that extend well beyond the life expectancy of some guitar makers. Manuel Reyes of Córdoba is said to have a waiting list that will take decades to complete.

Clearly, the most highly skilled guitar makers are keen to make an instrument less of a 'commodity', 'product' or 'thing' and more a statement of excellence and an embodiment of a life's work; however, they have to make a living and will sell an inferior guitar at a modest price. In many cases a top-of-the-range guitar can be seen as the culmination of several generations of guitar makers' work, descended along a family or master-apprentice-master line (for example, Manuel Contreras was an apprentice with the Ramirez company before setting up his own business). Guitar makers have always been quite secretive about particular aspects of their work, and have found that such secrets are best kept in the family. After all, such secrets may give makers the market edge; they may even tell outright lies about what they do to preserve such secrets. The guitars of different makers can look similar, as there is, after all, one principal design used by guitar makers. However, the identity of a guitar is given away by the unique branding of its headstock, rosette design (the mosaic-like work around the sound hole), and perhaps its colour (for example, the ruddy orange of Esteo, or the green entertained by Manuel Reyes, see David George 1969: 42). Ultimately, the sound of a 'good' guitar and its attendant meanings are rooted in life histories and life experience; it is something that a craftsman has taken pride in making.

Guitar makers in Spain are absolutely obsessive about the wood they use for their guitars, that is, old well-cured wood and spruce with estimable density (*con brisas* – subtle intercalations into the grain that curl about as if driven by the vacillating winds). Spruce was traditionally more desirable for guitar tops despite its longer break-in period than the more easily managed cedar. One guitar maker in Rhonda used to ransack old furniture shops for potential material. The new, manufactured guitars, are made with much less of a concern for the aesthetics of wood to the disappointment of many old *guitarreros*. There is also the debate about the what type of tuning keys should be used on the headstock, the *clavijeros clásicos* (wooden pegs) or factory-made machine heads, the former being lighter but more difficult to construct and then tune, the latter being heavier but less burdensome for the artisan to make and for the guitarist to manipulate. There is also a traditional popular preference for lightweight *flamenco* guitars that may be going by the boards with changes in construction techniques. Important and complicated debates surround the current challenge to traditional methods of construction that is, ultimately, a challenge to the identity and role of the guitar in Spain. In an interview with Manuel Contreras II we talked through some of these issues.

The Quest: Comments from Manuel Contreras II

Although they may differ in personality (Santos was secretive, Borreguero was a profligate, Gonzalez was an entrepreneur), all great *guitarreros* possess, or are possessed by a common trait – perfectionism. The endless quest for the great guitar . . . (George 1969: 53)

Manuel Contreras II studied guitar making with his father, Manuel Contreras I (1926–94) from an early age, the guitar consolidating family and kinship ties and establishing another dynasty of guitar makers. Manuel Contreras II studied law at university and is an amateur guitarist. He is driven, like his father, by a search for excellence in guitar construction and the accommodation of the demands of the many professional guitarists who play his guitars.

We began our interview with Manuel Contreras II by questioning if he thought that there was anything intrinsically 'Spanish' about the guitar. He said that the climate and the humidity of central and southern Spain might affect people and their character as well as their expressions of musicality and sociability through the guitar: 'The surroundings you live in affect your relationship with the instrument; many people come here to study and absorb the identity of this country, to study *flamenco* and classical guitar. The guitar is our main instrument, perhaps the only one that can express our musical identity. No other instrument is able to express Spanish music quite like the guitar.'

Manuel noted that the guitar lends itself to so many different styles and contexts. We discussed the fact that not only is the guitar played in musical traditions worldwide from Africa to Papua New Guinea, but that guitar making is also a worldwide phenomenon with a number of Spanish guitars being made in places as far apart as England and Australia. 'It is a Spanish guitar, but it is not a Spanish guitar', said Manuel: 'These makers have different concepts and different styles of guitar making in different places. It is Spanish guitar, but it is international.'

Most of the guitar makers try to develop their sounds and try new ideas. I asked Manuel the question: when does a guitar become something else? 'There is no limit, guitar players demand that changes are made. The sound of the guitar you have made is never enough to satisfy all performers, it is never loud enough or they want something more.' Players in different countries seem to have different approaches. The Japanese, for example, seem to want conventional guitars made to the Torres design, a design that goes back to the mid-1800s. 'Most of those who buy guitars want us to retain the *form* but build in new features, they sometimes ask the impossible. Guitarists want more and more.' Manuel is always experimenting. 'I have to devise new systems, where the guitar looks the same, but inside, the bracing for example, is quite different. We build guitars with additional resonators either inside the guitar or raised out from the back of the guitar. These provide more tone colour and a less aggressive sound.'

Manuel insisted that the more famous guitar makers, like Contreras, depend to some extent on the patronage of professional guitar players. Spanish classical guitar culture needs figureheads to draw and retain public interest, players of the calibre of Andrés Segovia, Julian Bream and John Williams. It is also vital to nurture and develop symbiotic relationships between players and makers, like the one that existed between Segovia and the guitar maker José Ramirez III. Such relationships have furnished the guitar world with new and innovative designs that help to meet the demands of professional performance (as noted by Steve Waksman elsewhere in this book). In contrast, the *flamenco* guitar has experienced an enormous growth in popularity with artists like Paco de Lucía playing across different styles and genres and with forms of *nuevo flamenco* created by groups like Ketama and Pata Negra. The classical guitar world remains small, its popularity fluctuating. Manuel noted that 'if people see John Williams appear at the BBC, the sales of my guitars increase a lot, even if John Williams is not playing a Contreras guitar on the night!' In the case of both the classical and *flamenco* guitar the sales and marketing operation remains small in comparison to that of the electric guitar. Predominantly electric guitar players such as Steve Vai and Joe Satriani are constantly appearing in music magazines that have a large distribution network and high sales; they also appear on TV, MTV and video endorsing Ibanez or other large guitar companies.

According to Manuel, 'the Spanish classical guitar continues to occupy a special place in musical culture worldwide, but not the one it deserves. There is not enough music for the classical guitar, it is a very demanding instrument to master and it just does not suit everyone. Most people can get something out of an electric guitar.' This point was made abundantly clear by the scene that met us outside in the main shop. A middle-aged man was seated with a bottom-of-the-range Contreras guitar. He struggled to play the opening guitar section to Led Zeppelin's *Stairway to Heaven* as we continued to reflect on the uncertain future of the classical guitar. The global and the local converged in unexpected ways as the Contreras workshop transformed itself into a scene from the film *Wayne's World* (1992) and one imagined generations of master luthiers turning in their graves. The man was not invited to try one of the backroom guitars.

The Great Magician of Sound: a Workshop in Granada

What with the guitar boom of the past twenty-five years, guitar makers have sprouted like mushrooms in a pine forest. What could be more pleasant than to create in the solitude of one's home or small shop and to make a good living at it to boot? (Pohren 1990: 204)

Without poetry, without *flamenco*, without the love for Andalusia, how can a man construct a true *flamenco* guitar? The feeling, the poetry, that is everything. (Manuel Reyes, quoted in George 1969: 47)

The musical infrastructure of a small city like Granada is, of course, extremely complex. There are twenty-four guitar makers listed on the official Granada website, although I have found evidence of up to thirty-one makers. The guitar makers that we interviewed in Granada were located along Cuesta Gomerez, the steep hill leading up to the Alhambra Palace.[14] Their workshops were dotted around a small section of the lower part of the hill, separated by and interspersed with restaurants and tourist shops. There was no question that this was a tourist trap and that the guitar makers based there had recognized this fact a long time ago. One stops for a rest (preparing to walk up the hill or having just come down it), a drink, a look at the souvenir shops or enters the guitar workshops.

To varying degrees, the guitar workshops we visited in Granada were arenas of spectacle and display. Undoubtedly, they were unusual, reflecting the personality and approaches to construction of the maker. The shop part of each establishment was often decorated with memorabilia, from personal photographs to signed portraits of famous guitar players. Here, the animated and sometimes serious discussions, negotiations and banter between the maker, his friends and his customers brought the whole workshop to life, providing a personal narrative that pulled visitors ever deeper into a particular kind of guitar world. [15] The 'wares' were as much the personal memorabilia on show as the racks of guitars and the rows of chisels – his 'tools of the trade'. These were his credentials. The memorabilia connects the maker to the world of the performer and to officialdom, and often to the local network of *artesanos* (craftsmen's guild) and the *Catedra de Flamencología* (Professorate of Flamenco Studies). Furthermore, these and other social relations that have come to be intimately involved in the material practices and rituals of guitar construction showed the workshop to be part of the local musical network of the city and a point in national and international musical networks. It was a social centre as much as a retail outlet.

De-constructing people

Francisco Manuel Díaz or 'Manolo' as he is known, was born in Granada (a *Granadino*) in the late 1940s. A respected guitar maker and performing *flamenco* guitarist he had won many awards for his work in both fields. Although he had travelled widely as a performer and considered himself 'a citizen of the world' he had a deep respect for the people and culture of Andalusia, and Granada in particular. He said that people are friendly in Granada, 'they speak to each other', unlike the

Figure 5.3 Manolo's workshop in Granada

bigger cities where, according to him, there is a lack of human contact. Indeed, in his contact with people it was important for him to be honest and sincere in both his personal and business dealings. A joker and storyteller, he acknowledged that he is 'good with people'. 'You have to be able to translate the spirit of making and constructing to people', he said.

Whilst many people do not want to know the fine details involved in guitar construction, many of Manolo's customers do have an idea of the type of sound they want to get from a guitar. The maker tries to translate his hard-won experiences of what makes a 'good' guitar and what differentiates one from another into layman's terms. Not all of us can tell that a particular grain or thickness in a guitar top will profoundly influence the control that one will have over the sound of a completed, or nearly completed, guitar. The maker may try to carry both process and product in mind; he can see how it all fits together.[16] He also has some idea of what makes a 'good guitar' for a particular individual. This picture is built up from many years experience of assessing customers' playing abilities, idiosyncrasies and personalities, as they visit him in his workshop or speak to him over the telephone. Manolo fits all the pieces together quickly in a mode of construction work that interfaces material-cultural and social-psychological worlds.

Figure 5.4 Manolo at work

A Poetics of Place

In trying to convey the rich tapestry of sounds that one can extract from a guitar, Manolo used powerful imagery drawn from the local surroundings. Like the sooth-ing fountains of the Alhambra Palace and its gardens, the guitar's sonorities are related to a rainbow-like continuum of colours and scents.[17] Aesthetics and wood ecology were combined in an elaborate poetics of the guitar in relation to the envir-onment in which it is found. This poetics, despite its almost mystical inflections, underlined the very real dependency of a guitar's tuning systems, timbre and sonorities upon weather, temperature, humidity and the quality of the timber from which it is made.

Manolo believed that guitars made in Granada lend themselves to personal interpretation and reflection; they are 'perfectly' constructed, like the gardens of the Generalife. In fact, the guitars of Granada and the gardens of the Palace were said to incorporate similar aesthetic and physical qualities. The Alhambra dominates the geographical landscape of the city and the surrounding area, a landmark of historical, social and economic importance. Similarly, the guitar dominates the local musical landscape, in performance, the media and in the iconography of advertising and display. Individuals appreciate the significance of these landmarks and landscapes in different ways, according to their personality and frame of mind. The guitar plays an important role in local people's sense of place, in the construc-tion of a local identity, and in the ways in which a place like Granada is presented to the outside world.

Gender and the Guitar

Guitar making appears to be an engendered occupation; we did not discover any women guitar makers on our travels, although in some of the workshops in Madrid women took care of enquiries and general front-of-shop matters. The subject of gender came up most forcefully in guitar makers' discussion of the *form* and *temperament* of their guitars. Manolo identified the guitar as 'totally feminine' given the shape of the body, with its shoulders, waist, soundhole and bottom, as well as its internal cavities. 'It is almost a woman', he said. This identification of the guitar with the body of a woman is a common notion expressed by guitar makers. This metaphor was developed by José Ramirez III whilst describing his choice of woods for guitar construction:

> I will limit myself to expressing my innermost feelings on the basis of my experience
> with these two types of wood. I regard both the Picea-Falso Abeto (German Spruce) and
> the Thuja Plicata (Red Cedar) as two beautiful sisters – one blonde and the other brunette;
> one European and the other American, although I have to confess that I have a soft spot
> for the brunette, and by this I do not mean to scorn the blonde. (Ramirez III 1993: 17)[18]

After making considerable technical adjustments to his guitars Gerundino Fernandez of Almeria was to note: 'It not only is still more feminine in looks than the traditional guitar, but has resulted in improved volume and tonal quality' (Gerundino, quoted in Pohren 1990: 208). Whilst Manuel Reyes remarked, 'she was a crazy guitar. She used to get very cold, and colder more often than most guitars' (quoted in George 1969: 47). Manolo regarded the guitar as 'a spirited woman', 'something alive', and the whole process of guitar making (in the sensual world of the workshop) as a process of giving life and giving birth – from selecting the wood to polishing the completed guitar. David George notes that Manuel Reyes used the term *dar a luz* (to give light, to give birth) to describe this process (George 1969: 54). The guitar breathes, its wood sensitive to temperature and humidity. So too, the player's senses become attuned to the guitar, he reacts to it. Don Pohren notes:

> A guitarist only has to open his case and smell the sweet dry-wood odour of an old guitar to feel a certain enjoyment. As he strokes the deep strings of a quarter-of-a-century old guitar, the sonorous, age-mellowed sound will give a thrill, a *jondo* sensation, a desire to play and to play well. (Pohren 1962: 73)

Manolo, like other luthiers and *aficionados*, is a poet of the guitar. His poetic language intersects with a long tradition of writings about the guitar by poets such as Lorca, with the language of *flamenco* lyrics and the anecdotes of Don Pohren and with a range of social and engendered practices, such as the banter between the guitar maker and his friends. Indeed, no opportunities for a jibe or a joke are lost in this predominantly masculine world; a world in which the guitar is usually the only 'woman'. The following examples illustrate how the members of this 'brotherhood of the guitar' interact.

Jokes and the Brotherhood of the Guitar

When guitarist Rafael (from Granada) and a *flamenco* singer (*cantaor*) spent a short time in the shop, Manolo enjoyed himself immensely by joking that the swarthy singer was from Costa Rica, perhaps an Amerindian. He was actually from the gypsy caves within the Albaicín quarter of Granada, but Manolo could not resist a good-natured jibe at his friend, pretending to confuse him with a Costa Rican tourist who had visited his shop that morning. The incongruity of the fact that 'locals' as well as 'global' travellers passed through his workshop had not been lost on Manolo and his sometimes black sense of humour. Whilst 'pulling the leg' of his customers, he worked on Rafael's guitar.

This leg-pulling was at its most intense when one of Manolo's best friends came into the shop. He was *flamenco* guitarist José Carlos Zarate. José enters the shop.

Figure 5.5 Manolo and Rafael

Manolo points to him and jests: 'I have no photo of him' (pointing to the photographs in the cabinet) 'He is not my friend.'

José: 'Hey, I have brought the guitar back because it has no sound!'
Manolo: 'What do you expect after 30 years?!'

The guitar needed new strings and adjustments to the nut. Manolo made the necessary adjustments and put new strings on the guitar. He then proceeded to tune it up. José tried the guitar and smiled. He called Manolo, 'el gran majo del sonido' ('the great magician of sound'). In his white coat, Manolo looked like a scientist or medical doctor treating his 'finely tuned' patients rather than a magician. However, even we could hear the difference Manolo's 'magic' had made to the guitar.

The rapid fire exchanges between Manolo and his friends and customers in the shop were more than just a show for us. Manolo liked to quip and tell a story, it was part of his 'fine tuning' (we relaxed and got to know him better) and a means of bringing the material culture of the shop to life. The stories came quick and fast. Whether it is the one about the master *flamenco* guitarist Manolo Sanlucár calling him 'racatripa' (tripe scrapings) or the one where he pondered on the reaction of cats seeing a violinist walking down the street whilst playing a tune upon cat gut strings. These stories and exchanges tended to bounce off the equally colourful walls of the workshop, which were decked out in eye-catching displays of guitar memorabilia. With the photographs that lined the walls of his shop, Manolo tried to create a faithful representation of his past, his achievements, and the people he had met and shared stories with (some of whom are now dead, so consequently particular photographs take on the role of a shrine). These pictures provided a visual counterpoint to the verbal exchanges going on in the shop.

Manolo between Worlds

Manolo continues to run a small one-man business in the tourist zone of Granada. Business is steady. He takes one month to make a guitar, after that there is a need to move on to the next to keep the business and the supply of guitars going. There were only three guitar makers in Granada when he began to make guitars in the 1960s. He joked that, 'there are 30 guitar makers in Granada, but I have been working for more years than the 32'. We think he meant that he had either been working for more years than he cared to remember, and/or there were two guitar makers in Granada who he did not regard as *real* guitar makers.

He said that all the main principles of guitar making were outlined by 1900 and that after this date there was a healthy rise in making, but a major decline in the 1930s due to the Spanish Civil War. In the 1950s guitar making in Granada began to grow again with the general interest in guitar music throughout the world. Nowadays, 90 per cent of those who buy Manolo's guitars, play the guitar purely for leisure. However, he was relieved that locals and not just tourists buy his guitars. This gave him some confidence in the future of guitar making in Granada. He was aware of the growth of guitar making worldwide, in places like Mexico, but did not rate these largely factory made guitars very highly. He thought that there would always be a need for *handmade* guitars, for the long-established traditions of guitar making in places like Granada, and for the personal service he could offer as the

Figure 5.6 Manolo's memorabilia

'great magician of sound'. Manolo did not labour a discourse of authenticity around the guitar as something uniquely Spanish or Andalusian, even if he regarded guitar makers in Madrid as being too commercial. It is clear that he provided us with a very local interpretation of the world of guitar making; a customized *modus operandi* with its own stamp of authenticity. However, for many years, 'the great magician of sound' had been all too aware that his livelihood was tied up with events in the national and even global economy, and at the mercy of world markets (from wood prices to global tourism).

Concluding Remarks

Global forces are increasingly impinging on what used to be or what is imagined to be a distinctly local musical world. Amongst the inhabitants of this guitar world there is a strong sense of a local musical identity that is clearly displayed in the workshops of guitar makers. Guitar makers are proud of a long and rich history of guitar making in Spain and are aware of the ways in which the guitar plays a unique role in the formation of city, regional and even national identities. However, there is also an almost melancholy realization amongst guitar makers that their art and craft is now an international concern with brilliant guitar makers of the Spanish guitar emerging in, for example, New York and Australia. There is also the constant threat of good quality factory-produced guitars being made in Spain and elsewhere. Guitar making as a profession is a highly competitive business. We were told by guitar makers and others that the *Spanish* guitar is something made best in Spain and even better, made by hand in Spain. There is often bitter debate about the move from traditional hand crafting to modern mass production. It is not clear how this will affect the identity and aesthetic value of the guitar in Spain.

The Spanish guitar, its sound, images, players and personalities continue to be woven into the fabric of Spanish life. There is no doubt that the guitar is more important to some people than others, however it is undeniably important in many areas of Spanish social, cultural and artistic life. From Lorca to Picasso, Espinel to Ramirez, Sor to Paco de Lucía, *flamenco* to the Córdoba Festival, the amateur to the professional, the art and times of the guitar form an impressive whole held together by an even more impressive sense of community and an all pervasive sense of place.

In this chapter we have begun to position our research on the Spanish guitar in relation to current cultural theory and recent work on the cultural study of musical instruments, their technology and the relationship between guitar crafts and guitar communities. We have tried to emphasize the importance of the role of instrument makers in the construction of musical culture. Much has been written about the world of the performer and the composer, whereas little attention has been paid to the world of the instrument maker. In an ongoing study of the role of the guitar in Spain, we hope to help to redress this imbalance.

Acknowledgements

We are indebted to the late José Ramirez IV, Manuel Contreras II and Francisco Manuel Diaz for their help and guidance. Thank you to John Flanigan and Sean O'Brien for helpful and informative discussion. Kevin Dawe's research was generously supported by The Open University Arts Faculty Research Committee.

Notes

1. In Arjun Appadurai (1990). See Slobin (1993) for a useful demonstration of how one might apply Appadurai's model to the cultural study of music.

2. Anthropologist David George's *The Flamenco Guitar* (1969) is the notable exception. The book includes a revealing interview with Manuel Reyes, a guitar maker based in Córdoba (see pp. 35–58). See also Romanillos (1987).

3. During the summers of 1995 and 1998 we travelled between the region of Andalusia and the capital Madrid in an attempt to discover more about the Spanish guitar – an acoustic instrument that exists in both 'classical' and *flamenco* forms. *In general*, classical guitars are larger, heavier and have thicker wood and bracing than *flamenco* guitars. They have mechanical tuning keys as opposed to the traditional wooden pegs of the *flamenco* guitar (although these pegs are now rare), have much higher bridges and no tapping plates on their soundboard (the right hand fingers of the *flamenco* guitarist constantly make contact with the top of the soundboard whilst strumming). Many of these factors naturally effect the sound of each instrument. Much has been written about the defining characteristics of each of these forms of the guitar but Pohren (1990) provides a useful and simple summary borrowed from Manuel Contreras.

4. Lorca's poetry provided the inspiration for British composer Reginald Smith Brindle's *El Polifemo de Oro* (The Golden Polyphemus), the title taken from Gongora's poem. Smith Brindle comments: 'Lorca attributes to the guitar occult powers, and returns again and again in his poems to the image of the strings spread out like the arms of Polyphemus, or the "great star" of a tarantula's web, waiting to trap our sighing souls within its "black wooden cistern" (Smith Brindle 1982). The composer also wrote a suite for classical guitar called *Four Poems of García Lorca* (Smith Brindle 1977).

5. 27 April 1927, Paris. Oil and charcoal on canvas, 81 × 81 cm. Picasso used the form of the guitar in many of his works and in different media (including paint-ings, collage and sculpture). I recommend the following books as starting points for studying the role of the guitar in Picasso's artworks: Robson (1991) and Harrison, Frascina and Perry (1993). I have also found Richard Leppert's work extremely helpful when studying music iconography (see Leppert 1989 and 1993). Grunfeld's history of the guitar contains a wealth of visual illustration (Grunfeld 1969). For an interesting discussion of the influence of Picasso's painting *The Old Guitarist* upon the poem *The Man with the Blue Guitar* by American Wallace Stevens and, consequently, upon the music of British com-poser Michael Tippett, see Tippett (1984).

6. Karl Neuenfeldt's skilful study of the *didjeridu* shows its importance in the iconography, symbolism and political economy of Australian Aboriginality (Neuenfeldt: 1997a; 1997b). Neuenfeldt cleverly uses Arjun Appadurai's work

on 'the social life of things' where material objects are described as having social potential and a social life (Appadurai 1986). Indeed, 'a thing' can have a 'career' (that has a particular trajectory or trajectories and a history or histories), which often involves it having a 'mutating role' as a commodity. See also Dawe (2001).

7. In *The Dilemma of Timbre on the Guitar* (1960), Emilio Pujol talks about the different ways in which the nails can be used to pluck the guitar strings to accommodate the extremes of musical styles. In his seminal thesis he says that: 'Each style, however, embodies a distinct mentality: the one spectacular and tending to exteriorise one's personality, and the other intimate and sincere, deeply penetrated by the spirit of the art' (Pujol 1960: 58).

8. Those Spanish guitarists that look destined to follow in the footsteps of Paco de Lucía include such notable young performers of *flamenco* as Gerardo Nuñez (b.1961) and Vincente Amigo (b.1967). These guitarists are building upon a rich legacy of guitar playing that stretches back from Paco de Lucía and Manolo Sanlucár (1943) to the first half of the twentieth century with Sabicas (1912–90) and Ramón Montoya (1880–1949) (to name but two) and further back to guitarists of the nineteenth century. See Mederos (1996) for an overview of developments in *flamenco*.

9. For reliable accounts of the history and development of the Spanish guitar and its music see Chase (1959), Baines (1961), Grunfeld (1974), Sadie (1980), Summerfield (1982)[1996], Turnbull (1991) and Ramirez (1993).

10. Segovia's life works are championed by Wade and Garno (1997). However, his technical ability as a performer, teacher and editor of a repertoire for the guitar is criticized by John Williams in Smith (1999).

11. John Hooper's *The Spaniards* is a useful account of the development of 'New Spain' after Franco's death (Hooper 1986).

12. This is the 'Spanish lute' ensemble comprising of a *bandurria*, guitar and *laude*. See the excellent book on this subject by Juan Jose Rey and Antonio Navarro (1993).

13. See MacFarlane and Marcos for reports on the Cordoba Festival in 1989 and 1991, respectively.

14. These were Casa Ferrer, Antonio Morales, José Lopez Bellido and Francisco Manuel Díaz.

15. This is quite unlike the world of Attilio, the Sardinian instrument maker interviewed by Lortat-Jacob. Attilio's workshop 'without being a completely secret place, had a more private character . . . Literally embracing nature, turning its back on social places and spaces for display, it confined Attilio in an industrious solitude' (Lortat-Jacob 1995: 43).

16. In one of his articles on guitar making in *Classical Guitar*, Trevor Semple notes: 'There is so much room to drift the sound of an instrument in any

particular direction. The important thing is to have a really clear concept of what you are aiming for, and the courage to develop bold and sometimes unorthodox ways of coaxing a particular sound from a sometimes stubborn piece of wood. All down the line you are forced to make highly subjective judgements about this desirable sound you carry round in your head' (Semple 1990: 25).

17. In his poem, *La Guitarra*, Lorca says that the guitar 'weeps for distant things. Hot southern sands, yearning for camelias' (1922).

18. Shirley L. Arora notes that 'Hispanic proverbs, riddles and folk verse offer numerous examples of metaphor in which a woman is compared – implicitly or explicitly – to a guitar or vice versa' (Arora 1995: 1). Arora draws on a large number of examples to support her thesis. I include one example here: *A quien tiene escopeta, guitarra, reloj o mujer, nunca le falta un traste que componer* ('he who has a shotgun, a guitar, a watch or a woman will never lack for something to fix') in Jara Ortega 1953: 105). See also *Receta para construir una guitarra* ('Recipe for constructing a guitar') by Luis Lopez Anglada, 1984, (in Leal Pinar 1989: 31–2). I also recommend classic studies on the subject of gender and sexuality in Spain by David Gilmore and Stanley Brandes.

References

Appadurai, A. (ed.) (1986), *The Social Life of Things: Commodities in cultural perspective*, Cambridge: Cambridge University Press.

—— (1990), 'Disjuncture and Difference in the Global Cultural Economy', *Public Culture*, 2 (2): 1–24.

Arora, S. L. (1995), 'A Woman and a Guitar: Variations on a folk metaphor', *Proverbium* 10, 21–36 (also in *De proverbio: An Electronic Journal of International Proverb Studies*, 1 (2), 1995, http://info.utas.edu.au/docs/flonta).

Baines, A. (1961/1966), *Musical Instruments Through the Ages*, Harmondsworth: Penguin.

Bourdieu, P. (1977), *Outline of a Theory of Practice*, Cambridge: Cambridge University Press.

Brandes, S. (1980), *Metaphors of Masculinity: Sex and status in Andalusian folklore*, Philadelphia: University of Pennsylvania Press.

Bream, J. (1985), Liner Notes to *Guitarra. The Guitar in Spain*. Two cassettes, RCA Records RK85417(2).

Chase, G. (1941) [1959], *The Music of Spain*, New York: Dover Publications Inc.

Clinton, G. (1989), 'Escuela Granadina de Luthiers' (Granada School of Guitar Making), *Guitar International* (series of articles from July 1989).

Dawe, K. (2001), 'People, Objects, Meaning: Recent work on the study and collection of musical instruments', *The Galpin Society Journal* 54: 219–232.

deWaal Malefyt, T. (1998), 'Gendering the Authentic in Spanish *Flamenco*', in Washabaugh (ed.) *The Passion of Music and Dance: Body, gender and sexuality*, Berg: Oxford and New York.

Garcia Lorca, F. (1922), 'La guitarra' from *Cante Jondo* in Leal Pinar (1989: 29).

—— (1954) [1922] 'Las Seis Cuerdas' from *Obras Completas* in Smith-Brindle (1982) and taken from *Die Dichtung vom Cante Jondo*, Insel Verlag, Frankfurt am Main (1967).

George, D. (1969), *The Flamenco Guitar. From its birth in the hands of the* guitarrero *to its ultimate celebration in the hands of the flamenco guitarist*, Madrid: Society of Spanish Studies.

Gilmore, D. (1982), 'Anthropology of the Mediterranean Area', *Annual Review of Anthropology* 11: 175–205.

—— (1990), *Manhood in the Making: Cultural concepts of masculinity*, Yale University Press.

Grunfeld, F.V. (1969) [1974], *The Art and Times of the Guitar: An illustrated history of guitars and guitarists*, London: Collier Macmillan Publishers.

Harrison, C., F. Frascina and G. Perry (1993), *Primitivism, Cubism, Abstraction*, New Haven and London: Yale University Press in association with the Open University.

Hooper, J. (1986), *The Spaniards: A portrait of the new Spain*, Harmondsworth: Penguin.

Jara Ortega, J. (1953), *Mas de 2.500 Refranes Relativos a la Mujer: Soltera, casada, viuda y suegra*. Madrid: Instituto Editorial Reus.

Leal Pinar, L.F. (1989), *Retazos de Guitarra*, Madrid: Editorial Alpuerto, SA.

Leppert, R. (1989), *Music and Image: Domesticity, ideology and socio-cultural formation in Eighteenth-Century England*, Cambridge: Cambridge University Press.

—— (1993), *The Sight of Sound: Music, representation, and the history of the body*, University of California Press.

Lortat-Jacob, B. (1995), *Sardinian Chronicles*, Chicago: University of Chicago Press.

MacFarlane, J. (1989), 'International Festival of the Guitar – Córdoba', *Classical Guitar*, (December): 20–2.

Manuel, P. (1989), 'Andalusian, Gypsy, and Class Identity in the Contemporary Flamenco Complex', *Ethnomusicology*, 33 (1): 47–65.

Marcos (1991), 'Cuaderno *Flamenco*: The 1991 *Flamenco* annual and a new *flamenco* bulletin from the *Flamenco* Foundation in Jerez', *Guitar International*, (October): 13.

Mitchell, T. (1994), *Flamenco Deep Song*, New Haven: Yale University Press.

Mederos, A. (1996), *El Flamenco*, (No. 37 in the Flash Series), Madrid: Acento Editorial.

Neuenfeldt, K. (ed.) (1997a), *The Didjeridu: From Arnhem Land to Internet*, John Libbey and Company Pty Ltd/Perfect Beat Publications.

—— (1997b), 'The Didjeridu in the Desert: The social relations of an ethnographic object entangled in culture and commerce', in K. Neuenfeldt (ed.), *The Didjeridu: From Arnhem Land to Internet.*

Pohren, D.E. (1962/1990), *The Art of Flamenco*, Madrid: Society of Spanish Studies.

—— (1992), *Paco de Lucia and Family: The master plan*, Madrid: Society of Spanish Studies.

Pujol, E. (1960), *El Dilemma del Sonido en la Guitarra* (The Dilemma of Timbre on the Guitar), Buenos Aires: Ricordi.

Ramirez III, J. (1993), *Things About the Guitar*, Madrid: Soneto Ediciones Musicales.

Rey, J.J. and A. Navarro (1993), *Los Instrumentos de Pua en Espana*, Madrid: Alianza Editorial, S.A.

Robson, I. (ed.), (1991), *Picasso Museum, Paris: The masterpieces*, Munich: Prestel-Verlag.

Romanillos, J. (1987), *Antonio de Torres, Guitar Maker,* London: Element Books.

Sadie, S. (ed.) (1980), *The New Grove Dictionary of Music and Musicians*, London: Macmillan Publishers Ltd.

Semple, T. (1990), 'The Craft of the Guitar Maker: 3. Soundboard materials', *Classical Guitar*, (October): 24–5.

Slobin, M. (1993) *Subcultural Sounds. Micromusics of the West*, Hanover and London: Wesleyan University Press.

Smith, M. (1999), 'Return of the Native', an Interview with John Williams (guitarist) in *BBC Music Magazine*, (May): 26–9.

Smith Brindle, R. (1977), *Four Poems of García Lorca*, (guitar score), London: Schott and Co. Ltd.

—— (1982), Notes to the Guitar Score of *El Polifemo de Oro*, (1956, revised 1981), London: Schott & Co. Ltd.

Summerfield, M.J. (1982) [1996], *The Classical Guitar: Its Evolution, Players and Personalities since 1800*, Milwaukee: Hal Leonard Publishing Corporation.

Tippett, M. (1984), Notes to the Guitar Score of *The Blue Guitar*, London: Schott & Co. Ltd.

Turnbull, H. (1974) [1991], *The Guitar: From the Renaissance to the present day*, Westport, Conneticut: The Bold Strummer Ltd.

Wade, G. and G. Garno (1997), *A New Look at Segovia. His Life, His Music*, New York: Mel Bay Publications (2 volumes).

Ward, P. (1978), *The Oxford Companion to Spanish Literature*, Oxford: Oxford University Press.

Washabaugh, W. (1994), 'The Flamenco Body', in *Popular Music*, 13(1): 75–90.

—— (1995), 'Essay Review' in *Popular Music*, 14(3): 365–71.

—— (1996), *Flamenco: Passion, politics and popular culture*, Oxford and New York: Berg.

—— (ed:) (1998), *The Passion of Music and Dance: Body, gender and sexuality*, Oxford and New York: Berg.

6

The Guitar as Artifact and Icon: Identity Formation in the Babyboom Generation[1]

John Ryan and *Richard A. Peterson*

> *Oh guitar which I had in my youth*
> *Sing that I might forget my grief*
> *Remind me of the winds of bygone days*
> *When art and music were always with us . . .*

(From the poem, *My Guitar* by Rabah Seffal 1998: 294.)

> *For me, I think the only danger is being too much in love with guitar playing.*
> *The music is the most important thing, and the guitar is only the instrument.*

(Jerry Garcia, quoted in Sudo 1998: 87.)

Each rising twentieth-century generation of youth has had a characteristic way of relating to popular music. Some times it has been through a new dance form such as the Charleston, the monkey, hip-hop, or rave. Some times it has been through a new electronic medium of communication such as the 78 rpm record, MTV or the Internet. Musical instruments in the hands of professionals have sometimes been emblematic for fans, but only in the era of the rising babyboom generation – roughly those born between 1956 and 1965 – did a considerable proportion of male teenage youth at least dabble with playing and performing with the instrument of their pop idols.[2] As one of our boomer interviewees put it, 'back then there was no variance in the "play guitar" measure because everybody played guitar (at least boys)'. Why did the electric guitar serve the boomer generation, both female and male, as what Steve Waksman (1999: 4) calls an 'instrument of desire'? Most generations give up their youthful enthusiasms as they mature, so why then have a goodly number of boomers returned to their love of guitars as they have reached their middle years?

Our examination of the place of the guitar in boomer consciousness considers four related topics in turn. First, through an extended life-history case study, we explore the evolving place of the guitar in the life of one boomer. Second, we report the findings of interviews with a number of boomer performers to show the common shared experiences of these members of the boomer generation. Third, we examine statistics, including an analysis of some previously unavailable data, showing the explosion of interest in guitars in the 1960s and 1970s and the transformation of this market since that time. Finally, we explore the electric guitar as a continuing icon of identity for boomers.

Extended Interview

We begin our exploration of the instrument's unique place in the babyboom generation's psyche with extensive excerpts from an interview with an aspiring professional guitarist who, by degrees, put his musical ambitions aside to become a professional academic, a person who, in his mid-years reconnected with his first love and now finds himself with eight guitars plus several more he believes are not worth mentioning.

The First Guitar

I was born in 1949 and I got my first guitar for Christmas in 1958 or 1959. I asked for it after seeing Rick Nelson sing on the Ozzie and Harriet show. Something about Rick on stage, his bobby-socked female fans swaying gently to the music from the front of the stage was appealing even then. And, don't let anyone tell you different, Rick Nelson was a *great* rock n roll singer. My guitar was a Western-style, steel-string acoustic with a brandy-and-black sunburst finish. I don't remember it having a brand name. I think it was made of plywood, I know it was virtually unplayable, but to be honest I don't think I tried very hard. For some reason I liked the idea of playing the guitar more than the effort it required. If I had taken it seriously I'd probably be pretty good by now. The only record of this guitar is a photo of my father on Christmas morning, dressed in his new smoking jacket, the guitar strapped around his neck. He's strumming with a silly look on his face. I think he's pretending to be Elvis. Funny to think that I'm older now than he was then. That guitar eventually disappeared. I don't know where it went, and I don't remember ever missing it until now.

Beatlemania

In 1963 the Beatles invaded America and I was in the ninth grade. Something about the response of their female fans was intriguing. My response, and that of many of my peers, was immediate – we needed to form a group of our own.

My friend Freddy Lindenberg and I formed the group. First we needed to buy instruments – an electric guitar for me, an electric bass for him – we were undaunted by the fact that neither of us could play. I talked my father into taking me downtown to one of the few music stores that carried guitars. He bought me a little white 1959 Danelectro 'Dano Convertible' single pickup, semi-hollow body guitar for about $50 and a cheap Kent amplifier for another $25. Still, it was a great guitar, and I lucked into it because of the expertise of the music store owner and my father's generosity. Of course I don't own it anymore, but, if you've got it, please send it back.

My little white guitar is now a classic. Today it fetches $450 to $550, and just recently a whole series of Danelectro reissues have hit the market. Here's an advertisement for the reissue:

> The popular convertible is now back on the street. One of the most in-demand Danelectros of its day, now reissued and ready to roll (and rock). Unplugged it has a resonant tone with excellent projection. Electrified it puts out the 'signature' Danelectro sound with an acoustic vibe. Fasten your seat belt and take it for a ride.

Recalling this has spurred me on to buy one of these reissues. They list for only $299, and I can probably buy one for $125 to $150.

Freddy and I added two other guys to the group. The drummer was the little brother of Freddy's girlfriend, I don't remember who the other guitar player was – I do remember that both of these guys could play some. However, it turned out that I was the only one who could sort of carry a tune, so I was the lead singer. We each tried to stand like one of the Beatles. I stood stage left and bow-legged like John, which seemed logical at the time. We combed our hair down and bought collarless jackets. None of this sat well with the Brothers of the Holy Cross at my High School.

The 'Gad Zeuks!' debuted in 1965 at Paula Chambers' fourteenth birthday party in the basement of her parent's home. I think Freddy got us the gig. We 'knew' three songs: the Rolling Stones' 'Get off my Cloud', and 'As Tears Go By' and the Beatles 'You've got to Hide Your Love Away'. We had no PA system; I sang through a mike plugged into my cheap little amp; that was not unusual then. I vaguely remember a look of confusion and horror spreading over the girls' faces as we began to play. I think the reception was decidedly cool. This was not to be the Beatles at the Cavern or even Rick Nelson playing at the frat house. I remember one guy accusing me of not really knowing the words to *Get Off My Cloud*. He was, of course, right. I didn't know the chords either.

The Gad Zeuks! made their second and final performance on the stage of the St Charles Borromeo Grammar School auditorium at a Brownie Troop Christmas party. We played our three songs and, though we were hardly any better, the eight, nine, and ten-year-old girls went crazy. I remember that several asked for my autograph after the show. I imagine them pulling this scrap of paper out of a desk drawer today and wondering . . .

The Folk Period

By late 1965 I had discovered Bob Dylan. Some kid had a copy of *Subterranean Homesick Blues* in study hall and something about that cover said I had to have it. I can't say I enjoyed the album at the time, but somehow I knew it was important. I quickly bought up the rest of the Dylan catalogue, plus those of Donovan and Joan Baez. I started writing songs about then, liberated somehow by my imitation Dylan style and working around the four chords I had learned (C, F, G, Am). At some point I saw a notice in the paper that the YMCA was sponsoring a national song-writing contest. Using my four chords I penned a new song, *The Time Has Come* inspired by a biblical proverb and an editorial I read in the paper. Here's a snippet:

> The time has come, the harvests are in
> Man has reaped what he has sown

Some time later I was notified on the phone by a YMCA representative that I had won the contest. This meant that, not only would my song be published in a YMCA campfire song book, but I also would be the headline act at a YMCA-sponsored hootenanny (sort of concert and sing-along wrapped up together). The latter did not strike me as particularly good news. Not only did I not have an act – this really was the only song I knew – but I only had my little Danelectro hollow-body electric guitar, not suitable for the genre.

As form follows function it was time to ask my father if I could trade in the electric for an acoustic steel string. The concept of keeping one when buying another was totally foreign to me and to everyone I knew at the time. That fact is a key ingredient in the vintage guitar market today. I knew a girl who could sing and play better than I could and enlisted her to form a duo with me. She had an Epiphone guitar, which seemed nice, so I decided that was what I would get. My father and I went down to the same music store and traded in the Danelectro. In those days Epiphone built high-quality guitars. I picked out of a catalogue the most expensive one we could afford, the Epiphone Texan. It cost $250 with case. While writing this I researched its current value using one of the vintage guitar online websites. Here's what I came up with:

> Current Market: 1965 Epiphone Texan, natural finish, excellent. Very rare! Just like Paul McCartney's. Single parallelogram inlays. Sensational sound! $2,595.

Armed with my new guitar and my new act we played the hootenanny. I really have no memory of how it went – I was too scared to remember. There was an article about me in the paper, with a photo of me sitting on the steps of my High

School, and I remember telling the reporter I planned to be an attorney. For a few months, I received a piece or two of fan mail every day. That freaked me out. It was not from girls but from people with 'problems' who were 'inspired' by the song. There really were some lonely people out there.

The rest of my high school career was spent honing my songwriting skills (later I went on to win the Kentucky Fried Chicken National Songwriting contest two years in a row) and my folk accompaniment skills. However, I only played two other public performances during that period. One was at a pep-rally[3] at my high school for which I was asked by the Brothers to write a song celebrating the exploits of various heroes on our football team, most of whom I couldn't stand to be in the same room with. The second was at a Sisters of Mercy convent during lunch. They had apparently been attracted by the sentiments of my inspirational song. I played it and followed with a searing rendition of Dylan's 'Positively 4th Street'. I think the nuns were horrified. Did I tell you that my singing partner was black? I think that scared them too – I know it scared my mother.

The Sundance Hangmen: College Years Success

I entered West Virginia University in 1967, and I quickly gravitated to a group of SDS radicals even though politics were not my passion, but for several of us, music was. After fantasizing about it for a long while in our sophomore year we decided to form a group. By this time I could play well enough to get by; my friend Frank was an excellent air drummer and Scott was willing to play bass. They each used money intended for books and living expenses to buy their instruments. We found a second guitarist who was actually pretty good and he joined as well. Our first gig was in a coffee house, The Potter's Cellar. My older sister and her husband, both Vista volunteers, drove over from Ohio illegally in a government vehicle that wasn't supposed to leave the state. As camouflage they threw mud over the license plate. They also carried an ounce of a controlled substance cleverly hidden in the wheel cover. I imagine that if they had been caught they'd still be in prison.

Our set consisted primarily of my original material – folk rock heavily influenced by the Byrds and Neil Young – and the music was well received. For some reason we named ourselves *Sundance Hangmen*, changed guitarists several times, and developed a respectable reputation and a local following. For a while I played with a D'Armond pickup attached to the Epiphone, but I felt the need for an electric guitar. I had my eye on a Gretsch Tennessean, the same model played by George Harrison, the problem was that I didn't have the $500 cash. Fortunately a fan of the band came up with a way for me to raise the money by selling produce from his indoor garden. This time I kept my other guitar, the Epiphone.

It was a great feeling to be playing the same guitar as George Harrison, but the instrument itself proved highly temperamental. While tonally rich, its movable bridge and general construction made it difficult to tune and keep in tune (I'm sure it wasn't just me; I've since heard others say the same thing). Looking for an instrument with a crisper sound, I settled on a Fender Telecaster. Since we now were essentially the house band at a local club, and needed a real PA system anyway, we headed back to our favourite music store over the border in Pennsylvania. There I spotted a blue paisley Fender Telecaster. It reminded me of a Telecaster that I had seen George Harrison play. I bargained with the store owner and ended doing an even trade of my almost-new $500 Gretsch for the $300 Fender.

Current Market: 1964 Tennessean, brown, plays & sounds great. $2,195.

Folkie Again

By 1971 John and Yoko were a couple and the Beatles had broken up, each having moved on to solo projects. Sundance Hangman began to break up as well. Other band members wanted to add their songs to the playlist, something I, on artistic grounds, wasn't willing to accept. At the same time one of the other band members began to bring around a girl folksinger who could sing and play pretty well. Shortly thereafter she became my girlfriend and singing partner, and a year later, my first wife. Sundance Hangman faded away. For reasons inexplicable to me now except that I was once again a folk singer, I sold the Paisley Telecaster to a former bandmate for a couple of hundred dollars at the most. Following the fashion of the moment, he sanded off the paisley finish to show the natural wood.

Current Market: 1968 Paisley Telecaster, excellent condition, lightweight, maple neck. $5,500.

I played a lot of music in the years immediately following graduation. After a short stint back in my hometown of Rochester, New York, I returned to West Virginia to hang with friends and get divorced. A former band member, Terry (the guy who introduced me to my first wife) and I formed an acoustic duo, performing songs I had written. We had a good and successful time playing the lively Morgantown folk scene. During graduate school I developed a solo act both in Morgantown and then in Nashville, wrote songs, and tried to get a publishing deal, but not too hard. The Epiphone was the only guitar I wanted or needed during that period.

Withdrawal and Return via Recording

I received my doctorate from Vanderbilt University in 1982. In part due to the rigours of an academic career, in part due to the fading of the dream of making a living in music, perhaps because of the security of family life – who knows why – I played less and less in the next few years.

However, about 1987 or so, I got interested in the new sophisticated home-recording technology. I think this was an outcome of my academic interest in the production of culture and of the effects of changing technology on the music industry. Another factor was encouragement from several friends. My friend Rick Shields had never stopped playing and had an impressive home studio. He encouraged me to set one up. Other friends, Tom and Jeannie Styron were always interested in what I'd been up to. It seems that unless someone else is interested, the enthusiasm just fades away.

I ended up buying a little Tascam four-track cassette deck for about $200. This turned out to be a major stimulus to playing. These were truly multi-track machines – meaning you could record a track, roll it back, add another – say a lead accompaniment to rhythm guitar, add another and so on until you had filled four tracks. 'Bouncing' or combining tracks was also possible – thereby increasing the number of tracks that could be recorded. Never before had such recording power been put in the hands non-professional musicians. Amazingly, these little machines have a recording capacity somewhat equal to that the Beatles used to make the path-breaking Sgt Pepper album.

But the effects were more than technical. In spite of the image of the young Eric Clapton wannabe playing for hours alone in his room, it turns out that playing music when you're young is primarily a *social* experience. There *are* the hours alone, but this is the backstage work necessary for a level of public competence. For me, I had stopped playing because the social context that gave it meaning disappeared as I immersed myself in the demands of my academic career. The home multi-track changed all of that. It was a true creative tool that mirrored, and in some ways surpassed, the exhilarating experience of playing with others (see Ryan and Peterson 1993). No longer were solitary performances simply sent into the air and lost. Now there was a canvas, so to speak, to paint on. Performances could be saved, improved, added to. You didn't have to be in proximity to others to create that stimulating environment. You didn't have to play live in order to amaze your friends. You could just send a tape – at least as long as someone was interested.

The recorder also turned out to be a stimulosus to further guitar purchases. I decided I needed an electric guitar to get the sound I was searching for on the tape. While visiting my parents for the holidays, my wife and I (I had since remarried) visited the legendary music store, The House of Guitars, in Rochester, New York. Seeking something with a lot of punch and on a limited budget, I picked out a Fender Japanese Squire Stratocaster for about $100. I still have it. It plays great.

Current Market: 1980's Squire Fat Strat; Made in Japan; 3 Individual Switches; 1 volume/1 tone; Rare Model; Cost: $295.00.

Home recording became a major hobby for me. Gradually I increased the quality of my equipment. And I was playing regularly – just not in front of other people. In the Epiphone and the Fender I had all the guitar I needed. But there were more to come.

The Vintage Turn

One of my biggest influences has always been the Byrds. I don't think I will ever tire of the first two albums. The Gretsch six-string, played mainly by David Crosby, was the same model (Tennessean) played by George Harrison and the same model that I had purchased in 1969 after seeing *A Hard Day's Night*. Central to my enjoyment, beyond Gene Clark's vocals and songwriting, beyond the beautiful harmonies, is the distinctive sound of the jangly high tones of Roger McGuinn's Rickenbacker electric twelve-string. I was stirred by that sound the first time I heard it and have been ever since.

In 1989 I saw an advertisement for a new Rickenbacker model: the 370-12 RM. This was a limited edition Roger McGuinn signature model. McGuinn helped design the guitar, basically a 370-12 like the one he used to play but with additional on-board electronics to capture the sound of his twelve-string on those original studio recordings. Hand made from the finest materials, only 1,000, were manufactured. They listed for $1,399 each, at the time a lot of money for a new electric guitar. My wife surprised me with one for my fortieth birthday. I've used the guitar some in home recording, but mainly I have been learning Byrd's songs note for note – I'm not sure why but it has nothing to do with recording or making it in the music business. I know it's a thrill to play those songs I've loved so much on an instrument that I've admired for so long. I guess when I play it I *feel* like Roger McGuinn. Oh, if you can find one for sale, it will now cost you about $4,000. I'll never sell mine. Not just because of the associations with McGuinn and the Byrds, although that is important; it's also because it is such a beautiful instrument to look at and hold.

There was one other guitar I always wanted. In 1966 I got interested in a songwriter, Eric Andersen. I remember taking the bus downtown to buy his album *'Bout Changes and Things* after reading a positive review somewhere. On the cover of this album he is holding a great big Gibson J-200, the biggest and fanciest Gibson acoustic guitar ever made (Roy Rogers, Gene Autry, and Elvis, played one too but that was of no importance to me). Emmylou Harris (quoted in Finster 2000: 36) has described the J200 as 'simply a thing of beauty – an American original with its shape and appearance. Nothing else even comes close.'

I thought it was the coolest guitar I'd ever seen – but way out of my price range. About 1994 I felt the need to get one. My practical justification was that I was playing and recording a lot, and I didn't want to wear out the Epiphone. But the other thing was I'd always wanted one and now I could afford it. I can't remember how much I paid for it – maybe \$2,000.

Current Market Quote: \$4,000

I also now own an Eric Clapton Signature Stratocaster. It doesn't mean that much to me; it just seemed like a nice thing to have, plays great and has an excellent sound. Besides, it's just like Clapton's. Oh, and beyond the eight I have noted, I have four more guitars, but they aren't worth mentioning.

I don't play it much now. In fact I play hardly at all. In 1995 my daughter was born. The time for playing (and especially recording) had evaporated. Now it's not just having the time but having it at the right time since not waking the baby became a major priority. The energy has dried up as well, along with most of the desire. When given a choice between playing the guitar or playing with my daughter, she wins every time. Turning fifty also has had an effect. In ones forties, these days, one can still harbour secret fantasies of 'making it' as a musician in some way. No one breaks in in their fifties. So now when I do play its mostly the Rickenbacker and it's mostly impersonating Roger McGuinn, and maybe impersonating a dream.

The Amateur Boomer Guitarist

The case just described, that of the first author, is unique in detail but representative in outline as we will presently show by reviewing the experience of other novice boomer generation guitarists. Our collective portrait of the young boomer guitarist is drawn from three sources. First, it is drawn from a snowball sample of would-be guitarists whose income does not now come primarily from music. Second, it is drawn from years of experience talking with guitarists in Nashville and elsewhere. Finally, the collective portrait is drawn from the quoted early experience of performers who have gone on to being well known.

In the Beginning

Our babyboomer informants report becoming aware of the guitar as part of the process of maturing. For some it came from their parents' involvement with the political folk movement of the 1950s. For more it began by seeing the reaction of girls their own age to Elvis or the Beatles. As one said, 'It was to get girls. I played football, but after I blew out my knee it had to be the guitar.' Suddenly it seemed to most that everyone was playing guitars.

Parents supported some budding musicians by buying or helping to finance the first guitar, but in more instances the family actively resisted the informant's involvement in music. One informant contrasts the encouragement of his estranged grandfather – a honky tonk country music singer who let him play his beautiful big Martin – with the trepidation of his mother – who saw his guitar playing as a possible sign of the bad seed. Interestingly, this is the only explicit mention of an informant's mother. Informants tend to talk about the feelings of their parents, and only male relatives are mentioned positively.[4]

Informants remember their first instrument with fondness or disgust, and radiate joy in talking about finding their first 'real' instrument. Most often this was like the one that their guitar hero was depicted as playing. They also talk about how their first 'real' band was formed and remember vividly their first few public appearances.

Modelling Success

An informant says: 'My friend Robby picked up the Washburn guitar, posed like Elvis, said we could be stars like Ricky Nelson, and we were on our way.' Beside Presley and Nelson, the older informants mention Leadbelly, Chuck Berry, and Buddy Holly. They report how important it was to see their heroes, to see what they wore and most importantly what guitar they used. Unlike older generations of apprentice musicians, this 'seeing' was never live, but took the form of photos, album jackets, movies, and television.

As the following quote from Roger McGuinn, member of the seminal 1960s group the Byrds, shows, those who went on to become very successful also began by modelling the success of others. McGuinn says:

> The Byrds were a folk-based band. (Roger) McGuinn, (David) Crosby and (Michael) Clarke all played 12-string acoustic guitars. (Chris) Hillman was learning on a cheap Japanese bass. Michael didn't have a drum kit, so he learned on a set of cardboard boxes with a tambourine taped to the top. He did have real drum sticks. The first practice recordings they made sounded very primitive. Dickson (their manager) decided to get a loan so that the band could get some real instruments. They all went to see the Beatles' movie 'A Hard Day's Night', and studied the instruments the Beatles were using. With a borrowed $5000 and with the trade-in of McGuinn's banjo and guitar they bought a Rickenbacker 12-string electric guitar, a Gretsch 6-string guitar, a Gibson bass, a set of Ludwig drums and three small Epiphone amplifiers. They also got some black suits with velvet collars just like their heroes the Beatles (McGuinn 1999).

As with many of our interviewees, some members of the band didn't really play their instruments when the group was formed, they bought new instruments by trading in old ones, and the new ones were those played by their heroes who were also the inspiration for their performance outfits.

Like Roger McGuinn and the author of the extended interview, some informants learned what guitar George Harrison played (as well as the extent of female enthusiasm) by seeing the Beatles' movie, *A Hard Day's Night.* Younger informants most often said they modelled their look and their guitars after Neil Young, Keith Richards, Stephen Stills, Jimi Hendrix, and Eric Clapton. Their training films were *Monterey*, the movie of the Monterey Pop Festival featuring Jimi Hendrix, *Woodstock*, and *Gimmie Shelter*, the Rolling Stones tour film that climaxed at the Altamont Festival. While real, the mimicry couldn't be blatant. As one informant notes, 'When I was putting a band together, we were opposed to guitar-heroes, so if someone started playing "Stairway to Heaven," or "Smoke on the Water" Hendrix style, it turned us off.'

Even established artists speak quite explicitly about the relationship between their early heroes and the instruments they chose to play. For example, Joe Perry of Aerosmith (quoted in Melhuish and Hall 1999: 229) describes how he came to play a Les Paul-designed guitar:

> . . . I had a Silvertone guitar, then I had some unknown Italian acoustic guitar that my parents provided me with. Then I got a Guild with F holes and semi-hollow body, then I went to see Jeff Beck play, in about 1968 . . . At that time I was working in a factory, in the foundry, and I can remember, after seeing him play, the next day I was sitting there thinking, 'Man, I just got to get a Les Paul'. So that next weekend I went out and found one. They were re-issuing Gold Tops then and I got one of those. That was it.

And here's Ron Wood of The Rolling Stones (quoted in Melhuish and Hall 1999: 293) talking about one of his favourite guitars:

> I've got this great old 'Cowboy' Gibson. I call it the 'Cowboy' one because it's like the one that Elvis played on in that film where he did, 'I just want to be your Teddy Bear'. He had a single scratch plate, where mine's got a double, but it's exactly the same coloring, the same wood, everything.

Withdrawal and Return

Several of our babyboomer interviewees still play music semi-professionally, but all came to a point in their twenties when they realized that they couldn't make a good living by playing. As one says, 'I knew my limits as a player because I had so many friends who were so much better', and 'I remember watching Keith Scott (now Brian Adams' lead guitarist) just blow away every single one of us'. A goodly number never seriously tried to make a career playing. As one said: 'Of course, I found women weren't moved by a hacker like me the way girls were back in high school when wearing tie dyeds and carrying a guitar was enough.'

Our informants have become successful professionals with a demanding range of family and community responsibilities. Most put their guitars in a back closet or sold them during their most stressed family- and career-building years. Like the first author, however, in recent years, a surprising number, have returned to their teen love. They have brought the guitar out of the closet to be refurbished and have purchased guitars of a quality they could never before afford. These latter, in most cases, are guitars of the sort played by their early idols. Asked why he spent so much money on a guitar, one informant offers: 'It's a (D-28) Martin – what every bluegrass picker yearns to own.' Some buy the re-issue copies but others have purchased originals at upwards of $6,000. A number of our interviewees have also acquired sophisticated equipment to record and multi-track their sound so they can accompany themselves. One said: 'I have an eight-track studio set up at home with all the corresponding electrical gagetry (including a drum machine). This allows me to be a one-man band.'

Though not making music professionally, many of our interviewees along with other boomers have kept something of their aspirations. For example one-time guitar playing boomer, Eric Nicoli, Co-Chairman of Warner-EMI, now plays a vintage Fender guitar. When friends kidded him that he had merged EMI Records with Time-Warner simply to meet Eric Clapton, he responded, 'I don't want to get close to Eric Clapton, . . . I want to *be* Eric Clapton' (Buckingham 2000). Puente (2001) reports on the large number of professional boomers who have acted on the passion to play regularly in their off hours.

Much has been made in the press about the financial speculation in guitars, most recently Eric Clapton's sale at Christie's auction house of 100 guitars that fetched from $14,000 to $450,000 (Wilson 1999; Sexton 1999). However, none of our informants evinced any interest in buying guitars as a speculative investment. One said: 'No. Actually the fact that some of them are worth a lot of money is a kind of frustration to me, since I feel constrained about taking them to gigs, parties, etc.' As importantly, informants do not publicly display their guitars at home or in the office.

Clearly, for our interviewees, having instruments is now largely a private passion. One informant says: 'I play in my bedroom or in my dreams'. Another said she recently bought a replica of the 1957 Danelectro that was made with lipstick tube pick-ups'. She says she 'wanted to have something fun-looking but not too expensive, [and adds] a search for lost youth, I would imagine'. About having a guitar now, another says simply 'my life depends on it'.

A number of our boomer informants now have growing children. Unlike most of their own parents, the informants are delighted with those who take an interest in music, although the delight is tempered a bit in most cases when the music becomes metal or rap. The kids are given instruments, lessons, guitar camp weeks and the like. As Kitman (1998: 17) notes, 'where previous generations of parents encouraged – even pushed – their offspring to go into the medical or legal profession, . . . rock music is no longer seen as a satanic calling; it's an approved career path, with parents footing the bill.' Is there a bit of projected wish fulfilment here? Kitman thinks so. Perhaps, but we didn't probe.

The Guitar Rules

The guitar bug may have lodged more deeply into the psyche of some boomers than others but, as we will show in this section, there was a phenomenal growth in guitar sales in the years of their youth. The piano, trumpet, and saxophone in turn had been the emblematic instruments of popular music in the first half of the last century, but for most of the second half, the prime instrument was the guitar. We cannot find a single pop hit record of the first forty years of the twentieth century that featured a guitarist (Whitburn 1986).[5] In the early years, the piano was used to accompany the voice, the trumpet dominated in the early jazz years, ceding to the saxophone by the 1950s. Only in the blues and in country music was the guitar-playing singer featured during the first half of the century. The best way to show the rise to dominance of the guitar in commercial music is to see, decade by decade, which instruments experienced the greatest sales. It is significant to trace the changes in the kinds of guitars produced and the growth of the trade in vintage guitars.

It is not as easy to document the relative importance of various instruments for amateurs, but trade association data does give suggestive hints. The American Music Conference (AMC 1973) published a set of figures showing the sales of the leading instruments from 1940 to 1972, and we can supplement these with the latest available figures from the National Association of Music Merchants (NAMM 1999).[6] In 1940, a transition year between Great Depression poverty and Second World War prosperity, 190,000 new guitars were sold, more than any other instrument. The only instrument that comes close to these sales figures in 1940 is the piano with sales of 136,332. Pianos, however, represented a much larger consumer outlay, $95 million as compared with $10 million.

It is revealing to trace the increase of new guitar sales from 1940 to 1972, the year when new guitars sold for $91 on average, and babyboomers (then 12 to 26) were arguably the prime market for the inexpensive instruments. Between 1940 and 1959 guitar sales doubled. By 1964 they had doubled again, and by 1970 they had more than doubled yet again. Thus in 1972 more than eight guitars were sold for every one sold in 1940. The 1972 figures also substantiate our observation that a goodly number were cheap imports. The AMC figures show that in 1972, 85 per cent of all fretted instruments sold in the US were imported, but they contributed only 48 per cent of aggregate dollar sales. Of course, by 1972, there had been three decades of national prosperity, and the population had about doubled, so a change was to be expected. The increasing importance of the guitar for American amateur musicians, however, becomes clear when the increase in sales is compared with that of the other instruments. By 1972 piano sales had not doubled the 1940 figures, and the same is true for woodwinds, brass, and accordions. Only non-fretted stringed instruments (violins, violas, cellos, and double bases together) doubled in sales, but they reached a peak sales figure of 80,340 in 1968 and fell back a quarter by 1972.[7]

Guitar sales, too, have not continued to rise in the years since 1972. The US sales of new guitars was 1,154,921 in 1998 (NAMM 1999), somewhat less than half the 1972 figure of 2,669,480 (AMC 1973). Hardly signalling the impending death of the guitar, however, it is important to note that new guitar sales were higher in 1998 than in 1988, and still more than double the sales of all pianos, brass, woodwinds, and drum kits combined (NAMM 1999).[8] Electric guitars accounted for 47 per cent of all new guitars shipped in 1998, that is down from 69 per cent in 1988.

Four-part Guitar Market

The numbers we have quoted are for new guitar sales, but most guitars are sold and resold numerous times, so there is now a lively trade in used instruments. These sales are difficult to enumerate because exchanges are made between individuals, through personal ads, in guitar stores, at pawn shops, and through the Internet. For our purposes, it is convenient to recognize four kinds of guitars.

Most mass-marketed beginner guitars are cheaply made. They are subject to warping and cracking, and many get rough use. These we call 'junk guitars'. Some used guitars, however, were well made and come to be recognized among guitar aficionados for their distinctive sound quality, their physical appearance, and for the famous guitarists who have played them. These are called 'vintage guitars'.[9]

It is also useful to distinguish two kinds of *new* guitars because they have a very different meaning for defining the world of guitar buyers. Most new guitars are priced according to their materials, sound quality, craftsmanship, and perhaps the endorsement of a current star guitarist. An increasing number of new guitars, however, are created as exact copies of renowned models or instruments played earlier by famous guitarists. These we call 'replicas'. Some replicas are made to sell relatively inexpensively, but some receive official endorsements and are made in a 'limited edition'. The John Lennon 'Casino' guitar is a case in point. The following advertisement from Epiphone shows the level of detail possible in creating such replicas:

In November 1997, a team from Epiphone visited 'The Dakota' (home of Lennon's widow, Yoko Ono) in New York to examine John's Casino. During the meticulous examination, countless measurements were taken, body tracings were done, and all components of the guitar were photographed. As a result, and in cooperation with Yoko Ono, Epiphone proudly introduces the Limited Edition John Lennon 'Revolution' and '1965' Casinos. The 'John Lennon 1965 Casino' is a reproduction of the guitar as John originally purchased it with the sunburst finish and stock hardware. The 'John Lennon Revolution Casino' is a reproduction of the 'stripped' guitar featuring one dull coat of lacquer, gold Grover tuners and the pickguard removed.

You can have (a copy of) John Lennon's Casino for $2,000, Stevie Ray Vaughn's Stratocaster for $1,159, or Jimi Hendrix' for just $949. The originals of these three are priceless, and the price difference between originals and replicas without a celebrity draw are considerable as well. For example, a 1950s vintage Fender Strato-caster can cost as much as $40,000 and even more depending on condition – the following advertisement for a vintage Stratocaster is typical:

> *1954 Stratocaster*, tremolo. This very clean early (6-54) example is in exceptionally clean and lacquer check-free 9.5 condition, pre-assembly-line contours and routing, ridiculously rare and perfect first generation Bakelite parts including short skirt knobs, football switchtip and salt 'n' pepper pickup covers, absolutely superb tone and a very clean formfit case . . . $25,000.

A brand new reissue of this guitar can be purchased for less than $500. Here is an advertisement from a popular retailer's catalogue:

> *'50s Stratocaster*. Enjoy a timeless classic. This reissue captures the feel of the Buddy Holly-era Strat. Its deep body contours, characteristic V-neck shape, vintage style hard-ware, classic colors, and aged plastic parts all lend authenticity . . . $489.

Developing the Market for Vintage Guitars

George Gruhn, owner of a vintage guitar store in Nashville, is one of the foremost experts on the subject. In a 1999 article in *Vintage Guitar* magazine (Gruhn 1999) he links vintage guitar sales to generational demographics. The vintage guitar market developed, he says, during the folk music revival of the 1959–64 period. Dedicated folkies recognized that older guitars were reasonably priced and of superior quality compared to the guitars being produced – a time widely recognized as the nadir of American guitar making.

In the late 1970s and all through the early 1980s, the market for vintage instruments was virtually stagnant. Gruhn reports that prices barely kept up with inflation, and he attributes this to economic recession, high interest rates, and also to generational life-cycle factors. He points out that, historically, young people aged 13 to 25 were the primary buyers of musical instruments and that males in this age range were the primary market for guitars new and old. By the late 1970s, babyboomers were moving out of this age range and into work and family obliga-tions. As Gruhn (1999: 12) puts it:

After age 23 to 25, a typical male acquires a wife, children, house, car, and upward mobility in his job. He is likely to come home at night tired. If he decides to relax by playing guitar, as soon as he opens the case, takes the instrument out and strums a few chords, the resulting sound wakes up the kids, which upsets the wife, who makes him put it back in the case.

Gruhn's long experience led him to believe that once people stop playing they would not return to the market in great numbers. However, by the mid 1980s, he noticed a change in his clientele – many individuals in their forties were buying vintage and collectable guitars, driving up prices in the process.

Three Kinds of Vintage Buyers

Guitar 'players' comprise one kind of vintage guitar buyer. Their numbers are relatively few, however. The successful and well-to-do professional musician can afford a vintage guitar, of course, but they are priced out of the market for the vast number of beginning players. Players are most likely to buy vintage instruments that are acoustical. These are made of wood and retain or improve their quality with age.

Even players who can afford one may not buy a vintage electric guitar because the sound reproduction and processing technology is inferior. In the 1950s and 1960s dedicated PA systems were a rarity. Musicians often sang through their guitar amplifiers or, alternatively, through poor quality house systems. Today it is common to run the guitar sound through a bank of special effects units, two amplifiers (for a more stereo sound), through a mixing board, and into a high-quality PA system. There are two consequences of this set up. One has to do with the clarity of modern sound systems. Even the best older electric guitars tend to create considerably more background noise, and this can be problematic when played through relatively quiet sound systems (Gruhn 1999). Conversely, the wealth of signal processing equipment today makes the intrinsic tone of the instrument less important. As Gruhn (1999: 189) writes, 'many modern players spend a few hundred dollars on an instrument that is played through several thousand dollars of outboard gear.' This is even true of acoustic guitars, which today typically have built-in pickups for amplification. In either case, because of background noise or the effects of signal processing, the vintage instrument is not always the most practical choice for the modern player in a performance situation.

The second type of vintage guitar buyer is the 'collector'. These are non-players who buy vintage guitars just to posses them and perhaps also on the speculative chance that they may appreciate in value. Some collectors enjoy a solitary hobby but others regularly attend meetings organized at holiday convention centres. For example, 1500 people from around the world attended the Nashville 1999 meeting of the 'Chet Atkins Appreciation Society' at the Opryland Hotel. According to the *Nashville Tennessean* of July 10, guitars, guitar books, and old records, and other memorabilia were on sale. There was a performance showcase including an appearance by Atkins himself. Collectors are most visible at guitar auctions like the one held at Christie's art auction house in 1999 for one hundred Eric Clapton guitars. Of course, some of the collectors acquiring a guitar at the auction – most notably Michael J. Fox – are players themselves (Wilson 1999: 2). Those who are 'mere trophy hunters' are hated by all who value vintage guitars as musical instruments, because they are seen to be responsible for the astronomical prices paid for the instruments of great guitarists and pop music stars (Roche 1999; Wilson 1999; Sexton 1999). Their effect on high quality but not-famous guitars is less clear.

For the third type of vintage guitar buyer who plays but not professionally and collects but not as a speculative venture, we use the term 'player-collector'. They comprise the large majority of vintage guitar buyers (Gruhn 1999). Sean Roche, owner of Guitars for Stars, a company that acquires and authenticates guitars for artist management companies (1999: 12) agrees. He writes:

> If you want to find out who is scooping up all the vintage instruments, go bang on your neighbor's door. What was a 'musician's habit' has become a 'hacker's' paradise as well-heeled middle-age 'suits' live out their youthful fantasies of being rock-and-roll stars by scooping up vintage instruments.

Alan Greenwood, publisher of *Vintage Guitar* magazine echos this opinion:

> For the most part, people collect guitars they had, or wish they had, during their teen years, when their musical tastes were formed. We figure that most people don't have the bucks for things like old guitars until their late 30s. (Greenwood 1999)

Identifying the Player-Collector

Evidence from guitar enthusiasts suggests that many people now interested in vintage instruments are middle-aged babyboomers. Readership data collected in 1999 by *Vintage Guitar* magazine, and provided to us by the publisher, Alan Greenwood (1999), is instructive. The target reader can be read clearly from the magazine's content. Issues are devoted to articles on particular vintage instruments – their tonal and playability qualities, articles on the care and repair of instruments, interviews with well-known artists about vintage instruments they own and play, and lots of advertising from dealers listing vintage instruments for sale.

Greenwood reports that the average age of the *Vintage Guitar* subscribers is forty-three years of age. Ninety-nine percent of the readers are males. They have been playing an average of 27.3 years – having begun in their teens. Ten per cent of the readers are professional musicians, 41 per cent define themselves as semi-professional, and 49 per cent classify themselves as an 'amateur/hobbyist'. Informants typically own more than one type of guitar, but the readership is skewed toward interest in electric guitars with 93 per cent owning a solidbody electric, 68 per cent owning a hollowbody electric, and 82 per cent owning an acoustic guitar. The data also suggest that readers are active in the vintage guitar market – 47 per cent had purchased at least one vintage or replica instrument in the past twelve months. Greenwood (1999) sees this as a new phenomenon:

> Boomers are very active in the guitar market. At no time in history have so many people in their 30s, 40s, and 50s been buying guitars. In the past, if you were even still playing guitar at that age, you were most likely playing the old one you bought as a teen. At no time has there been so much money floating around either!

Further data on player-collectors are provided by Paul Kotapish, assistant editor of *Acoustic Guitar* magazine. *Acoustic Guitar* is a monthly magazine devoted to amateur acoustic guitar players. More so than in *Vintage Guitar*, the editorial emphasis is on playing. Typically each issue contains a variety of lessons on playing styles, interviews with professionals about their playing techniques, guitar tablature of songs, and advertisements from dealers of primarily new instruments.

In 1999 the magazine conducted a mail survey of a sample of subscribers. Five hundred surveys were distributed and 348 completed for a response rate of 69.6 per cent. The results indicate that the average age of the *Acoustic Guitar* subscriber is 48, or only one year younger than the reader of *Vintage Guitar*. Nearly 95 per cent are male, and almost 87 per cent own their own home. Nearly 70 per cent have at least a Bachelor's degree, and, of those, over 30 per cent have a postgraduate degree. Their average annual household income is $86,450. This is a well-educated, high-income group of males in their forties.

According to the *Acoustic Guitar* data, 65.1 per cent of informants either have performed live in a band or group or plan to, and nearly 51 per cent performed live as a solo act or planned to do so. Another indicator of serious music activity is the fact that over 62 per cent of the informants record their own music. Of those who record their own music, nearly 72 per cent have a personal recording studio. Finally, just like the *Vintage Guitar* readers, the readers of *Acoustic Guitar* magazine are active instrument buyers. At least a third of the informants were planning to buy an instrument in the next year, and consistent with their high socio-economic status, the average amount they were planning to spend on an acoustic guitar was $2,823, and the average amount they planned to spend on an electric guitar was $1,371. Clearly these enthusiasts are serious about their relationship with guitars.

Icon and Identity

No one has made a census of instrument owners in the US, but it seems most likely that, of those people with multiple instruments of one kind, more non-professionals own five or more guitars than own any other musical instrument.[10] It is, however, simplistic to say this is just because there are more guitar players. In this final section of the chapter, we explore the meaning of the guitar particularly to those of the babyboom generation. In the light of the unprecedented success of Elvis Presley and the Beatles, the answer may seem self evident, but back in the big band era of the 1930s not many teens strove to be swing trumpet or saxophone players like their pop idols.[11] What is more, as late as 1954 most of the rhythm and blues-based singers were backed by sax, brass, and piano-based bands. So going back to the mid-1950s, what was it about the guitar that made it so attractive to those who would make the rock revolution, both those who went on to careers in music and those whose fortunes eventually lay elsewhere?

Why did Guitars Become so Popular?

To begin with, the guitar fitted well with the 'do it yourself' ethos of the youth of the day. Relative to other instruments (other than the piano), the guitar is easy to play well enough to pick out a tune, and (unlike the piano) it is portable. The guitar (unlike brass, or reeds) sounds well played solo or in a group, and unlike these instruments one can play a guitar while singing. So the guitar is arguably the most versatile of instruments fitting into many different kinds of music aggregations. In addition, a beginner's guitar was cheap relative to the cost of a beginner's piano, brass or woodwind instrument. Finally, access to these other instruments was primarily through lessons and bands, places where adults' aesthetics ruled. The self-owned guitar became a symbol of generational freedom with folk music over-tones for the young player and his/her audience.

If the guitar is so attractive, why did it take until the 1950s to become widely popular among would-be musicians? Of course this was a period of new-found affluence for young people, but perhaps the most important factor was the coming to prominence of the electrified guitar. There had been experiments with amplified guitars in the mid-1930s, but it was only in 1948 that a solid-body guitar, Leo Fender's Broadcaster (soon redubbed Telecaster), went into production (Bacon and Day 1999). These were first popular among country music and rhythm and blues artists, the solid-body Fenders entering pop music through the fusion of country and rhythm-and-blues called rockabilly. With the unprecedented popularity of Elvis Presley in the mid-1950s the guitar became *the* instrument to play, and with Beatlemania a decade later the guitar *band* became the focus of youthful attention.

Talkin' 'Bout my Generation

In 1955 Bill Haley and the Comets topped the charts for ten weeks with *Rock Around the Clock*, and that same year Chuck Berry's first record, the guitar-driven *Maybellene*, was a top-ten hit and the first crossover rock hit from black to white audiences. In 1956, Elvis' fifth single, *Heartbreak Hotel*, began his domination of the charts, and, by 1957, Buddy Holly had cut *That'll be the Day*, the Everly Brothers had started their long string of hits with *Bye, Bye Love*, and *Wake up Little Suzie*, while Rick Nelson's rhythm and blues-derived tunes were springing up on TV as well as radio. Thus, for all those who wanted to play youth-oriented pop music, the guitar had become what Rebecca McSwain (1995) terms a 'cultural imperative'. As Peterson (1997) has noted for country music, the guitar became the symbol of 'authenticity' in rock music.

When the guitar-based rock became dominant in pop music even the oldest boomers were only twelve, thus it is not surprising that rock 'n' roll had a powerful effect on so many of the babyboomers. Researchers have posited a strong role for media, especially popular music, in adolescent identity formation (see, for example, Frith 1981, Roe 1987, Arnett 1991, Larson 1995). As Roe wrote in 1987:

> More and more studies show that the whole adolescent milieu is penetrated at many levels by an active interest in music; that a great deal of adolescent discourse centers around the language and terminology of rock; and that music provides the core values of numerous adolescent subcultures. (1987: 215)

A significant dynamic in this process is identification with celebrities. Frith describes the particular power of rock 'n' roll to accomplish this identification:

> The young had always had idols – film stars, sportsmen, singers like Frank Sinatra and Johnnie Ray; the novelty of rock 'n' roll was that its performers were the same age as their audience, came from similar backgrounds, had similar interests . . . (1981: 203).

And Todd Gitlin describes it this way:

> Rock announced: Being young means being able to feel rock. Whatever it is you're in, kid, you're not in it alone; you and your crowd are where it's at; spirited or truculent or misunderstood, and anyone who doesn't get it is, well, square (1987: 37).

When in 1965 Pete Townsend sang about 'my generation', he did so with a guitar in hand, and a defining event of the generation was the Woodstock Rock Festival whose enduring symbol is a dove of peace perched on a guitar.

Meaning for Boomer Vintage Guitar Buyers

The guitar may have symbolized the babyboom generation in its youth, but why should those boomers who have grown up to have jobs outside music and have marriages, houses, and children now comprise the bulk of vintage and replica guitar buyers?

George Gruhn (1999: 12) offers a psychological explanation: 'babyboomers had a mid-life crisis when they hit age 40 and bought little red sports cars, tennis and racquetball equipment, and guitars.' He sees affluent babyboomers as spoiled and self-indulgent, able to afford the 'luxury' of a mid-life crisis. If babyboomers want to indulge themselves, and undoubtedly many do, crisis or no crisis, the key question is, why *guitars?* After all, there are lots of things people can spend their money on. The return of middle-aged baby boomers to the guitar, and especially vintage or expensive reproductions, seems to be more than simply acquiring another possession like a little red sports car, an expensive stereo, a make-over face, or an Armani suit. As one of our interviewees put it: 'I never stopped being interested in guitars. It's just that now I can finally afford some quality', and another adds player-collectors 'just like having that Les Paul sitting in the corner. It's beautiful to look at, wonderful to hold, and *means* something that you shouldn't try to simplify too easily.'

Nonetheless, historically this pattern is unusual. Earlier generations typically left behind their youthful enthusiasms as part of 'growing up'. Those born in the 1930s and 40s adored swing and may still respond to Glen Miller records, but few have collected the instruments of their youthful heroes. Some commentators have said that boomers are being childish in collecting the guitars played by the idols of their youth. Cintra Wilson of the online magazine *Salon*, for example, writes about the Christie's auction of Eric Clapton guitar's this way:

> The room at Christie's was packed to bursting with middle-aged rich people full of adolescent pre-concert adrenaline. Most of the buyers seemed to be fat old rock 'n' rollers, gray-haired balding boys with ponytails wearing Hawaiian shirts and prescription sunglasses – Christ, maybe 200 of those (Wilson 1999: 1).

Like a Victorian moralist, Wilson seems to think these men should grow up and 'act their age'. What she saw at Christie's is new, of course; this sale of used guitars would have been unthinkable before the boomers. It is, we suggest, just one small example of shifts taking place in the way cultural taste works. Through the first half of the last century, middle-class people were expected to leave behind their 'childish' teenage popular culture-based enthusiasms and 'mature' into tastes for the what were then called the 'high' or 'fine' arts, including classical music and opera. Such highbrow snobs looked askance at the expressions of what they disparagingly called 'mass culture' (Gans 1974). But the boomers followed Bob Dylan's dictum that the 'times are a'changing' and new standards apply. In the years since popular culture has become valorized. Rather than aesthetic exclusiveness, the moral imperative has become inclusiveness and a postmodernist willingness to mix and match a range of alternatives in all aspects of life, a pattern that has been called omnivorousness (Peterson and Kern 1996). The new orientation has meant that people can valorize ideas and practices of their youth. For many boomers, as we have seen, this means sustaining the fascination with the symbol of their youth, the guitar.

Will the Fascination with the Guitar Continue?

New guitar sales continue to be much higher than for any other instrument and a goodly number of these fall into the hands of young people. George Gruhn (1999) asserts, nonetheless, that young players do not share the enthusiasms of their boomer elders. Today's youth don't turn to vintage guitars the way young boomers did, he says, for four reasons. First, the price of such guitars has become prohibitively high. Second, new guitars are of higher quality than they were in the 1970s when the quality of new guitars deteriorated substantially.

Third, like boomers, when young people buy up, they chose instruments similar to those of *their* generation's guitar heroes. And many performers today have endorsement deals with manufacturers other than Gibson, Fender, Gretsch, or Martin and the other major manufacturers known from the boomers' youth. For example, Richie Sambora of Bon Jovi plays a Kramer guitar, Steve Vai, once of David Lee Roth's band and Whitesnake, plays an Ibanez, Garth Brooks plays a Takamine acoustic, Paul Crook of the heavy metal band Anthrax plays a B.C. Rich guitar, and Randt Rhodes of the same band plays a Jackson guitar.

Fourth, as Gruhn points out, old electric guitars tend to create considerably more background noise, and this can be problematic when playing through the new quieter sound systems. Conversely, the wealth of signal processing equipment today makes the intrinsic tone of the instrument less important, so long as it is clean. In consequence, as noted earlier, many players today spend a few hundred dollars on an instrument that is played through several thousand dollars of outboard gear. In either case, because of background noise or the effects of signal processing, today's amateur player is not likely to hold vintage guitars in the same high esteem as have baby boomers.

Mention of 'outboard gear' brings to mind another reason guitars may hold a lesser place in the affections of the rising generation of amateur musicians as they age. Today a keyboard can be used as well as a fretted instrument to generate 'guitar sounds' and these are routinely manipulated and sampled together in infinitely varied ways to make today's rap, techno, alternative, and house music. It is thus arguable that the emblematic 'instrument' of today is the personal computer, processor, MIDI and the other digital equipment used to generate and manipulate sound (Ryan and Peterson 1993). When the youth of the millennium reach middle age they may well scour used equipment stores and attend swap sales to find the 'antiquated' MIDI instruments, mixing boards, and CD burners of their youth so they can recall their teen years and make music for themselves and their friends in what they identify as the good old authentic way.

The Iconographic Meaning of the Guitar

Essayists have sought the symbolic import of the guitar in Western society. Most have focused on recent decades (Frith 1996; Waxman 1999) but Rebecca McSwain (1995) gives one of the broadest readings. She says: 'The guitar has become a potent 20th-century cultural artifact because the electric instrument preserved the meanings of the ancestral instrument while adding new and important meanings' (1995: 30). In the time of the thirteenth-century troubadours, says McSwain, the guitar symbolized spirituality, sexuality and seductiveness. By the seventeenth century the guitar was associated with secular seductive sensuality and by the early nineteenth century with passion. She also suggests that the guitar was associated with the 'everyman', ranging from gypsies, ethnics, and poets to earls and bourgeois ladies. In the last century, Picasso and other cubist painters used the guitar to symbolize humankind. McSwain cites Wallace Stevens' 1937 poem, *The Man With the Blue Guitar*, as an example of the guitar and the guitarist as symbolizing the struggle of individual craftsmanship against the machine age.

The marriage of the guitar and electricity, McSwain (1995) asserts, added new meanings. In the early twentieth century, electricity was associated with progress and was a metaphor for mental power, sexual attraction, overstimulation and danger. In addition electricity symbolized progress and urbanization–a sense of the cutting edge and the possibilities of the future, and these meanings attached themselves to the electric guitar as well. For McSwain, part of what is unique about the electric guitar is its ability to graft such meanings onto the older tradition of craftsmanship, fine woods, and tradition.

Most interpretations of the meaning of the electric guitar have focussed on it as a phallic symbol (cf. Frith and McRobbie 1978; Butler 1993), but Steve Waksman (1999) provides a much wider interpretation – one that includes issues of race, generation, the power of sound, modes of interaction, creativity, competition, musical quest, and the guitar as a technological object. To a greater extent than other commentators, he suggests the time-bound nature of the electric guitar's potent iconography. Citing Simon Reynolds (1998), he notes that while rock is built around telling a story in words and gestures where the iconic babyboom-generation guitarist, wringing in sweat, is the focus of attention, contemporary techno music, freed of lyrics and the physical act of using instruments to make music, constructs meaning in the sweated bodies of the dancers.

Conclusion

We have shown the place of the electric guitar in the lives of the babyboomer generation from the inside out. First we explored the evolving place of guitars in the life of one member of the generation. Then we showed that this case is not unique by quoting from our interviews with boomer amateur guitarists and citing the published statements of a number of established professional rock guitarists. We then examined the evidence showing the explosive growth of guitar sales in the boomers' formative years and the more recent development of the market for vintage guitars. Finally, we examined the symbolic meaning attributed to the guitar and to guitarists of the boomer generation and noted the recent waning of the symbolic power of the guitar for the younger generation who gravitate to electronic music.

Contemporary pop music may no longer speak to the lives of the boomer generation, but the guitar still figures prominently in the identity of a number of the would-be boomer guitarists we interviewed. One succinctly expressed his generation's continuing identification with the guitar. Asked how often he plays now, he replied:

> Not nearly as often as I would like. Plans to play more, play in public again, and so forth have come and gone with regularity the past few years as professional respons-ibilities have crept into the space opened up by my son's going to college.

Nonetheless, guitars still figure prominently in his life:

> Recently I found on the web the exact same model and style and color Hagstrom hollow-body bass that I played as a band member at University. It wasn't mine, and I could have bought it for $100 but didn't have the money, so it passed out of my life, mourned and gently remembered. Then, in 1999, for $550 I was able to get one just like it – maybe the same one, who knows! [and in answer to the probe – you could have spent your money on other things, why did you buy it?] Because music remains very important to me, I guess because it remains a central element in how I define myself in terms of maintaining continuity between my youth and my current state of mind. Plus, it's a challenge to resuscitate old skills and rewarding to find out they can be revitalized.

Notes

1. Acknowledgments: We wish to thank Karen Campbell, Alan Greenwood, Paul Kotapish, Dan Miller, and Jon Weisberger for the information they provided and to thank Claire Peterson for her editorial assistance. Among those who have shared with us their experience with the guitar we especially want to thank Chet Atkins, Scott Baretta, Andy Bennett, William Bielby, Scott Bills, Harold Bradley, Robert Burnett, Jeff Burroughs, John Corner, Don Cusic, Paul DiMaggio, Terry Fain, Bruce Feiler, Danny Finley, Aidan Foster-Carter, Patricia Francis, David Goodman, John Johns, Dave Laing, James McCobbin, Jan Murdoch, Brian Murphy, Keith Negus, David Pankratz, Ruth Peterson, Keith Roe, Neil Rosenberg, Todd Russell, Rick Shields, Mats Trondman, and Charles Wolfe.

2. In the early years of the twentieth century before the advent of the phonograph, the piano had been widely played by young people.

3. A pep-rally is an attempt, through songs and chants, by fans and cheerleaders to invoke the necessary spirit to spur their team to victory.

4. In contrast, country music artists coming up before the Second World War often talk of being taught the guitar by an older female relative. Back then the macho instrument was the fiddle. In Bill Monroe's family, as in many others, the oldest brother got to play fiddle (Peterson 1997).

5. The guitar was of course central in the blues and in country music by the 1930s when Jimmie Rodgers, Gene Autry, and Roy Rogers gave it greater national visibility. The hit jazz offerings of Django Reinhardt and Charlie Christian came before mid-century but as one soloist among several others, and neither led a group on a charted record (Whitburn 1986).

6. The categories used in the two data sets are the same, and the American Music Conference is an umbrella organization of music industry trade associations including the National Association of Music Merchants. In addition, the NAMM provided both data sets, so we take these two data series on instrument sales to be comparable.

7. 'Drums sold' increased from 9,000 in 1958 to a high of 60,000 in 1966 and fell to 41,856 in 1972. These figures are not included in our discussion because it is notoriously difficult to interpret the meaning of these figures. In practice, 'drums sold' sometimes refers to the sale of a complete drum kit or to one of its numerous components.

8. NAMM reports that 252,360 brass instruments, 382,730 woodwind instruments, 106,759 pianos, and 93,950 drum kits were shipped to US distributors in 1998. Guitar units outnumbered all of these instruments combined (NAMM 1999).

9. Of course, the designation vintage guitar is subjective and doesn't always neatly fit our categories. For example, a 1948 $4 Sears and Roebuch 'Roy Rogers'

guitar in good, if not playable, condition would fetch a hundred times its original cost. The same is true of the otherwise unremarkable first guitars of B.B. King, Chet Atkins, Eric Clapton, or Stevie Ray Vaughan.

10. Amateur musicians who play two other stringed instruments, the bluegrass banjo and mandolin, also tend to have a number of instruments, but there are far fewer players of these instruments than there are guitar players.

11. Why is the Guitar so collectable? Unlike most other instruments where players seek out the one model with which they feel comfortable, there are a wide number of basic types of guitars each of which has its uses for a single player. When a trumpet player comes to a recording session, for example, she/he brings a trumpet. When a guitarist comes to most sessions, the assistant wheels in a portable closet full of instruments and electronic equipment for manipulating the instrument's sound. Likewise most serious amateurs feel the need for a number of instruments in order to play a variety of music styles. One needs an acoustic and an electric to begin with, and the differentiation works out from there as manufacturer, model variant, and other factors are taken into consideration. Stylistic variation also fostered guitar collecting. Along with the other fretted instruments, guitar manufacturers have offered otherwise identical guitars with distinctive woods, decoration, or body colour and they long have made slight stylistic changes year after year. This has created a profusion of variants that are recognized by afficionados. The ads for guitars, as can be seen from those quoted above, standardly identify the musical quality by the manufacturer and model and stress the stylistic features.

References

Acoustic Guitar Magazine (1999), 'Subscriber Profile', San Anselmo CA: Acoustic Guitar.

American Music Conference (AMC) (1973), *Music USA: 1973 Review of the Music Industry and Amateur Music Participation*, Chicago: AMC.

Arnett, J.J. (1991), 'Adolescents and heavy metal music: From the mouths of metalheads', *Youth & Society* 23: 76–98.

Bacon, T. and Day, P. (1999), *The Fender Book: A complete history of Fender electric guitars* (2nd edn), New York: Miller Freedman Books.

Becker, H.S. (1982), *Art Worlds*. Berkeley: University of California Press.

Buckingham, L. (2000), 'Playing God with British Music', *The Guardian*, 29 January: 23.

Butler, J. (1993), 'The Lesbian Phallus and the Morphological Imagery', in *Bodies That Matter: On the discursive limits of sex*, New York: Routledge.

Frith, S. (1981), *Sound Effects: Youth, leisure, and the politics of rock 'n' roll*, New York: Pantheon.

Frith, S. (1996), *Performing Rites: On the value of popular music*, Cambridge: Harvard University Press.

Frith, S. and McRobbie, A. (1978), 'Rock and Sexuality', in S. Frith and A. Goodwin (eds) (1990) *On Record: Rock, pop and the written word*, New York: Pantheon Books.

Gans, H.J. (1974), *Popular Culture and High Culture*, New York: Basic Books.

Gitlin, T. (1987), *The Sixties: Years of hope, days of rage*, New York: Bantam.

Greenwood, A. (1999), Personal communication.

Gruhn, G. (1999), 'Gen X, Gen Y, and the Vintage Guitar' *Vintage Guitar*, (July): 12, 189–90.

Kitman, J.L. (1998), 'Stethoscope or Stratocaster?' *New York Times*, November 14.

Larson, R. (1995), 'Secrets in the Bedroom: Adolescents' private use of media', *Journal of Youth and Adolescence*, 24(5): 535–51.

McGuinn, R. (1999), 'Welcome to the BYRDS FAQ Version 1.4.2.0: Frequently Asked Questions about the music group The Byrds Adapted for the World Wide Web' available:.http://users.aol.com/McGuinn742/ByrdsFAQ.html#inst

McSwain, R. (1995), 'The power of the electric guitar', *Popular Music and Society*, 19(4): 21–40.

Melhuish, M. and Hall, M. (1999), *Wired for Sound: A guitar odyssey*. Kingston, Ontario: Quarry Music Books.

National Association of Music Merchants (NAMM) (1999), Music USA: Statistical Review of the US Music Products Industry, Carlsbad CA: NAMM.

Peterson, R.A. (1997), *Creating Country Music: Fabricating authenticity*, Chicago: University of Chicago Press.

Peterson, R.A. and Kern, R. (1996), 'Changing Highbrow Taste: From snob to omnivore', *American Sociological Review* 61: 900–7.

Puente, M. (2001) 'Boomer rockers reelin' in the years', *USA Today*, June 7.

Reynolds, S. (1998), *Generation Ecstacy: Into the world of techno and rave culture*, Boston: Little Brown.

Roche, S. (1999), 'Where has all the Vintage gone?' Vintage Guitar, November: 12–13.

Roe, K. (1987), 'The School and Music in Adolescent Socialization', in J. Lull (ed.) *Popular Music and Communication*. Beverly Hills: Sage.

Ryan, J. and Peterson, R.A (1993), 'The Electronic Musician: New technologies in the music industry', in M. Cantor and C. Zollars (eds) *Current Research on Occupations and Professions: Creators of culture*, Vol. 8, Greenwich, CT: JAI Press: 173–201.

Seffal, R. (1998), Poem: 'My guitar', *The Literary Review*, 41(2): 294.

Sexton, P. (1999), '100 Clapton axes up for auction'. *Billboard*, (June): 19(1).

Waksman, S. (1999), *Instruments of Desire: The electric guitar and the shaping of musical experience*, Cambridge: Harvard University Press.

Wilson, C. (1999), 'The Emperors New Guitars', June 30. Available: http://www.salonmagazine.com/people/col/cintra/1999/6/30/clapton/index1.html

Whitburn, J. (1990), *Pop Memories 1990–1954*, Menomonee Falls WI: Record Research.

7

Into the Arena: Edward Van Halen and the Cultural Contradictions of the Guitar Hero

Steve Waksman

What Becomes a Hero

In 1984, Van Halen broke through to the top of the pop charts with one of the catchiest singles of the year, *Jump*. An upbeat, tuneful number, the song was seen as a breakthrough for the band on several counts, not least in that it featured the musical leader of the band, guitarist Edward Van Halen, abandoning his usual instrument in favour of the lush-sounding synthesizer chords that defined the song. For Edward, the success of the song was especially sweet, because he had fought with his bandmates – especially then-lead vocalist David Lee Roth – over the inclusion of *Jump* on the band's album, *1984*. At the heart of the conflict was an issue dating back to the band's third album, *Women and Children First*, released in 1980. The lead track, *And the Cradle Will Rock*, sounded like a solid, guitar-heavy, more or less typical Van Halen track, but underneath the flanged and distortion-laden textures of the tune was a secret weapon, a Wurlitzer electric piano that Edward had camouflaged by playing through his Marshall guitar amplifiers. So effectively disguised, the inclusion of the keyboard posed no serious problem with regard to the recorded version of the song. Playing the cut live, though, was a different matter. As Edward recounted in a 1985 interview: 'That was my first encounter with the band not wanting me to play keyboards – when we did the song live, Mike [Anthony, Van Halen's bassist] played it. They didn't want a "guitar hero" playing keyboards, and that kind of ties in with why they didn't want *Jump*' (*Guitar World* 1997: 40). For all his widely admired virtuosity, Edward Van Halen was expected by his bandmates, and perhaps by many of his fans, to adhere to an ethos of rock 'heroism' that tethered him to his principal instrument, the electric guitar.

Though a small episode in the broad course of Edward Van Halen's career, the tension surrounding the guitarist's use of a keyboard in concert and, later, on record testifies to the power that the image of the guitar hero has wielded over the past three decades of hard rock and heavy metal history. Edward's desire to use the keyboard, and his willingness to be seen performing upon it, would have stirred no controversy if he were not widely considered perhaps the pre-eminent electric guitar virtuoso of his time. The techniques that Van Halen has exhibited in his approach to the electric guitar since the release of the first Van Halen album in 1978 have wielded an undeniable influence upon the recent development of rock guitar styles, and have been commented upon at length within the proliferating number of guitar-oriented publications and even within academic scholarship. As Robert Walser noted in his study of heavy metal guitar styles, Van Halen's emergence as guitar hero was a culmination of the process whereby 'the electric guitar acquired the capabilities of the premier virtuosic instruments of the seventeenth and eighteenth centuries: the power and speed of the organ, the flexibility and nuance of the violin' (Walser 1993: 68–9). While Edward Van Halen's musical prowess has drawn considerable scrutiny, however, other aspects of his status as a uniquely visible and influential rock guitar hero have received far less attention. Walser's discussion of the 'potency' embodied in the stance of the guitar virtuoso, and the contestation over musical authority involved in the appropriation of 'classical music' rhetoric by Van Halen and other heavy metal guitarists marked a significant move towards understanding the extra-musical dimensions of rock guitar virtuosity. Nonetheless, much remains to be explained regarding Edward Van Halen's long-standing status as a figure of uncommon power within the world of rock guitar.

Most notably, the model of guitar heroism into which Van Halen has been cast needs to be understood historically, not just as part of a centuries-long development regarding the prominence of virtuosic display, but more narrowly as an outgrowth of changes within the cultural and economic position of rock music that took hold during the 1960s and 1970s. These were the years when the rock music industry forged a new economy of scale, expanding its economic reach in dramatic fashion. Although record sales were an important component of this development, perhaps the most charged symbol of the changing cultural and economic position of rock was the growth in the format of live performance. Spurred by the success of the great music festivals of the late 1960s, rock concerts were increasingly housed in large venues initially designed not as concert halls but as sports facilities; and with this shift in the mode of live presentation, the phenomenon of 'arena rock' was born.

Van Halen, the band, was a full-fledged product of the era of arena rock. Although they got their start playing on the Los Angeles club circuit, they made the move to arenas almost immediately upon the release of their eponymous debut. By the mid-1980s the band had one of the largest stage productions of any act touring in rock, and during the summer of 1988 Van Halen headlined the most expensive tour in rock history, the heavy metal-oriented Monsters of Rock. Discussing the initial stages of that tour, *Rolling Stone* writer Steve Pond described Van Halen as 'the biggest hard-rock band of our time; the band that includes the genre's most envied and emulated guitarist but sometimes sounds more like a Top Forty pop-rock band; the band that replaced a flamboyant, seemingly irreplaceable lead singer [David Lee Roth] with a journeyman singer-songwriter [Sammy Hagar] and kept right on rocking; the Ultimate Party Band, riding on years of stories about backstage excesses and hotel-room bacchanalias' (Pond 1988: 41).

Such is the legend that has revolved around Van Halen for so much of the band's career. From the end of the 1970s and throughout the 1980s in particular, the band was considered the state of 'arena rock' art, the standard bearer in a style of rock presentation that drew thousands upon thousands of fans into its scope. And yet it was precisely the scope of arena rock that made it a controversial phenomenon, and a less-than-satisfying representation of rock's power to move an audience for many commentators. Especially for those who viewed rock to be the province of an oppositional or resistant spirit relative to mainstream values, the magnification of the rock audience that arena rock effected appeared too much like the homogenization of musical taste about which critics of popular culture had warned since the advent of the Frankfurt School critique of the 'culture industry' in the middle of the twentieth century. Arena rock, for these critics, was all too successful at creating a 'mass' of musical consumers who were led by the illusion of rock rebellion to subordinate their individual differences to the collective, undifferentiated pleasures of a massive hard rock spectacle.

It is within this changing context of mass participation in rock music that the full significance of the guitar hero takes shape. The dedicated artistry and drive for individualistic self-expression embodied in the figure of the guitar hero has worked as a crucial counterweight to the suggestion that arena rock represented an endpoint in the process of absolute commodification where rock was concerned. Reflecting for many the potential for authentic artistry within a mass cultural phenomenon, the guitar hero also stands at the cusp of a much more slippery and dynamic boundary between audience and performer within the sphere of rock performance. From one perspective, the electric guitar virtuoso does indeed represent a new degree of hierarchy in the world of rock, a celebration of musical mastery that upholds a staunch division between fans and their favourite icons. At the same time, though, there is a strain of intimacy running through the relationship between the guitar hero and his audience that problematizes any overly rigid understanding of this boundary. The tension between these effects defines the place of the guitar hero in recent rock culture, and Edward Van Halen's career as a celebrated guitarist offers a rich base from which to examine the emergence of the guitar hero out of the space of the arena.

Atomic Punk

In his 1985 journalistic account of the rise of Van Halen to the height of hard rock success, J.D. Considine remembered his first brush with the Van Halen attitude. It came over the radio while driving the streets of Baltimore in 1978. The song was *You Really Got Me*, a cover of the 1960s two-chord Kinks classic. Considine was struck by the difference between the version of the song now playing before his ears and the original: 'what I heard was guitar playing that bristled with confidence, sneaking slick asides in behind a singer who infected the lyrics with a degree of snideness that made the tame put-downs my friend and I were tossing off moments before seem goofily polite by comparison' (Considine 1985: 7). Most of all, though, Considine was 'appalled' by what he heard, appalled that a band of young kids from L.A. had the audacity to haul out time-worn and supposedly outdated conventions of arena rock as though they still had life and energy left in them. After all, the end of the 1970s was rapidly approaching, and mainstream hard rock had been left fossilized by the brash anger and simplified structures of the new breed, punk, and its less confrontational cousin, new wave. Such were the governing assumptions of any self-respecting rock critic of the time; but Considine was not content to leave it at that. Van Halen's version of *You Really Got Me* chafed against his new-found sense of musical propriety, but it also sounded too good to dismiss. Thus was he left to observe, 'despite the fact that diligent listening to the Ramones had left me murmuring the mantra "less is more" every time I heard Van Halen, a voice deep inside me seemed to snicker, "Yeah, but bigger is *still* better"' (Considine 1985: 8).

Heavy metal excess, punk simplicity: such has become one of the definitive aesthetic divisions in the recent history of popular music. Over the years metal and punk have fused together and split apart in all manner of ways, such that any rigid distinction between the two necessarily dissolves upon close inspection. Ideologically, though – for musical distinctions are always infused with ideology – what 'metal' and 'punk' signify tend to remain at odds; and in the 1970s, when both forms essentially emerged as distinct entities, they were certainly viewed in opposition to one another. Edward Van Halen's emergence as a visible and influential guitar hero occurred at this moment of musical and ideological division in rock; and even though he has certainly been placed more on the metal side of this opposition over the years, the value assigned to Van Halen's virtuosity was shaped by the broader aesthetic and discursive struggle over the purpose of rock performance at the end of the 1970s and into the 1980s.

When punk burst onto the rock scene in the mid-1970s, it was widely understood to represent a refusal of rock conventions. At that time, many commentators perceived rock to have lost the critical edge that it had carried during the 1960s, to have sacrificed the intensity and commitment that had made it a key form of countercultural expression in favour of expanding its consumer base. In his comprehensive account of 1970s rock, *The Noise*, Robert Duncan voiced this notion of rock's decline in social engagement, especially as it bore upon the arena rock phenomenon. For Duncan, heavy metal was the quintessential music of the arena, 'the paradigm of the counterculture into the mainstream' (Duncan 1984: 37). The key to heavy metal's cultural impact and success lay for Duncan in the music's prioritization of technology, which in turn manifested itself most notably in the heavy metal fascination with volume. Duncan explained that 'rock 'n' roll had always liked *loud* . . . because *loud* meant passion, *loud* meant the pent-up anger of the age, and loud rock 'n' roll thus became an acting out of that anger and so some sort of return to the senses in the time of the rational, the technological' (Duncan 1984: 46). In virtually the same breath, though, he issued a warning that the loudness of metal, if pushed too far, negated the legitimate enactment of passion. What Duncan calls the 'loud*est*ness' of heavy metal took shape in the context of the arena as a 'series of sonic body blows, true violence and trauma', and a set of effects within which 'there was no acting *out*, just the being acted *upon*' (Duncan 1984: 47). For Duncan, therefore, the issue of technology in heavy metal music came back to the matter of political economy. The electric guitar and its attendant technologies of amplification had promoted a jarring commodification of musical space within which any possibilities for meaningful participation had been overwhelmed by the massive sound and spectacle of the arena rock show.

Punk may have continued heavy metal's fascination with 'loud', but it rejected the notion that 'loud' had to be encased within a mode of presentation that matched the scope of the sound with spatial, physical and economic grandiosity. Just as importantly, punk rejected, at least in theory, the elevation of the performer onto an almost sacred terrain that had become a prominent feature of commercial hard rock, and that manifested itself in the figure of the guitar hero. Within the setting of the arena, the guitar hero, as an exemplary virtuoso, served a crucial ideological function, offering the appearance of individual achievement and mastery in the face of the growing crowds that occupied the spaces of rock performance (Waksman 1999: 266). In punk rock, by contrast, such unfettered virtuosic display was considered a means of elevating the performer above the audience in a way that went against the populist grain of the music. Writing about punk *avant la lettre*, Lester Bangs powerfully articulated this aspect of the punk ethos:

> What we need are more rock 'stars' willing to make fools of themselves, absolutely jump off the deep end and make the audience embarrassed for them if necessary, so long as they have not one shred of dignity or mythic corona left. Because then the whole damn pompous edifice of this supremely ridiculous rock 'n' roll industry, set up to grab bucks by conning youth and encouraging fantasies of a puissant 'youth culture', would collapse, and with it would collapse the careers of the hyped talentless nonentities who breed off of it. (Bangs 1987: 34)

In Bang's estimation, only by bringing themselves down to the level of their fans could rock 'stars' earn their position at the head of the stage. He celebrated figures like Iggy Pop who deliberately upset the boundary between the stage and the floor, and the performer and the audience, through a performance style that was at once confrontational and self-mocking. Punk rock would seek to capitalize, artistically and politically, upon the spirit of negation described by Bangs and embodied by Iggy, and to renounce the inflation of contemporary rock stardom in favour of more ordinary styles of creativity.

By 1978, when Van Halen rose into the national rock spotlight, the core values of punk had made a deep impression on rock music as a whole, such that J.D. Considine could not register his response to the band's first single without taking the punk critique of arena rock into account. For a time in the latter years of the 1970s, it seemed as though punk had driven an irrevocable wedge through the climate of rock opinion, demystifying some of the music's cherished mythology and disturbing the assumption that rock was the expression of a unified youth culture (an assumption also unsettled in a different manner with the surge in popularity of disco). Within this climate of opinion, Van Halen was widely perceived as something of a throwback – what Mikal Gilmore called 'the inevitable progeny of yesteryear's metal epoch' – and much of the sense of anachronism stemmed from Edward Van Halen's apparently enthusiastic embrace of the trappings of the guitar hero in a manner that echoed earlier rock guitarists such as Eric Clapton and Jimmy Page (Gilmore 1998: 196).

As much as punk represented a crisis in the perpetuation of hard rock conventions, however, it also set a backdrop for Edward Van Halen's virtuosity against which the guitarist's achievements seemed, to many, all the more daring. Dan Hedges, for instance, began his 1986 pop biography of 'Eddie' Van Halen with a meditation on the current state of rock guitar that addressed, and refuted, the supposed obsolescence of the guitar hero. 'Not long ago, someone had written [guitar heroes] off as an extinct species – what with most of the Titans of the sixties either fried-out, semiretired, or dead' (Hedges 1986: 3). This perception was but a superficial judgement, according to Hedges, for while guitar heroes might have been harder to locate in the popular music of the day, 'the closet *axemeisters* never really died out. They've been there all along . . . Honing their riffs and fire and flash in garages, basements, and ten-bucks-an-hour shoebox-size rehearsal rooms all across the land' (Hedges 1986: 3). For Hedges, Eddie Van Halen is the paradigmatic 'closet *axemeister*', a high-school underachiever who spent his study time playing and replaying his copy of Cream's *Disraeli Gears* 'just trying to get the licks right' (Hedges 1986: 3). Such humble origins lend an air of Algeresque struggle to Van Halen's subsequent rise to success. Moreover, the portrait drawn by Hedges of a musical world in which the guitar hero had receded from view bears distinct if subtle traces of the punk renunciation of virtuosity. The supposed scarcity of visible guitar heroes within Hedges' narrative makes Edward Van Halen seem like a phoenix rising from the ashes of arena rock to restore the electric guitar to its rightful place at the pinnacle of rock achievement.

For his part, Van Halen himself seemed duly aware of punk's presence and impact, and his awareness left some ambivalent traces around his discussion of his music and of rock and roll in general. When Edward referred to himself casually as 'just a punk kid trying to get a sound of a guitar that I couldn't buy off the rack', one could hardly help but discern an edge of punk sensibility underlying the guitarist's approach to music (Obrecht 1980: 78). Similarly, Edward asserted in *Rolling Stone* that he was 'a kid just as much as the kids who come to see us . . . I like loud guitar; I like to play real loud onstage' (Atkinson 1979: 14). This desire to portray himself as just another 'kid' who was into rock and roll echoes Dan Hedges' preceding portrait of Van Halen as just a more successful version of the rock-and-roll kids who were playing their guitars in bedrooms and garages; for Edward, such comments were a means of asserting his connection to his audience at a time when his status as guitar hero promoted a greater sense of distance between his persona and that of the average fan.

But punk informed Van Halen's outlook on music in other ways, as well. The punk aesthetic of aggressive simplicity, which was renewed in the 1990s through the rise of grunge and the spread of 'indie rock', has been an important point of reference for Van Halen with regard to discussing the value of musical technique to the making of popular music. Discussing the music on his band's 1995 album, *Balance*, Edward reflected upon the 'rawness' of Van Halen's sound relative to other bands of the day:

> The songs on our new record are really raw, but sometimes they don't seem as raw because we know how to play our instruments. I think a lot of people get 'raw' confused with [a lack of] musical ability. If you can't play, then it's raw. But that's not true. The energy is what I mean by raw – just three people blowing, making music. And if you can play well, it doesn't sound 'raw' in one sense, but it has a raw energy to it because there's not a bunch of other crap in there, like synth pads and shit. (Zappa 1995: 116–17)

Edward Van Halen here works to authenticate his band's sound in a manner that cuts in at least two directions. With his closing reference to 'synth pads and shit', he voices the stock rejection of 'synthesized' music that had become an embedded aspect of rock culture through the 1970s and up to the present, when hip-hop, techno and electronica have generated a crisis of sorts for the continued vitality of guitar-based rock and roll. Just as significantly, though, his efforts to defend the rawness of his band's sound in defiance of common assumptions about the connection between rawness and musical ability tacitly acknowledge the extent to which 'punk' values had placed the sort of virtuosity associated with the guitar hero into a defensive position.

Edward Van Halen, then, has over his career often positioned himself, and been positioned by others, as a great defender of the continued value of virtuosity and musical technique in the face of those who have downplayed or even renounced those aspects of musical performance. For Van Halen, though, more than sheer technique was at issue. Especially as his style of electric guitar performance became widely copied in many of its details, the main issue surrounding Van Halen's status as guitar hero became not only virtuosity but *innovative* virtuosity, for technique without originality of conception would merely create a mechanical reproduction of musical effects. Edward voiced his concern with these matters in a 1980 interview with *Guitar Player* magazine:

> I guess they always say that imitation is the highest form of flattery. I think this is a crock of shit . . . What I don't like is when someone takes what I've done, and instead of innovating on what I came up with, they do my trip! They do my melody. Like I learned a lot from Clapton, Page, Hendrix, Beck – but I don't play like them. I innovated; I learned from them and did my own thing out of it. Some of those guys out there are doing my thing, which I think is a lot different. (Obrecht 1980: 99)

The conflict between imitation and innovation outlined in these comments by Van Halen touches upon one of the major contradictions running through the figure of the guitar hero: the guitar hero, as a representative icon of individual creative expression, also fosters a certain standardization of instrumental technique as patterns of influence are enacted through emulation or outright imitation. This contradiction parallels the ambivalent location of the guitar hero within the space of the arena as a symbol of individual achievement who legitimized a new stage in – or a new way of staging – the mass commodification of rock music. In both instances, the supposed artistic freedom that the guitar hero embodies exists in tension with the economic imperatives underlying the hard rock/heavy metal form. The guitar hero therefore stands as a quintessential example of the more general phenomenon within consumer-oriented capitalism whereby the creation of a mass audience involves not simply the cultivation of homogeneous taste patterns among fans and consumers, but the belief that products of culture permit free individual expression even as they standardize artistic tastes and practices.

How this counterpoint between personal innovation and cultural standardization has taken shape around the career of Edward Van Halen can perhaps best be observed through the running concern with the guitarist's choice of instrument. Even before the time of the Gibson Les Paul, the endorsement of notable guitarists has been a significant marketing tool among guitar manufacturers for cultivating interest in their products. In the advertisements that circulated through the pages of *Downbeat* magazine in the 1930s, and in the advertisements that circulate through the pages of *Guitar Player* and *Guitar World* today, aspiring guitarists and other professionals alike are counselled to heed the advice and follow the choices of a range of guitar luminaries. For guitarists, in turn, an endorsement deal brings not only added income but certification that one has earned the reputation and the notoriety to serve as an example to others. Perhaps the ultimate prestige in this regard is the 'signature' guitar, in which a famed guitarist lends his name to an instrument in exchange for having some input on the design and some economic investment in the final product. The Gibson Les Paul and the Gretsch Chet Atkins are only two of the most well-known and enduring such models, but in recent years signature guitars have proliferated dramatically as manufacturers have sought any possible avenue to distinguish their product from those of their competitors.[1]

Edward Van Halen has been a prominent endorser in the years since he first rose to public acclaim. Throughout the 1980s he was featured in a series of advertisements for the Kramer guitar company, and in the 1990s he made the move into the signature guitar realm through deals with Music Man and then with Peavey. At the centre of the Van Halen mystique, though, is the story of his expertise with modifying guitars and his early rejection of the standard guitar models that were readily available on the market. Against the tide of reverence for vintage instruments that has risen within the recent guitar market (see Chapter 6), Edward placed a priority upon crafting his own piecemeal instruments in a desire to carve out a shape and a sound he could call his own. The Les Paul was 'just the cliched guitar, the rock and roll guitar', and while Edward liked the sound the guitar generated, he wasn't happy with aspects of the design, especially the lack of a tremolo bar that would allow him to creatively bend and tweak the notes of his instrument (Obrecht 1980: 75). Stratocasters featured the tremolo bar, but the sound of the single-coil pickups was too thin for the tastes of both Edward and his bandmates.[2] Unsatisfied with the leading electric guitar options, Van Halen set about creating his own hybrid object that blended the sound of the Les Paul with the functionality of the Stratocaster.

The impulse to tinker with the electric guitar, to modify its specifications to suit one's personal tastes, is long-standing. Early figures in the history of the instrument such as Les Paul were tireless tinkerers; and for Paul in particular, involvement with the technological dimensions of electric guitar design accentuated his image as a premier virtuoso during the 1950s (Waksman 1999: 36–74). Some thirty years later, Edward Van Halen came to represent a similar combination of technical virtuosity and technological resourcefulness. In his first major profile with *Guitar Player* magazine in 1978, Van Halen outlined the process and the principles that characterized his experiments in electric guitar design while he described his main guitar, an instrument he assembled with parts he bought from the Charvel guitar company:

It is a copy of a Fender Stratocaster . . . I bought the body for $50 and the neck for $80, and put in an old Gibson patent-applied-for pickup that was rewound to my specifications. I like the one-pickup sound, and I've experimented with it a lot . . . I like [the pickup] towards the back – it gives the sound a little sharper edge and bite . . . There is only one volume knob – that's all there is to it. I don't use any fancy tone knobs . . . give me one knob and that's it. It's simple and it sounds cool . . .

Nobody taught me how to do guitar work; I learned by trial and error. I have messed up a lot of good guitars that way, but now I know what I'm doing, and I can do whatever I want to get them the way I want them. I hate store-bought, off-the-rack guitars. They don't do what I want them to do, which is kick ass and scream. (Obrecht 1978: 29, 58)

Through Edward's account, individual experiments with guitar design intersect with and reinforce the ideology of innovative virtuosity that underlies the image of the guitar hero. The quest for a unique instrument goes hand in hand with a rejection of 'off-the-rack' guitars. Edward refuses the notion that he has to be satisfied with the standard choices available to guitar consumers. However good the Les Paul or the Stratocaster might be, they don't live up to Van Halen's personal standards of how a guitar should play, or how it should sound; and this wilful search for a guitar that matches his personal ideals and desires sets Van Halen apart as a musician of uncommon creative control.

From this vantage point, Van Halen's tinkering in pursuit of the perfect sound might be understood as a form of resistance to the conventions of electric guitar consumption. However, when one situates these qualities of inventiveness and individualism within the context of Van Halen's career as an influential guitar hero, the implications of his activities assume a different cast. Van Halen's cut-and-paste approach to guitar construction laid the groundwork for a new aesthetic of electric guitar design that had a considerable impact upon the guitar industry in subsequent years. British guitar historian Paul Trynka, for one, has noted the influence of Van Halen's desire to combine the best features of Gibson and Fender instruments: 'In essence, Van Halen popularized the concept of the "superstrat," building up his own design from Boogie Body, Fender and Charvel parts' (Trynka 1995: 104). Over the course of the 1980s, a host of upstart guitar companies such as Jackson/Charvel, Aria, Kramer and Ibanez turned this "superstrat" design into the staple of their production lines, and such guitars became widely used among hard rock and heavy metal players. Kramer guitars, which featured a newly-patented Floyd Rose tremolo device, became the best-selling models in the US during the 1980s, not least due to the endorsement of Edward Van Halen.

In 1991, Van Halen pushed this process one step further by striking a deal with the Music Man company to produce a guitar carrying his signature line of approval. The Music Man Eddie Van Halen model was a modification of the 'superstrat' guitar style that Edward had been working with for years. Journalist Dan Amrich observed about the deal, 'For a tinkerer like Eddie, creating a production instrument represented the ultimate thrill' (*Guitar World* 1997: 6). It also represented a way to standardize details that he had previously had to obtain through personal effort, and to reap further financial reward. When interviewed about his new guitar, Van Halen went to great pains to assert that it was still effectively *his* instrument: 'I wanted it like, if my main guitar gets ripped off and I have to go to the store and borrow one, it will be identical' (Wheeler 1991: 89). That Van Halen had displaced his former disdain for 'off-the-rack' guitars with a desire to have his own guitar take its rightful place 'on the rack' can be taken as a ready indication of the growth in power and prestige that he had experienced over his career. Yet Edward also asserted that the goal of his collaboration with Music Man was not sheer mass production; he was attracted to the company in part because they envisioned making only about a thousand instruments per year 'instead of like other companies that make 25,000 in a month' (Obrecht 1991: 70). The scale of production gave Van Halen a feeling that he would be able to exert a high measure of quality control: 'That way each guitar will be exactly the way I want it'. More importantly, though, it meant he could enter the field of mass production while still maintaining an aura of personal identification with his namesake instrument.

When Edward Van Halen transferred his signature line from Music Man to Peavey in 1995, it was because the former company couldn't produce enough guitars to keep up with consumer demand. Prospective buyers were kept on waiting lists for the Music Man Eddie Van Halen model that were anywhere from ten to eighteen months long (*Guitar World* 1997: 146). Peavey was a larger company that could meet demand for the instrument while still upholding the quality; moreover, they were already involved in producing a line of Edward Van Halen 5150 amplifiers, named after the guitarist's home recording studio. The move to Peavey marked another step in the consolidation of the process whereby Van Halen's name and reputation as a guitar hero have assumed significant commodity value in conjunction not only with the band's music but with the electric guitar and its accessories. That Van Halen inhabits his role as perhaps the most influential and, indeed, economically powerful guitarist in rock with a certain discomfort only enhances the sense of contradiction that revolves around his public persona. Matt Resnicoff's description of Edward in a 1991 *Musician* magazine feature is especially telling in this regard: 'There's terrific pressure on Ed to be a superhuman soloist, and he wears it in the way he's so scattered, so insulated even within an insider-only environment where everybody loves and respects him not only as a music hero, but as an unlikely industry kingpin' (Resnicoff 1991: 57). Despite this sense of discomfort, Van Halen has continued to appear as a figure of real authority and stunning virtuosity on record and in performance with his band. The arena remains, in a sense, the true 'home' of Edward Van Halen, guitar hero, despite the reticence that often hovers over his image.

The Solo

It is the moment for which much of the crowd has been waiting. Lead singer Sammy Hagar ceremoniously hands the stage over to one of the most celebrated instrumentalists in rock, guitarist Edward Van Halen. The Solo is about to begin. Van Halen concerts are known for the extended solo spots given to each of the band's members; bassist Michael Anthony and drummer Alex Van Halen each take their turns, and even singer and occasional rhythm guitarist Hagar might pull out his acoustic guitar for an 'unplugged' solo moment. But for most Van Halen fans, Edward's solo is The Solo, the one that aspiring guitarists and non-playing admirers alike have come to watch and to hear. As such, The Solo represents a peculiar brand of hard rock ritual that demonstrates the intense priority placed upon the electric guitar as an instrument of virtuosic display in recent hard rock and heavy metal performance.

Videotaped during the band's 1986 tour, Edward starts his solo in a strikingly casual manner for someone playing to an arena full of people. He sits on a low riser near the front left side of the stage, dragging heavily on his cigarette and blowing a series of smoke rings into the air before launching into his music. What follows over the next fifteen minutes is a series of extended riffs and reworkings of some of Edward's solo compositions from the band's various albums. The opening segment is a subdued and rather pretty set of guitar chords hovering around the key of A that Edward would later record as *316*. Tapping out a series of lightly rendered harmonics with his right hand, the guitarist stands up and raises the volume and distortion levels significantly. This change in sonority marks Van Halen's segueway into the next section of his solo, derived from his groundbreaking 1978 recording, *Eruption*. Edward stretches the structure of the original recording through an ear-blurring sequence of staccato picking and his trademark two-handed tapping,[3] spinning rapid lines that are periodically punctuated by trem-bar mutations. Pausing to move across the stage, he self-consciously plays to the crowd, lending a certain dramatic flourish to the cascading finger-tapped arpeggios that climax this segment of the performance.

Edward's performance next moves back to more subdued musical terrain. Lush, echo-laden chords rise and fall with the turn of the volume knob on Van Halen's guitar, announcing the shift into *Cathedral*, a piece from the band's 1982 album, *Diver Down*. Almost classical in tone, 'Cathedral' is a tune on which the guitarist sticks fairly close to the recorded version aside from a few stray arpeggios, growls and harmonic squeals. Edward achieves a violin-like tone through his combined manipulation of the volume knob with well-timed echo effects. Concluding the piece, he moves onto a riser on the right side of the stage, and enters a much coarser musical segment more in keeping with the speed and flash of the *Eruption* interlude, the basis of which is a series of rapidly tapped harmonics that echo the opening strains of the band's 1981 album, *Fair Warning*. As Edward stretches out from this starting point, he moves into some of the more blues-inflected phrases of his solo, using pentatonic structures as the launching point for his self-styled bends and tapped-harmonic chord patterns.

The Solo's climax consists of another passage of two-handed tapping, this time derived from the nylon-string, quasi-*flamenco* instrumental piece, *Spanish Fly*, first heard on Van Halen's second album. Edward electrifies the formerly acoustic series of harmonically shifting arpeggios, creating an effect similar to the last section of the 'Eruption' solo. Relocating to the centre of the stage, the guitarist seats himself on the riser housing his brother's drum set, where he settles upon a pattern of hammer-ons and pull-offs that he repeats with escalating speed, the roar of the crowd mounting at each step along the way. Standing once again, Edward moves to the front of the stage, where he plays a final set of ascending, high-pitched, swiftly picked notes, ending at the very bottom of his fretboard with a single note that he picks into oblivion as Sammy Hagar returns to the stage, calling out 'Edward Van Halen' to the crowd to announce that The Solo as such has come to an end.

The musical montage that is Edward Van Halen's in-concert guitar solo has undergone many changes over the years. When I first saw the band in 1984, with original lead singer David Lee Roth still acting as head ringmaster, Edward's solo was less premised upon his recorded solo compositions. There was more room for improvisation, for stretching out, and his two-handed technique was more squarely at the centre of the performance; he even had a special plastic attachment added to his guitar, enabling him to poise it flat on its back and play in a pianistic manner. Meanwhile, the version of The Solo released on Van Halen's 1993 live release, *Right Here, Right Now*, follows the basic structure of the 1986 performance described above, but with the parts rearranged, and accorded different degrees of attention. In concert these mini-compositions, which work to ease the flow from song to song on the band's various albums, are instead compressed into a single segment in which the internal sequence is not so smooth; and the overall place of The Solo in Van Halen's live show is markedly, and perhaps deliberately disruptive. The flow of songs is suspended as Edward Van Halen takes his place alone in the spotlight, exhibiting for all his fans the techniques that have made him one of the most widely influential guitarists of the past quarter-century.

Of course, the specific musical content of Edward Van Halen's live solo is only part of the story. And a story is indeed what Van Halen's performance appears to be. As his extended solo performances have become an enactment of the guitarist's diverse solo compositions, so have they also become an occasion for the Edward to re-enact the various phases of his career as an electric guitar virtuoso. In a sense, then, the story told by Edward Van Halen every night onstage is akin to the story told in a different fashion by Dan Hedges in his popular biography of the guitarist, of an electric guitarist who 'hasn't necessarily put rock guitar back on the map . . . but rather has redefined the instrument and its potential' (Hedges 1986: 4). But this is not the end of the story. Writing in a manner designed to appeal to the 'average' Van Halen fan, Hedges recognizes that the story of Edward Van Halen, guitar hero, is also necessarily a story of the relationship between the hero and his audience. It is here, in the imagined connection between the sound and spectacle of the lone performer onstage and the mass of individuals who comprise his audience in the context of arena rock performance, that the contradictions inherent in The Solo come to the fore most strongly.

Representing these matters, Hedges follows his observations concerning Van Halen's importance as a latter-day guitar hero with a fictionalized sketch of a night at the arena, centred around an idealized fan he calls 'the Kid'. The setting is Madison Square Gardens, a regular stop on any arena rock tour. The Kid and his friends have travelled all the way from 'the dog's end of Pennsylvania' to see this show, and as much as they admire the other members of Van Halen, for them, 'Eddie is clearly The Man. The *real* show' (Hedges, 1986: 7). This opposition between 'the Kid and 'The Man' establishes a gendered pattern of identification wherein the guitar hero stands for an idealized form of masculinity that, in turn, lays the basis for a bond 'between men' that takes shape around the electric guitar.[4]

More important for my present purposes, though, is the way in which the bond between the Kid and his guitar hero, Edward Van Halen, works to undo some of the distance imposed by the boundary between arena rock stage and arena-sized audience. Sure, the Kid admires Van Halen with a sort of worshipful reverence, but he also experiences an intense connection with his hero onstage that is forged and solidified through a simple object: Edward's guitar pick. The Kid has the good fortune to catch one of the picks that Edward routinely flips into the audience over the course of a Van Halen show. And it seems more than mere coincidence that this pick landed in the hands of the Kid; as Hedges would have it, 'This one was *aimed*, Jack. No doubt about it . . . Eddie *looked straight at the Kid* before giving that 35-cent sliver of plastic that funny little flip with his thumb' (Hedges, 1986: 7). Now that the pick rests in the Kid's hands, Edward appears as more than a star onstage. He appears as friend, brother; Edward and the Kid are now 'Partners in Rock'. Even though Edward seems lost in his guitar playing for the rest of the show, the pick allows the Kid to dwell on a fantasy of intimate but innocent companionship with his favourite guitarist: 'Maybe he and Eddie'll hang out together . . . Eddie might even give him a guitar or two that he doesn't need anymore. Or *build* him a guitar'. Whatever happens, the Kid remains satisfied that his bond with Edward will endure, for 'when you're Partners in Rock, you don't even have to be in the same room to keep in touch . . . [for Edward's] guitar picks are coated with ESP' (Hedges, 1986: 7–8).

'The Kid' of Hedges' account cannot be made to stand in for Edward Van Halen's fans in any simple manner. However, the narrative that Hedges spins around this emblematic Kid – this young white teenage male who forms a partnership with his idealized hero – sheds light upon an aspect of the guitar hero that is rarely acknowledged. If many of the trappings of hard rock guitar heroism reinforce an image of individualist power and hierarchical devotion, those trappings are framed by a cultural fantasy of genuine, almost utopian connectedness between the guitar hero and his fans. Although Hedges is writing not as a critical commentator but as a popular biographer seeking to justify and reinforce Van Halen's mystique, he is perceptive enough to recognize that fans rarely participate in music only to subordinate themselves to their favourite artists. From this perspective, Van Halen's guitar pick becomes a charged and unique symbol of the complex lines of desire that run between the guitar hero and his audience. The pick tokenizes the embodied presence of Edward's virtuosity, making it accessible and containable, and in so doing momentarily collapses the scale of the arena into a '35-cent sliver of plastic'.

* * *

Reporting on the road with Van Halen in the early 1980s, journalist Mikal Gilmore was overwhelmed by the enormity of the band's arena rock spectacle. 'Everything about this show – from the titanic, military-motif stage to the overhanging rainbow-spectrum light system . . . is designed to search out even the most narcotized kid in the furthest reaches of Cobo's [Detroit's Cobo Hall's] three-tiered balcony, and thump him in the chest, good and hard' (Gilmore 1998: 198). Gilmore's observations bring us back to Robert Duncan's concern with the deadening effects of 'loud*est*ness'. As both writers acknowledge, the means of musical production assumed more than instrumental significance within the changing context of rock performance during the 1970s and 1980s. The trappings and the effects of technology (in the form of microphones, amplifiers, speaker cabinets, and of course, electric guitars) in the arena rock setting had significant implications for how a band related to its audience, and vice versa. Excessive volume ran the risk of overshadowing any possibility for meaningful participation even as its use was meant to maximize the excitement and build upon the celebratory ethos that rock and roll had cultivated for the better part of three decades. The guitar hero inhabited a two-pronged role in this context: he exhibited an ability to harness the power made possible by technological enhancement, and he gave that power a human face.

Edward Van Halen's long career as a notable guitar hero has embodied and been shaped by the tensions residing within arena rock. For most of that career, Edward has been cast as the musical cornerstone of a band that, without him, might have descended into the worst sort of hard rock pandering. Mikal Gilmore, again, portrayed Van Halen as a reluctant virtuoso, a guitarist almost too aware of the reverence that others hold towards him: 'I don't know shit about scales or music theory ... All I know is that rock & roll guitar, like blues guitar, should have melody, speed, and taste, but more important, it should have emotion' (Gilmore 1998: 200). Such self-effacing rhetoric might give a clue as to why Edward Van Halen found large arenas and stadiums a safer place to play than smaller venues, in a sense: 'It's more difficult to play to one person. They're either going to like it or not like it. Your chances of having your whole audience hate you is 50-50. But, if you're playing for 80,000 people, at least half are bound to like it. That's 40,000 people behind you. A bigger audience increases the odds of having people on your side' (*Guitar World* 1997: 135–6). It is in this tangled web of individualized achievement and mass adulation, of personal desires and standardized appeal, that Edward Van Halen's career assumes its contradictory character and its principal significance for understanding recent developments in rock history.

Notes

1. In my recent book, *Instruments of Desire: The electric guitar and the shaping of musical experience* (Cambridge MA: Harvard University Press, 1999), I cover the development of the Les Paul and Chet Atkins guitars in some detail. For the Les Paul, see pp. 39–53; for the Chet Atkins, pp. 97–100. Tom Wheeler's *American Guitars: An illustrated history* (New York: HarperPerennial, 1992) remains probably the best single source for the history of guitar manufacturing in the US, and includes lengthy discussions of both the Les Paul and Chet Atkins guitars and the companies that produced them, Gibson and Gretsch, respectively.

2. For an elaboration of the basic principles of pickup design, and the difference between the single-coil pickups found on most Fender guitars and the double-coil, or 'humbucking', pickups used on the Gibson Les Paul, see Paul Trynka (ed.), *The Electric Guitar: A illustrated history* (San Francisco: Chronicle Books, 1995): 155.

3. Two-handed tapping is the guitar technique for which Edward Van Halen is best known. At root, it is a technique that undoes the opposition between the fretting hand (the left hand for a right-handed musician) and the picking hand (the right). Using the right hand to strike notes on the fretboard along with the left, the guitarist uses various combinations of right- and left-hand hammer-ons and pull-offs to extend his normal reach and thus to expand the harmonic and melodic possibilities available at a given moment. Van Halen offers a detailed

hands-on account of his two-handed tapping style in 'My Tips for Beginners', *Guitar Player*, 7 (July 1984): 52–60. Meanwhile, Robert Walser offers an extended analysis of the tapped section of 'Eruption', including transcription, in *Running with the Devil: Power, gender, and madness in heavy metal music* (Hanover, NH: Wesleyan University Press, 1993): 68–75.

4. I have explored the gendered dimensions of electric guitar performance in much greater detail in the final three chapters of *Instruments of Desire*, on Jimi Hendrix, the MC5 and Led Zeppelin, respectively. See especially the discussion of 'cock rock' involving the music of Led Zeppelin pp. 244–57. On the more general significance of homosocial relationships between men, see Eve Sedgwick, *Between Men: English literature and homosocial desire* (New York: Columbia University Press, 1985).

References

Atkinson, T. (1979), 'Van Halen's Big Rock', *Rolling Stone* 293 (June 14): 11, 14.

Bangs, L. (1987), *Psychotic Reactions and Carburetor Dung*, New York: Knopf.

Considine, J.D. (1985), *Van Halen!*, New York: Quill.

Duncan, R. (1984), *The Noise: Notes from a rock 'n' roll Era*. New York: Ticknor & Fields.

Gilmore, M. (1998), *Night Beat: A shadow history of rock & roll*. New York: Doubleday.

Guitar World Presents Van Halen (1997), Wayne NJ: Music Content Developers, Inc.

Hedges, D. (1986), *Eddie Van Halen*, New York: Vintage/Musician.

Obrecht, J. (1978), 'Eddie Van Halen: Heavy-metal guitarist from California hits the charts at age 21', *Guitar Player* 12 (November): 28–30, 60.

—— (1980), 'Eddie Van Halen: Young wizard of power rock', *Guitar Player* 14 (April), 74–102.

—— (1991), 'Eddie!', *Guitar Player* 25 (August): 66–70.

Pond, S. (1988), 'Van Halen Feels the Burn', *Rolling Stone* 530–1 (July 14–28): 42–7, 154.

Resnicoff, M. (1991), 'Jamming with Edward', *Musician* 151 (May): 48–63.

Sedgwick, E. (1985), *Between Men: English literature and homosocial desire*, New York: Columbia University Press.

Trynka, P. (ed.) (1995), *The Electric Guitar: An illustrated history*. San Francisco: Chronicle Books.

Van Halen, E. (1984), 'My Tips for Beginners', *Guitar Player* 18 (July): 52–60.

Waksman, S. (1999), *Instruments of Desire: The electric guitar and the shaping of musical experience*. Cambridge MA: Harvard University Press.

Walser, R. (1993), *Running with the Devil: Power, gender, and madness in heavy metal music*, Hanover NH: Wesleyan University Press.

Wheeler, T. (1991), 'Eddie Gets a New Axe to Grind', *Guitar Player* 25 (May): 26–30, 89.

—— (1992), *American Guitars: An illustrated history*, New York: HarperPerennial.

Zappa, D. (1995), 'Sorcerer's Apprentice', *Guitar Player* 29 (March): 96–100, 110–19.

−8−

The Guitar Cultures of Papua New Guinea: Regional, Social and Stylistic Diversity

Denis Crowdy

A form of guitar- and ukulele-based popular music known as 'stringband' has developed since the Second World War in Papua New Guinea (PNG). Stringband ensembles consist of a combination of voices, guitars, ukuleles and sometimes a bass instrument. Unique regional styles and dynamic performance contexts are associated with stringband music. Differences in language, vocal timbre, melody, rhythm and guitar parts contribute to define these styles. This chapter explores the development of stringband music and its performance with a focus on the guitar. My aim is to articulate some important issues regarding global and local culture flow with music in which the local aspect is a significant factor.

My interest in the stringband music of PNG started while working as a guitar tutor at the University of Papua New Guinea, where I taught for eight years in the 1990s. That role mainly involved teaching styles that Papua New Guinean students were less familiar with, and included jazz, blues, and classical. An interest in stringband and other local popular music led to a series of field trips, the purchase of numerous commercial recordings, and many informal sessions playing with, and observing, stringband musicians.

Starting in the late 1940s and early 1950s the number of stringbands in PNG grew rapidly, and by the 1960s stringband was a significant part of village music making. By the 1970s a number of the distinctive regional styles mentioned previously had developed. A number of local guitar playing techniques featured tuning the instruments in unique ways, and the resultant styles have been a central focus of my musicological research in this area. With the development of the cassette recording industry, stringband has moved out of the mainstream of popular music making in PNG, though it still has an important stylistic influence on new music.

This paper attempts to demonstrate that a detailed examination of particularly 'local' examples of musical practices can provide an important view from which to critically consider notions of global and local flows of music, information, capital and resultant power. Stringband has developed with strong global influences, both in terms of the instruments used (guitars and ukuleles), and musical style. The way in which numerous local styles have developed is explored, including a discussion as to how those styles are used at various layers of regional and cultural perception; from village, to provincial and national levels. Popular music in PNG has embraced a certain degree of innovation and cross-cultural influence throughout its development over a fifty-year period. How stringband impacts on the modern scene is discussed to demonstrate this dynamism further. I then suggest some wider issues regarding the need for a critical view of the global and local in popular music that arise as a result of this study.

Hesmondhalgh (1998) argues that an older 'cultural imperialist' approach to mass communication, cultural and economic flow offers a useful critical position to consider relationships between local and global musical forces. This is offered in response to criticisms of such ideas from the perspective of globalization – where local and global interactions are posited as being more significant considerations than nation-state relationships. Some of Hesmondhalgh's points are reinforced here, as I am concerned with issues regarding the flow of cultural products (such as music) as a result of discussions on globalization. Also of concern is the notion that this is somehow a recent phenomenon; or that it results from recent developments in communications technology. The reality for people in places like PNG is that they have successfully negotiated global and local concerns in culture production for most of the twentieth century, and not just as a result of new technologies they have had little or no access to. Allied to this is the danger of a perception of a relatively even flow of cultural products and economic empowerment. This has the potential to be a dangerous side-effect of power imbalances ever present in the growing world music market of the West. Finally, I argue that such studies of local practices and their relationship to a wider global scene indicate that, at least in some circumstances, regional boundaries are no less important than they have ever been for those unable to easily traverse new forms of interaction as a result of such imbalances.

Papua New Guineans use the Tok Pisin term *lokal* to describe practices local to PNG, though more specifically those with village origins. *Lokal musik* is described by Webb (1993) as: 'the mildly self-deprecating term many Papua New Guineans use to describe music (usually guitar- and ukulele-based) of village origins' (Webb 1993: xix). This includes not only stringband music but is extended by Webb (consistent with local usage) to embrace PNG music for mass consumption, and so takes into account more rock and reggae based styles using electric instruments of the classic rock ensemble (electric guitars, bass, keyboards). There is no obvious Tok Pisin term for global, although music from outside PNG is described as *ovasis* (overseas).

Background

Papua New Guinea is the largest land mass of the South Pacific region excepting Australia. There are about four and a half million people in PNG, with approximately 85 per cent living in villages, and the rest in towns and cities. Over seven hundred languages are spoken, and there are three *linguae francae*: Tok Pisin (sometimes referred to as pidgin), Hiri Motu (developed from local Papuan languages and now much less used than in colonial times) and English. Diversity of culture is perhaps the most striking aspect of PNG. Although urban development has diluted this to a certain extent, issues of cultural identity based around regional criteria are ever-present and significant in many aspects of daily life.

Papua New Guinea still tends to suffer from the largely Western perception that it is the 'last unknown', obscuring the fact there are a number of towns and cities with the various utilities and lifestyles associated with those of urban areas in most parts of the world. Rugged terrain and isolation, however, have hampered efforts at establishing and maintaining a reliable and comprehensive road network. As a result, flying by light aircraft and walking are still the most effective means of travel in many remote areas. There are significant differences between urban areas, provinces, and regions within them in the development of health, education and other important public facilities. While, for example, Papua New Guinean students can submit assignments by e-mail, drawing from material on the Internet, they may then return to villages with no electricity amongst a population of subsistence farmers. This is the reality of life for many Papua New Guineans who hail from various backgrounds and traverse the spaces between town and village lifestyles. The development of popular music provides an important lens to view this urban-village divide, and the complex ways in which people navigate this space.

Colonization and subsequent political independence has occurred relatively recently in PNG. The first European missions established centres in the area in the late nineteenth century. Traders and business people established copra, oil palm and coffee plantations, and miners moved through at various times in search of gold and other minerals. Prior to the First World War, Germany laid claim to and administered New Guinea, while Britain controlled the Papuan area (north and south respectively of an imaginary line running roughly east to west, bisecting the country). Australia then took colonial control of Papua and New Guinea until accession to independence in 1975. Throughout this period, the indigenous people have experienced and adapted to varying degrees of change in their societies and musical change formed an important part of this.

Musical Change

In providing an historical overview of Papua New Guinea music, Webb and Niles (1987) have organized PNG music history into three main categories; pre-European contact, post-contact and late post-contact. They detail significant historical and musical events that have occurred in those periods. Pre-European contact music includes *singsing tumbuna*, a Tok Pisin term for traditional music, and usually refers to music that is not influenced by European contact. Although the idea of an unbroken musical tradition passed down through many generations has been shown to be somewhat inaccurate (Mclean 1994: 62–70 and Niles 1994: 84) its characterization in relation to non-Melanesian influence is significant in defining the extent and type of musical change. The impact of Christian missionary activity has led to a number of prominent music types that were developed prior to The Second World War, such as *kwaia* (Tok Pisin for choir) (see Webb 1993: 102–3 for a summary of suggested PNG text/ music types). These exist in a number of forms bearing varying degrees of incorporation of specifically indigenous elements (see Niles in Zahn 1996: xvii–xciii). The Second World War marks an important historical point in the PNG music scene, as guitars, ukuleles, and stringband ensembles spread in popularity following social change brought by the war.

In examining the effects of the Second World War in the South Pacific, Lindstrom and White (1990) describe the impact of this contact and the spread of instruments in influencing local musical practices.

> The convulsions of battle troop concentrations, population movements, and new musical technologies shook up once insular musical traditions. Instruments such as the harmonica, guitar, ukulele, and electric organ became more widely used. (1990: 157)

The large numbers of mainly US and Japanese military personnel generated and were supported by a comprehensive formal and informal recording and performance network. This support included cinema, plays, shows, radio networks and recording projects all supported by a formidable influx of performance technology such as gramophones, projectors, radio transmitters and receivers. Relationships with servicemen were significant in that their contacts were closer than those Papua New Guineans had experienced with other people from outside the country. Rather than just hearing music of the colonial 'masters', local people and servicemen engaged in musical and other activities for entertainment together. Such opportunities must have been welcomed by locals undergoing considerable upheaval in their lives, and they were in marked contrast to the realities of forced labour and the possibility of imprisonment for refusal to co-operate in the War effort. Without wanting to add to an already over-glorified view of local, apparently philanthropic participation in the War, the main point to emphasize is that there were changes in previously established relationships between Papua New Guineans and outsiders, despite turbulent circumstances.

Towns and plantations were important centres for the start of stringband ensembles and music. An early overview of introduced music forms in PNG is provided by Sheridan who describes urban stringband parties or 'Cup-tea sing-sings'[1] as 'a town version of the traditional village feast with songs telling of modern life and guitar substituted for the old drums' (1972: 819). Discussing local music styles using guitars built by villagers from local materials he states:

> This background of inventiveness is usually paralleled by an ability to experiment with chords and rhythms not always conventional but often interesting. With the trend towards the adoption of standard Pacific styles in the tavern bands of the urban areas, it may be that village guitarists will eventually produce the only local forms of guitar playing in New Guinea. (Sheridan 1972: 820)

This was an astute observation made at a time when stringband was moving towards its peak as the most prevalent form of popular music making. As it has turned out, regional styles that have developed outside of the main urban centres are the most distinctive, although the interactions between village and urban music making have been more complex than notions of a simple village-town dichotomy can express. The most common form of popular music since the early 1980s has been bands using electric instruments, and there are many examples of the incorporation of these local guitar styles into their repertoire and style. An understanding of the process of guitar diffusion is important in considering this later style development, and some examples will illustrate this.

In Babaka village, in the Hood Lagoon area of the Central Province, guitars became common from the 1950s onwards. In the 1960s numerous stringbands composing songs in the vernacular were active, and the performance scene was vigorous. I met with a group of village elders from Babaka in December 1996 who described the introduction of ukuleles to the village:

> In 1952 and 1953 we were living in the village and a man called Koneva Monse came to the village. We were small children at this time when this music was taught [when the knowledge/skills came to the village]. At this time there was no road. There were only canoes and not many motor boats. Koneva Monse lived at Korobosea/2 mile [in Port Moresby] at this time and he met one of our villagers who had leprosy at Kemo hospital. This villager bought Koneva to the village in 1952/53. At this time we started to make round ukuleles with wood from the bush and a round tinned meat can. There were no ukuleles at that time so we made them ourselves like this. Two men from here already knew how to play the ukulele, Kila Loia, who was shot dead by a Cook Islands man in Irupara, and Renagi Galewa. Those two men showed the rest of us how to play.

(Interview with Babaka villagers, 18 December 1996. Translated by Gere Rupa)

From this discussion it is evident that ukuleles pre-dated guitars in the village, at least on a widespread basis. Ukuleles can be made relatively easily with coconut shells and available timber. Guitars became more numerous in the village during the 1960s, no doubt as a result of the increase in employment amongst Papua New Guineans in the area and their increased financial power in the growing indigenous cash economy. While guitars are far more available today, they are still most likely to be bought by people in town who are employed and then brought to the village. A villager dependent on gardening, fishing and relatives for survival is unlikely easily to have the cash available for a guitar, and this would have been more of an issue in the 1960s and 1970s with a less developed cash economy in comparison to today. As songs were composed for ukulele and guitar accompaniment and became more popular, particularly amongst younger people, these ensembles became part of various village group events such as weddings, celebrations marking new buildings or roads and events celebrated annually such as Christmas and New Year.

Similar processes of development and influence were active throughout the area. A group of relatives from Paramana village, some 80 km further south-east from Babaka on the coast, formed a band called The Paramana Strangers in 1967. They recorded a number of albums and became quite famous throughout PNG and the Pacific through their tours and recordings. Singer Kiki Geno, in an interview in Paramana village in 1995, spoke of the importance of radio and live bands that were heard on occasional visits to Port Moresby in their formative period. Later, instruments were obtained, original songs in their language were composed and they embarked on a career recording numerous albums and touring throughout PNG and the Pacific.

From the 1950s onwards, a system of dance events known as *patis* (Tok Pisin for party), and six-to-six dances evolved. *Patis* generally consisted of dances in an enclosed area with one or more stringbands performing. Admission fees were often charged and refreshments made available. Six-to-six refers to the approximate times at which such events would start and finish - sunset to sunrise. The expression *pilai i go tu lait* (play until it becomes light) is very common in relation to string-band performance, both in organized and informal events, and refers to playing all night until the sun rises. Stringband music also accompanied other village events such as weddings, Christmas and New Year celebrations. Some traditional rituals and events have incorporated stringband performances in or around them. Anthropologist Michael Goddard, who carried out field work in the Western Highlands in the early 1980s described to me the incorporation of stringband music into a *singsing* in the village he lived in (personal communication, February 1997). Old men taking a break from performing traditional dancing and singing in the men's house would move to the opposite end to watch a stringband performing. He describes the same process as occurring in reverse when the stringband rested. At times both groups would be performing simultaneously.

This idea of a link between the performance contexts of traditional music and a newly developing popular music is important. Stringband only became popular, or can only be defined as such, because of its widespread use and acceptance in communities. This acceptance came about largely through incorporation into, and modification of, existing cultural systems and practices. An historical view of musical change, and particularly one dealing with socially relevant popular music, must be qualified with the notion that a certain amount of change represents a state of equilibrium, albeit a dynamic one.

An example suggesting links between traditional music concepts of form and texture and stringband is described by Feld (1988) where he details a significant socio-musical and stylistic concept for the Kaluli people of the Southern Highlands Province, and compares this with stringband texture as performed by people from the same area. This concept is translated from the vernacular *dulugu ganalan* as 'lift-up-over-sounding' and is 'the Kaluli sound, a local gloss for social identity articulated through human sonic essences' (1988: 76). He points out aspects of 'lift-up-over-sounding' evident in the way guitars and ukuleles are played, pointing out sound cluster strumming rather than conventional chords and a dense overall texture with the addition of continuously overlapped voices. Feld has suggested a useful general description of stringband music as '[b]lended voices in interlocked and overlapped polyphonies, in-sync and out-of-phase with strongly metric guitar or ukulele strums . . .' (1988: 96). Webb quotes the same passage and suggests that: 'Such features can be readily identified in numerous early and current string-band recordings' (1993: 6).

The introduction of another instrument in more recent times offers an interesting perspective from which to view the introduction and diffusion of guitars in PNG. Lengths of bamboo with intervening nodes hollowed out are struck with a pair of rubber sandals to produce a resonant bass sound with a percussive attack. The instrument is known as *mambu* (Tok Pisin for bamboo) and they can be played separately or in ensemble. The resulting sound is powerful and distinctive, and has been representative of certain areas of stringband performance in the North Solomons and Madang provinces since the early 1970s. Two accounts of the intro-duction and spread of this instrument follow.

In early 1997 I spoke to Alvis Grumar, member of a current stringband, who had performed in a number of stringbands in the 1960s and 1970s in the north coast Madang area. He described the playing of bamboo as having originated in the Solomon Islands. He explained that it was then brought to Madang by two musicians from Siar Island, Aksim (other name unknown) and Wesley Dag, who had travelled to the Solomon Islands for employment and education respectively. Starting on Siar Island a stringband style associated with the use of bamboo subsequently spread to other areas. At first permission was sought by neighbouring areas to use this style, consistent with traditional music borrowing practices, but as time went by this broke down. This was because the idea of using bamboo, and some of the styles associated with it, had already spread so rapidly and widely.

A musician active in the neighbouring village of Bomase in the village group known as Rempi (about 25 km north of Madang on the coast), Joseph Madako, related a similar story regarding the early introduction of bamboo style into the Madang area. He also stated that during the 1960s and early 1970s bands in Madang used only guitars and ukuleles. Madako pinpointed Dag and Aksim as the two men who introduced bamboo bands to Madang, and stated that the first bands to use these were based in Siar village and Krangket village. Later, other groups adopted the style and modified it for their own use. He also stated that permission was sought at first, but after a while groups from all over the province adopted bamboo without seeking permission and it became widespread. Madako further stated that bamboo was used by some groups prior to this innovation as stamping tubes, but commented that the pitch was the same throughout, and the bamboo did not match the guitar chords, indicating a primarily rhythmic function. The use of a number of tubes tuned to three or four primary chords allowed a better fit between the guitar and bamboo, and it took on a significant melodic function in the bass region of the musical texture.

Kemoi (1996) discusses the development of the bamboo band, which became popular from the 1960s in the North Solomons Province, with a particular focus on the islands of Bougainville and Buka. As the ensembles became more wide-spread on the island changes were introduced and developed:

> Because of the level of competition, the people of Buka came up with major changes in the way the bamboo instruments are made and played. Originally, the bamboo band from the western Solomons did not have sharp or flat notes on the instruments. They had only diatonic notes which were used to play a boogie-woogie type rhythm. Nevertheless, when it reached Buka, the Buka people incorporated sharps and flats, allowing minor chords and a greater range of notes for creating melodies with their bamboo band. In addition, instead of boogie-woogie sounds, rock 'n' roll music was introduced due to Western music influence. (Kemoi 1996: 35)

The growth in popularity of stringband music led to stringband competitions called *resis* (Tok Pisin meaning races or competition) where a number of string-bands perform to an audience and a group of judges who award prizes. *Resis* were at their most popular in the late 1960s and 1970s, and were often organized as events in themselves, rather than just at cultural shows which is more the case today. These cultural shows usually consist of a performance arena for traditional dance groups, a stage for power bands and an area for commercial displays. Based on Australian rural shows and instigated and supported by the Australian admin-istration in the 1950s and 1960s they have become an important part of cultural production in PNG, with a considerable degree of kudos associated with participation, by both traditional and popular music groups, and results in their competitive sections. The desire of bands to succeed at such competitions has had a significant impact on the development of stringband music, with groups practising for months in advance, hiding songs from public performance and carrying out rituals of isolation and magic to ensure the best possible result.

Although village parties have become less common, stringband *resis* have become an integral part of cultural shows and Independence celebrations. The Goroka Show in 1994 consisted of a large oval with numerous traditional *sing sing* groups performing simultaneously, an adjacent stage area for live band performances run by a recording studio and an area for commercial stalls, food and drink vendors. Between the traditional performance area and stage a number of stringbands gathered, honing their acts before performing at scheduled times in a stringband competition interrupting the live band performances. Most of the stringbands were from different areas of the highlands and the groups generally consisted of young men with one or two older men as musical leaders or managers. There were anything from three to eight guitars, some of which were amplified by re-wiring portable stereo cassette player/recorders. Some groups had bass instruments similar to *mambu* but made of PVC pipe. The players wore various body decorations including leaves, grass skirts, face markings, arm bands and head dresses. One band had several women with them who danced as the band played. Each band had a placard displaying the band's name and area of origin. It was clear that a number of relatives and friends had travelled with the bands or met with them in town to build a considerable entourage. Most tourists at the show were attending the traditional group performances, while a predominantly young Papua New Guinean crowd attended the performance of power bands on a stage nearby.

Before examining stringband style in more detail, an attempt at summarizing the development of stringband music will be made. Webb (1995), in studying the musical culture of the Tolai people of north eastern East New Britain Province, details and suggests a four-phase process in the development of stringband music in the area. These phases may be summarized as:

1. Learning a new repertoire of songs (mostly Polynesian).
2. The development of stringband ensembles and the *pati* system; original songs composed.
3. Aspects of traditional music practice incorporated; establishment of Radio Rabaul in 1961; diversification of fine points of musical style; the emergence of an identifiable Tolai stringband sound.
4. A period of creativity and innovation; search for personal styles; commercial recordings become common; gradual decline of stringbands in relation to power bands.

These phases are evident in other areas of PNG as well, and a rough chronology of musical change based on these brief musical examples is useful. In the 1940s and early 1950s there were isolated examples of guitar and ukuleles in towns and some villages; these became widespread later in the 1950s with overseas songs and early PNG composed songs forming the main repertoire. Gradually songs in the vernacular and lingua francae were composed, and as stringband became tightly integrated into village life through the *pati* and *resis* scene there was an efflorescence in the development of local styles. These musical changes were embedded in an over-arching theatre of social change on a wider geographical scope involving the development of a cash economy, perception of the potential for significantly different social relationships involving greater independence and a loosening of ties of servitude characteristic of labour relations with the colonial powers.

Stringband Style

During the late 1960s and early 1970s the stringband scene was at its most active. By then, specific regional styles had developed. These styles are usually described in terms of province;[2] many Papua New Guineans distinguish between Manus, Central and Madang Province styles for example. Finer regional discrimination is also made; people from Madang might be able to describe a band as being from the north coast of the province. Some of the characteristics that define these local musical styles include language, vocal style, melodic shape, rhythm, and guitar and bass styles.

Webb summarizes this, stating:

> Consensus recognition of stringband styles was originally confined to the following provinces, or culture areas within provincial borders: Manus, Kavieng (or northern New Ireland), Tolai (eastern Gazelle Peninsula, East New Britain) Central Province, and Madang. By the mid-1980s representative recordings of many other areas within the country had been released, though general public awareness has remained confined to the areas listed above. In addition, recordings from a wider sampling of villages within former delineated regions indicate that a more subtle discrimination of style-areas is possible. (Webb 1993: 6)

The guitar plays an important role in defining stringband style. This is perhaps most evident in guitar parts featuring a series of figures, picked rather than strummed, that recur throughout many songs in a band's repertoire. Often the guitars are tuned differently to the 'standard' tuning.[3] These different tunings are often described as open tunings by guitarists because the open strings form a chord, or part of one, when the open strings (not fretted) are played. Such tuning systems are a common feature of guitar playing in the Pacific area.

Perhaps the best known of Pacific guitar music involving such tuning changes is Hawaiian 'slack key'. Tatar describes features of slack key guitar playing as:

> . . . a predominantly plucked, rather than strummed, melody accompanied by a plucked bass. Constant repetitions of abbreviated melodic and rhythmic patterns form the basis of the musical piece. Because of the tunings, the harmonies center strongly on the tonic and dominant. Improvisation of melodic and rhythmic patterns in both bass and upper strings is a rule. Syncopation is common, as are triplets and also dotted eighths with sixteenths . . . (1979: 354)

The main difference between PNG stringband style using open tunings is that there is more repetition of a set of commonly recurring phrases, or minor variations of these. There is also less focus on development of a melodic line and more on providing a consistent accompanying texture. Similarities include the two part nature of melodic lines and figures over a constant bass, and extensive use of syncopation in the upper parts. In PNG guitar playing a guitar tuning is often referred to as *ki*, a Tok Pisin term most likely derived from the English musical term 'key'. Different keys are given distinctive names such as *Samoan ki*, *Faiv ki*, *Blu Mounten ki* and so on. In PNG, the use of the term *ki* extends beyond the meaning of a key centre and associated diatonic relationships however, and is frequently used to describe differences in guitar style that are associated with different tunings.

Some interesting changes and distinctions in stringband style are illustrated by musicians from Rurunat village, located about 100 km north-north-west of Madang town. In January 1997 I spent some time with musicians in the village discussing stringband music in the area and recording a number of groups from the village. The session was organized by Jeff Sawai, an active musician who has been involved with stringbands since the mid 1960s. He co-ordinated rehearsals featuring a number of older musicians, many of whom had not played the guitar for twenty years, to represent different periods and styles of stringband from the village over the years.

In an interview prior to performances by the different groups Sawai described the various bands and styles chronologically, defining them in terms of the way the guitar was picked or strummed, and an associated *ki*. The players took a considerable time to tune the guitars to their satisfaction, and there was much comparison between guitars, checking pitch, and discussion. Though many people recognise different *kis*, and will readily engage in discussions of style comparison and musical history, I have encountered few people capable of tuning the instruments easily. This is perhaps indicative of the reduction in use today of such open tunings, and the tendency of Sawai and other musicians in the area to associate particular tunings with different historical periods reinforces this notion.

Sawai describes the mid 1960s as being the height of the stringband *pati* and *resis* era. He cited the example of a wedding party in a neighbouring village in the mid 1960s where a band from Rurunat performed with other local bands until dawn. He recounts that stringband *resis* were regularly held locally, and that bands from the region mainly performed within these boundaries, only occasionally travelling to larger centres such as Madang or Bogia. Rurunat demonstrates a series of style changes, and that the *ki* used was significant in defining the nature of the texture and overall sound of ensembles performing in those styles, and in the description of the styles. The stringband *pati* and *resis* scene was also significant in the performance and development of these different styles and no doubt played an important part in bands and musicians obtaining new ideas and incorporating them into their own musical compositions.

This notion of *ki* is important as it binds the notion of style difference directly to guitar technique and style. This aspect of style difference (by no means the only one – just important for the sake of this discussion and the focus on guitar) is investigated in the following section, where some brief examples of this open tuning and style relationship will be demonstrated. Guitar tunings have played a role in defining specific styles that are associated with particular regions of stringband practice. Guitar style plays an important role in the stringband ensemble texture, and bands tend to maintain the essential features of that texture throughout their repertoire. Open tuning and playing techniques contribute to establishing the main phrases that define individual guitar style. These concepts are best understood through musical examples, and a discussion of two different tunings known as Samoan, and *Faiv-ki* will attempt to illustrate these main points.

Samoan and *Faiv-ki*

Samoan is a tuning that consists of the strings being tuned to scale degrees 451513 (from lowest to highest strings respectively) of a major key.[4] Bands from numerous villages in the Port Moresby area and further east along the coast often use this tuning. A good example of this demonstrated by a popular band from Babaka Village in Central Province, known as the BB Kings. The name is a play on the name of the village[5] and the American blues singer and guitarist. Recently, young relatives of BB Kings band members started a group called the Young BB Kings, who have continued in this style, performing original BB Kings songs and their compositions. I recorded a number of songs in Babaka village in December 1996, and these were performed by a mixture of original BB Kings and Young BB Kings members. The style consists of a rich three- and four-part vocal texture accompanied by several guitars and a ukulele, instruments that have clearly defined rhythm or lead functions that remain constant throughout each song. The lead guitar starts with a solo, and then continues with similar, though slightly simpler phrases throughout the piece, coming into prominence when the voice drops out between repeats of verses. The lead guitar part involves picking bass notes with the thumb and alternating this with picking by the index and second fingers of the right hand, resulting in rapid, arched, arpeggio phrases. Samoan is mainly played in the open position and there are certain combinations of open and fretted notes common to each chord. The simplest phrases in Samoan are those that occur under the singing and they are the most common and fundamental in terms of under-pinning the vocals and in their contribution to the overall texture of the songs.

The most common phrases played by lead guitarist Gele Leana have been extracted from a field recording of three songs. Floating bars above the lead guitar staff have been separated into notes played by the thumb (stems down), and those played by the fingers (stems up). This represents the resultant two part nature of

Figure 8.1 Guitar piece in Samoan tuning

the guitar playing, and it is the upper most part that is heard as a melodic line with regular bass accompaniment. Below the lead guitar staff is guitar tablature notation, which indicates the six strings (one to six from top to bottom) and the frets where notes are played. These phrases tend to be slightly more elaborate between verses, when the instrument takes on a prominent role due to the change in texture as the singing drops out.

Sixths and ninths form an essential part of the harmonic and melodic texture. There is an almost complete absence of the seventh degree (G) in the lead guitar part, and minimal use of it in the melody (just a couple of times as quick unaccented passing notes). This harmonic or tonal palette is quite common in much Pacific music; what characterizes this style is the repetition and elaboration of certain key phrases played in the open position relying significantly on open notes. This same principle of individual characterization of style applies to other tunings – they are characterized by guitar playing technique, open tuning and the resultant combination of phrases. A contrasting style demonstrative of this is the use of the *Faiv-ki* from East New Britain Province.

The use of the *Faiv-ki* tuning has been widely distributed in the New Guinea Islands area and north coast of the New Guinea mainland, and to a lesser extent other areas such as Central and Milne Bay provinces. *Faiv-ki* generally employs one of two tonal centres a perfect fourth apart, which are sometimes described as *G-ki* and *C-ki* respectively. These may be regarded as sub styles of *Faiv-ki* playing and different bands are associated with these substyles.

Webb has observed the importance of tunings on guitar technique and the determination of musical style in stringband. In discussing a song by John Wowono he states:

> ... it can be seen that this is very much a 'five key' melody, that is, the melodic sequencing is determined by the tuning, and more specifically, the position and hence melodic possibilities of the chord-fretting hand on the guitar.

Lead guitarist in the popular group Quakes, and skilled exponent of *Faiv-ki* guitar playing in the East New Britain style Anthony Taule describes the use of the *C-ki* centre as mainly associated with older bands from the 1970s such as the Devils band, whereas the *G-ki* is used by more recent groups. A similarly structured transcription of the lead guitar part from a field recording of a song called *Ia Desi* illustrates the contrast with Samoan. This song has been a part of stringband repertoire in the East New Britain province and according to Taule was composed by Richard Tokuraeba from Ratung village in the Pila Pila village area. It has been recorded by the Moab Boys stringband and most recently by Telek on his album recorded in 1997.

The most essential aspects of the guitar texture rely on a number of similar versions of phrases built from a selection of notes in a certain area of the fret-board. The thumb plays the tonic of the chord the chord on dotted crotchet beats 1 and three as notated into 12/8 meter here, and plays either the tonic or third on beats 2 and 4 depending on the chord (tonic for chords I and V, third for chord IV). The first and second fingers of the right hand alternate on the third quaver pulse of each dotted crotchet beat, and occasionally fill in with triplet figures for decoration. The movement in this upper part between the tonic (G) and third (B) creates a pendulum-like aural effect, and the triplet figures always move down from the

Figure 8.2 Guitar piece in *Faiv-ki* tuning

third to tonic. The figures at the end of these tonic chord phrases are known as 'warnings' as they mark movement to chord IV and consist of three diads of a major third descending in parallel chromatically from the tonic and third, through the chromatic F sharp and A sharp, to the F natural (forming the dominant seventh chord I) and A natural. The figure then shifts to the fifth string bass (C root of chord IV) while the fingers of the RH pick out patterns based on the first inversion of the chord. Similar figures contribute to phrases that are common throughout much of the stringband repertoire in East New Britain, and they constitute a clearly recognized guitar style that in turn assists in the recognition (and definition) of the stringband style known as *Faiv-ki*. Interestingly, the same tuning is used in various parts of the New Guinea islands and mainland, and differences in the essential figures used mean that the region of origin of the band is important in defining style difference.

These brief analyses indicate important features of local Papua New Guinean guitar styles that developed in the late 1960s and through the 1970s. With the rise of the cassette recording industry in the mid to late 1970s, the popular music scene changed considerably, leading to a wider distribution of music from around the nation, and what Webb (1998: 153) describes as the fostering of 'a national or generic culture'.

Stringband and Musical Change

Musical innovation is highly prized in Papua New Guinea, particularly amongst younger people. As a result, the growing numbers and influence of power (electric instrument) bands and nationally distributed commercially produced cassettes have become the centre of the popular music scene since the 1980s. Stringband has been far less popular in terms of cassette sales for instance, and performance contexts have changed considerably. Some examples are offered here to illustrate these changes.

In Baiteta village in Madang Province, up until the late 1980s the main stringband in the village, the Baiteta Bushband Boys (BBBs) would have provided the music for village dances or *patis* as described previously. A few weeks before I arrived in the village in January 1997 a dance had been held in a similar outside venue, walled with coconut fronds, but a PA system powered by a generator provided the music which consisted of local live band (commercial) recordings and overseas rock, pop and dance styles. Today, the BBBs occasionally play at a nearby resort hotel and that is their main performance opportunity. They are paid to perform for tourists staying there and dress in a slight modification of traditional dress and body decoration. They perform a complete gig of about three hours. Few other bands in this north coast region seem to use bamboo and perhaps this is one of the reasons they are hired by the hotel. From my experience and discussions with numerous people in PNG, stringbands using bamboo are generally associated with the Madang and North Solomons provinces, although I have observed bands from other regions such as the Highlands using the instruments. This association has been used by a hotel in Madang town who regularly hire a band known as 'The Melanesian Bamboo Band'. The use of the BBBs by a resort further out of town is a similar arrangement and involves the representation of Melanesian culture to tourists. This is an interesting situation given that locally the band is seen to represent Baiteta village, performing in a style that is no longer in the mainstream of popular music consumption in the late 1990s.

More and more frequently stringbands appear at formal functions with players dressed traditionally as cultural groups. The primary aim of these seems to be to present an image of Papua New Guinean-ness, with much in common with the way cultural groups are brought in to various events to give a Papua New Guinean 'flavour' in situations that have little (usually) to do with PNG culture other than setting up business in the country. In 1997 I attended the Mobil company Ball at a large hotel in Port Moresby with a friend employed by the company. Prior to a series of speeches focusing on the financial success of the company, a stringband from a nearby village in Central Province performed. The group presented themselves in traditional dress, then proceeded to sing a guitar and ukulele accompanied song that was about Mobil, and had been composed by one of the band members to words written by one of the employees from the same village the stringband was from. The purpose of the group seemed to be primarily ceremonial, with the audience politely watching and applauding. After a couple more songs (all accompanied by young women dancing, wearing grass skirts) the group left, the dance music provided by a session band from a local recording studio took over and the event transformed into a party that continued until the early hours of the morning.

Stringbands have provided an important part of urban and village social structure, particularly for male youths and young men. An example of this is provided by the members of the Mokinnies Stringband, who come from Toto and Medebur villages in the Madang Province. They released several popular albums and still perform today, though some members have left the original group to form another band. I recorded the band at a *haus simok* (Tok Pisin term for a small building for drying copra) between the two villages where young men gather to fish, cook and practice. The name Mokinnies is a concatenation of a vernacular expression used by the family of band members to express their annoyance at the amount of time spent in this isolation from village life. Young men in the area have been expected to live in a different house from their parents from their early teens as part of a process of attaining independence. Stringbands provide an important social pursuit for male youths and have become part of the social structure of village life in many respects. In an interview in January 1997 members described a plan to save enough money to buy instruments and amplification equipment with the aim of becoming a live band and recording commercially. They expressed the view that being a successful live or power band was an important goal and represented their idea of musical success. As a result members describe a conscious style change that has occurred in the last few years to accommodate the potential movement to power band.

The growth of the recording industry has created an interesting situation with the composition and performance of new songs. The Mokinnies are very protective of new songs in the fear that they may be used by an already established live band for recording, and therefore profit. Copyright law has yet to be implemented in PNG and though there have been methods of dealing with the ownership of music traditionally, in the context of the mass media and a national market these systems are ineffective. Power bands are seen as more powerful in their potential for popularity and commercial success, and these stringband musicians are attempting to protect their own interests from a relatively weak position in relation to the industry.

The use of stringband style in power band music is extensive, and indeed has enjoyed a considerable revival in the late 1990s with bands such as the Quakes who fuse distinctively East New Britain *Faiv-ki* guitar style with PNG reggae keyboard chanks, dance rhythms using MIDI instruments and other more widely used instrumental styles. This coexists with bands who have continued a stringband style into the power band genre (particularly bands from the Sepik and Central Provinces) and rely heavily on the regional distinctiveness of those styles to state their identity within the PNG popular music scene.

Conclusion

The development of stringband music has involved a complex series of events, where change and adaptation have been more predominant than stasis and resistance. Initially, the introduction and spread of guitars and learning of a new repertoire preceded exploration and innovation in local regional styles. Once these had developed, the use of stringband style in modern electric instrument groups created a distinct regional flavour in the newly developing popular music and commercial recording industry. As well as this, stringband music has been used almost in a customary or traditional sense, and often operating to represent different levels or layers of cultural identity, from regional to provincial, and even national.

The development of regional styles tends to imply movement from relatively homogenous origins (overseas music heard on radio and seen in towns) to more heterogenous results (distinctive regional styles). That the guitar, with no prior stringed instrument tradition in PNG, has played an important part in that process is significant in considering the interplay between notions of global and local. Popular musics such as stringband coexist with traditional music, though there is little doubt that amongst a younger generation it can largely replace it. The argument here is not that PNG is a more musically heterogenous place because of popular music. The notion of such musical diversification as affirming local cultural resistance to global musical influences needs to be tempered as it tends to 'risk confusing the flow of musical contents and musical expansion with the flow of power relations' (Feld, 1994: 263). There is, however, little doubt that the kinds of musical diversity, and their relative isolation from each other that existed even fifty years ago have changed dramatically. More importantly, the realisation that musical change has been, is, and will most likely continue to be the norm must be considered as a primary research perspective as the pace of change continues.

Perhaps this study will assist as one of the components in a response to Hall (1991: 33) when he asks 'What has been happening out there in the local? What about the people who did not go above the globalization but went underneath, to the local?' Rather than the development of local stringband styles being a defensive response as Hall (1991: 33–4) suggests, I suspect it is simpler than that, and more a result of the reality of being so far at the periphery of globalization. One of the things that is happening 'out there in the local' is the reinforcement, if anything, of complex layers of local boundaries, with village identity at one end of the scale, and national at the other. This results from the differences between the local and global as a result of the 'flow imbalance' previously discussed.

Although there has been some inclusion of stringband music in the more recent world music scene, as exemplified by collaborative projects between Australian musician David Bridie and PNG musician George Telek, the fact that there have been obvious musical choices in conforming to 'a new global aesthetic' (Hesmondhalgh 1998: 171) through the use of percussion and textures not usually associated with stringband music, ensures that it maintains a more central place in the world music market. This is not intended as a criticism of such collaboration – I don't wish to contend that any movement away from 'pure stringband' is problematic – merely that such local forms require extensive mediation to conform to textures, sounds and mixes percieved as appropriate for the world music market.

As Feld points out:

Even if local musicians take control in remote locales, how progressive can the world of popular music be when the practices of a transnational culture industry steadfastly reproduce the forms and forces of domination that keep outsiders outside, as 'influences' and laborers in the production of pop? (1994: 263)

Papua New Guinea stringband music, as an example of complex local style development, offers more than an exotic journey in syncretism. It can provide another perspective with which to view notions of global and local as they relate not only to guitars and musical style, but wider social concerns as well.

Notes

1. Singsing is a Tok Pisin term that refers to a gathering for the performance of (usually) traditional music, and is generally village based.
2. Papua New Guinea is divided into nineteen provinces for political and administrative purposes.
3. Standard here refers to the most common tuning of the guitar – the notes EADGBE from sixth to first strings respectively (perfect fourth intervals between all strings except for a major third interval between the third and second strings).
4. In the music I recorded the strings of the guitar were tuned to the notes D, E, A, E, A, C#, from sixth to first strings respectively.
5. Concatenating words by removing the vowels and referring to the acronym-like result is common throughout PNG. Irupara, a neighbouring village is often referred to as IRP (each letter pronounced as in an acronym) or IRPR. 'BBK' is therefore commonly used to refer to Babaka village. This has been extended in Babaka to BB Kings, and sporting teams are commonly known by this in sport competitions outside the village, such as local area tournaments or those in Port Moresby.

References

Feld, S. (1988) 'Aesthetics as Iconicity of Style, or 'Lift-up-over-Sounding': Getting into the Kaluli groove', *Yearbook for Traditional Music* 20: 74–113.

—— (1994) 'From schizophonia to schismogenesis: on the discourses and commodification practices of "world music" and "world beat"', in C. Keil and S. Feld (eds), *Music Grooves*, Chicago: The University of Chicago Press

Hall, S. (1991) 'The Local and the Global: Globalization and ethnicity', in A. King (ed.), *Culture, Globalization and the World System: Contemporary conditions for the representation of identity*, New York: Macmillan

Hesmondhalgh, D. (1998) 'Globalisation and Cultural Imperialism: A case study of the music industry', in R. Kiely and P. Marfleet (eds), *Globalisation and the Third World*, London: Routledge

Kemoi, N. (1996), 'The History of the Bamboo Band in Bougainville', *Kulele: Occasional papers on Pacific music and dance*, No. 2, Port Moresby: National Research Institute.

Lindstrom, L and White, G. (1990), *Island Encounters: Black and white memories of the Pacific War*, Washington: Smithsonian Institution Press.

McLean, M. (1994), 'Diffusion of Musical Instruments and Their Relation to Language Migrations in New Guinea', *Kulele: Occasional papers on Pacific music and dance*, No.1, Port Moresby: National Research Institute.

Niles, D. (1994), 'Religion, Media and Shows: The effects of intercultural contact on Papua New Guinean musics', in M. Kartomi and S. Blum (eds), *Music Cultures in Contact: Convergence and collisions*, Sydney: Currency Press.

Sheridan, R. (1972), 'Music (2)', in P. Ryan (ed.), *Encyclopaedia of Papua and New Guinea*, Melbourne: Melbourne University Press.

Stella, R. (1990), *Forms and Styles of Traditional Banoni Music*, Port Moresby: National Research Institute.

Tatar, E. (1979), 'Slack Key Guitar', in G. Kanahele (ed.), *Hawaiian Music and Musicians*, Honolulu: The University Press of Hawaii.

Waiko, J. (1986), 'Oral Tradition Among the Binandere: Problems of method in a Melanesian society', *The Journal of Pacific History*, 21(1): 21–38.

Webb, M. (1993), 'Tabaran: Intercultural exchange, participation and collaboration', *Perfect Beat*, 1(2): 1–15.

Webb, M. (1995), '"Pipal Bilong Music Tru"/"A Truly Musical People": Musical culture, colonialism, and identity in northeastern New Britain, Papua New Guinea, after 1875', PhD thesis, Wesleyan University.

Webb, M. (1998), 'Popular Music: Papua New Guinea', in A. Kaeppler and J. Love (eds), *The Garland Encyclopedia of World Music*, 9, Garland Publishing.

Webb, M. and Niles, D. (1987), 'Periods in Papua New Guinea Music History', *Bikmaus*: 7(1), 50–62.

Discography

George Telek, *Telek*, Origin OR030 (1997).

Hybridity and Segregation in the Guitar Cultures of Brazil

Suzel Ana Reily

Hoje, quase eu não entendo	Today I can hardly understand
essa linguagem que falas!	this language you speak!
És o instrumento das salas,	You are the instrument of parlours,
pois trocaste, ó meu violão,	for you have exchanged, oh my guitar,
pelos palácios dos nobres,	the palaces of noblemen,
que agora te dão açoite,	who now flog you,
a majestade da noite,	for the majesty of the night,
tua glorificação.	your glorification.

(Catulo da Paixão Cearense 1924: 214)

Musical instruments and styles – clear public indicators of 'cultural capital' (Bourdieu 1979) – are often closely linked to status positions (see La Rue 1994), and in Brazil, musical symbols have constituted strong markers of class and racial affiliation. In the nineteenth century, for example, the French painter, Jean Baptiste Débret (1940 [1834–9]: vol. 2: 108), who arrived in Rio de Janeiro in 1816 with the 'Artistic Mission' recruited to teach at the newly founded School of Fine Arts, remarked:

> It is a fact that in Brazil the cottage and the palace are common cribs of music. For this reason one hears day and night the sound of the marimba of the African slave, the guitar and the *cavaquinho*[1] of the common man, and the most proficient harmony of the piano of the rich man.[2]

Débret's observations certainly reproduce the dominant stance on the associations between instruments and social classes in Brazil at the time, but in actual practice the guitar refused to be confined to the 'common man': it could be found alongside drums amongst blacks and mulattos as well as in the drawing rooms of respectable households. This disjuncture between discourse and practice highlights a contradiction common to the 'hybrid cultures' (Canclini 1998 [1989]) of Latin America. Like the rest of this region, Brazil has been a space for the continuous and systematic encounter of diverse social and ethnic groups, leading to the development of a myriad of syncretic cultural expressions. The very threat of this proximity, however, also generated powerful mechanisms to preserve the segregation of these groups, amongst which one can include the construction of discourses identifying particular instruments and musical styles with specific social groups. The intermediary position of the guitar within the Brazilian social hierarchy placed it at the very crossroads of the tensions generated by the two opposing forces of syncretism and segregation. In a manner unmatched perhaps by any other musical instrument, the guitar moved with relative ease from one social sphere to another, such that it frequently mediated the country's processes of cultural hybridisation. This flexibility, however, often made it the focus of heated debates, and it became the target of hardened discourses aimed at fixing its social boundaries.

With the emergence of the nationalist-oriented modernist movement in the early twentieth century, it was the very hybridity of the guitar that was heralded, instigating a drive to transform it into the national instrument (Naves 1995: 25). In flagging hybridity as a cultural ideal, the traditional mechanisms for promoting social segregation were challenged, requiring the intelligentsia to engage in a reassessment of their conceptions of 'the popular', without, however, compromising their aesthetic ideals. Indeed, the modernist project envisaged an ennobled popular guitar, which could be proudly paraded as Brazil's contribution to the 'concert of nations'. During the 1930s, the guitar did indeed emerge as the Brazilian national instrument through its centrality to *samba*. Although *samba* cross-cut the country's social and racial divides, the carnivalesque associations it evoked did not exactly cloak the guitar with a serious image of nobility. It was not perhaps until the rise of *bossa nova* in the late 1950s that an internationally recognized, sophisticated – yet popular – guitar style emerge within the Brazilian musical scenario. The degree to which this hybrid genre promoted national integration, however, is questionable, as it had but tenuous links with the 'common man' (Reily 1996; Treece 1997).

In Brazil, then, the guitar provides a privileged means of addressing the tensions and contradictions of a hybrid culture. Through an historical overview, I shall outline the major fluctuations in the social spheres to which the guitar gained access, highlighting the processes of syncretism they generated as well as the discursive reactions they evinced. The chapter is divided into four sections: the first discusses the emergence of the hybrid cultures generated by the encounters between the diverse social sectors in colonial Brazil; the second focuses on the tensions between syncretism and segregation in the musical life of the nineteenth century; the third discusses the contradictions in the representations of the guitar amongst early twentieth-century Brazilian modernists; and the fourth addresses the impact of modernism and modernization upon the articulation of the guitar up to the present.

Prototypes and Trajectories: Guitars in Colonial Brazil

Records from the colonial period tend to be rather imprecise in their references to the guitar-like instruments used in Brazil, and this has hindered the study of their historical trajectories in the country. It must be remembered, however, that this problem is hardly unique to Brazil, for on the Iberian peninsula itself these instruments were far from standardized at the time; there was considerable variation in terminology, design and tuning as well as in the social contexts in which such instruments were used (Montanaro 1983; Lima 1964). There are, however, at least four Iberian prototypes from which the contemporary Brazilian instruments of the guitar family developed: the *viola de mão* (hand *viola*), or simply *viola*; the lute; the *machete* (also known as *descante*); and the *guitarra*.[3]

References to the *viola* prototype begin to emerge in the thirteenth century, and these documents suggest that the instrument was used primarily by troubadours. By the fifteenth century it had clearly become a common instrument of the Iberian popular classes in both urban and rural settings, and the dangers it presented – particularly in the urban context – were evoking strong reactions. In 1459, for example, state officials made a complaint to the court of Lisbon, claiming that bands of musicians playing *violas* used the distraction of their music to rob their audiences. This led to an edict determining that, unless there was a festival, anyone found in the streets with a *viola* after nine o'clock at night would be imprisoned, and the instrument and any other possessions would be confiscated (Lima 1964: 30). By the sixteenth century, however, the *viola* had gained favour in the Iberian courts, where it was plucked to produce a melodic line, distinguishing the techniques of palace musicians from the cruder strumming styles used by popular performers (Oliveira 1966). Although it was probably more widely used in Spain than in Portugal, the Portuguese court could boast musicians of high standard, such as the renowned Garcia de Resende (Tinhorão 1990: 26), and in 1535 Luís de Milan dedicated some pieces for the instrument to Dom João, then King of Portugal (Lima 1964: 29). While the *viola* managed to gain access to the courts, the *guitarra* remained an outcast of lowly associations (Oliveira 1966: 183).

Due to its noble links, the term *viola* came to be used generically for instruments of the guitar family in the colony of Brazil. A number of early colonial references indicate that *violas* were widely used by representatives of the church, especially the Jesuits, from the mid-sixteenth to the late-seventeenth centuries, in their endeavours to convert the natives (Leite 1937: 49). While the missionaries drew upon a repertoire derived from both the official church and the popular domain, many felt that popular instruments – such as *violas*, bagpipes, drums and tambourines – were particularly well suited to the enterprise of conversion; like Amerindian ritual life, the Portuguese folk traditions in which the popular instruments were employed were marked by a participatory ethos, such that the natives seemed more readily inclined to engage with them.

Although cultural exchange within the missions was essentially unilateral, signs of syncretism did emerge within them. It has been claimed that the *cateretê* was a dance that developed from native prototypes within Jesuit coastal missions amongst the Tupinambá (Andrade 1933: 173). It seems clear that the name of the dance derives from the Tupi language, but no descriptions of the mission dance have been discovered that might attest to its native links. However, a double line dance called *cateretê*, which is commonly accompanied by *violas*, is still widely practised in rural areas of south-eastern Brazil. While the choreography of the contemporary dance may no longer bear any relation to its mission counterpart, it stands as testimony to encounters between natives and colonists. Indeed, many missions were strategically located near Portuguese settlements, serving as a supply of Amerindian labour (Karasch 1992), and the clergy serviced both communities, albeit separately. Interestingly the *cateretê* has a devotional counterpart, in which a similar choreography is performed in honour of Saint Gonçalo of Amarante (c.1250), the patron saint of *violeiros* (*viola* players), and in Brazil Saint Gonçalo is typically portrayed playing the instrument (A. M. de Araújo 1964: 26–7; Reily 1998: 311).

While this may be pure coincidence, early documents regarding religious life in the colony indicate that carnivalesque forms of popular devotion derived from Portuguese prototypes were widespread, often with direct clerical support (Leite 1937–49). Given the frequency with which they are mentioned, it is safe to say that the favoured instruments of the colonists were the *viola* and the *guitarra*, and they were used to accompany both religious festivals promoted by church officials as well as secular entertainment.

Toward the end of the seventeenth century, references to *violas* within the official religious sphere begin to diminish in favour of instruments associated with the 'modern style', and what came to be known as 'Brazilian baroque' began to take shape. The focus of these musical developments were the mining regions, which were blossoming overnight into populated urban centres. Along with thousands of African slaves brought in to the region to work the mines, around 800,000 metropolitans came to the colony attracted by the Brazilian gold (Zemella 1990: 52). This invasion heightened existing social divisions, and they were particularly marked within the ecclesiastic sphere: Church activities were organised along racial lines, with separate congregations for whites, *pardos* (people of dark skin) and blacks. Attendance to orthodoxy focussed upon the devotional activities involving whites, which was also the sphere in which the prestigious new instruments were most prevalent. Although the modern style was associated with the colonial elites, the performers were frequently less privileged mulattos in the employment of well-endowed confraternities (Lange 1966). Through their activities, popular styles insinuated themselves into respectable circles; indeed, at the height of the Brazilian baroque period, church concerts in the mining regions often included pieces with risqué lyrics reminiscent of popular *modas de viola* (secular songs accompanied by *violas*) set to chamber orchestras in the 'modern style' (Tinhorão 1990: 91–2).

With the rise of the new repertoire, the *viola* came into disrepute, with clerical objections directed at the instrument's carnivalesque and secular associations. Yet, the Church was only partially successful in ousting the instrument from the religious sphere. Even one of the Church's most ardent defenders in the early eighteenth century, the Bahian layman Nuno Marques Pereira (1939)[4] was himself a *viola* player, a talent he employed at pageant plays and church festivals. This did not prevent him from claiming that the devil was a *violeiro* who invented profane *modas* (generic term for secular songs) to seduce his victims. There were also *viola* players amongst the clerics. In the latter part of the seventeenth century, for example, a mulatto priest by the name of Lourenço Ribeiro is said to have entertained the Bahian elites in their drawing-rooms with *modas de viola* (Tinhorão 1990: 48). In popular catholic activities – particularly those that took place in distant rural communities – the *viola* took pride of place, and it would eventually emerge as the quintessential peasant instrument.

Although the *viola* lost ground in the urban religious sphere, it remained the primary instrument for secular entertainment, both amongst the wealthy and the not so wealthy. The English traveller Sir George Staunton, who visited Rio de Janeiro in 1792, claimed that, along with the harpsichord, it was an acceptable parlour instrument for women to play (Staunton 1797: 161). But he also noted that 'the black drivers of hackney chaise at Rio, in the interval of leisure, are often heard playing on the guitar upon their stands' (Staunton 1797: 174). A late seventeenth-century Bahian performer of *modas de viola* about whom there is considerable information is the Gregório de Matos Guerra (c.1635–95), though all the work attributed to him is contained in epigraphic documents. Gregório de Matos, who came to be known as the 'Mouth of Hell', drew the attention of his contemporaries because of the wittiness of his lyrics and the sharpness with which he commented on the customs and morals of the time. The lyrics of many of his songs vividly describe the hybrid character of the musical expressions of Bahia at the time, noting particularly the strong African influence upon dance styles, in which 'the bum always dances'.

The continuous encounter between socially and ethnically diverse sectors during the colonial era produced a highly hybrid cultural environment, but it was not perhaps until the late eighteenth century that particular music and dance forms began to be identified as distinctly colonial inventions. The genres most commonly viewed as the first 'authentically Brazilian' musical expressive forms are the *modinha* and the *lundu*; while these styles followed distinct processes of historical development – the first 'Afro-Brazilianizing' a European form, the later 'Europeanizing' an African-Brazilian form – they eventually fused in the parlour context, to the point of becoming practically indistinguishable from one another, both encompassed by the generic term *modinha*.[5]

In both Portugal and Brazil the term *moda* was used to refer to any type of folk song, but by the late eighteenth century its diminutive form, *modinha*, had become associated in Portugal with a particular type of operatic parlour love song. Although there was also a Portuguese form of the *modinha*, it was clearly distinguished from the more rhythmic and syncopated – that is, hybridized – Brazilian *modinha*. Received accounts of the development of the Brazilian *modinha* typically begin with Domingos Caldas Barbosa (1738–1800), a native of Rio de Janeiro who emerged in the Portuguese parlours around 1775 with his *viola de arame* (wire-strung guitar), which he used to accompany a vast repertoire of morally questionable tunes which he called *modinhas* and *lundus*.[6] His performances caused shock waves – as well as considerable fascination – in the polite society of the metropolis, heightening notions of the rusticity and degenerate morality of the hybrid colonials. António Ribeiro dos Santos (quoted in M. de Araújo 1963: 39), for example, had this to say of Caldas Barbosa's impact on Lisbon parlour life:

[At an assembly I attended], young men and women sang such shameful love songs that I blushed with embarrassment, as though I were suddenly in a brothel or in the company of women of ill repute . . . Today, one only hears love songs with whimpering, lascivious dancing, open courtships, garishness. It is this that lulls the babies; that they teach to children; that young men sing and that women and maidens carry in their mouths. What lack of modesty, of temperance and of virtue one learns from these songs! This disgrace has become general since Caldas began introducing his ballads and singing to the women. I know of no poet who is more harmful to private and public behaviour than this troubadour of Venus and Cupid; the dandiness of love, the simplicity of Brazil, and the general American laziness which, in his songs, only breathe the shamefulness and liberties of love, and the voluptuous airs of Paphus and Citar, and casts spells of venomous filters on the fantasies of young men and the hearts of women. I admire the ease of his style, the richness of his innovations, the variety of motifs in his songs, and the sharpness and grace of the refrains with which he brings them to conclusion; but I detest his themes and, even more, the way he treats them and sings them.

António Ribeiro dos Santos's account would suggest that, at least for some members of Portuguese polite society, the colonial imprint on Caldas Barbosa's *modinhas* was most noticeable in their unpolished thematic material. Gerard Béhague (1968: 68), however, has claimed that a Brazilian character is also evident in the music; drawing on extant scores of late eighteenth century Brazilian *modinhas* produced in Lisbon, some – if not all – by Caldas Barbosa, he noted that the early Brazilian *modinha*, unlike its Portuguese counterpart, made extensive use of syncopations, a feature attributed to the African legacy in the colony. Along with these 'Brazilian' characteristics, the highly ornamented melodic lines of these early pieces evince the strong influence of Italian *bel canto*, which was greatly appreciated amongst the Portuguese elites at the time. Not surprisingly, it has been suggested that Caldas Barbosa created the Brazilian *modinha* by fusing the embodied musical practices he had assimilated in Brazil with the dominant parlour styles he encountered in Lisbon (Kiefer 1977: 15).

Caldas Barbosa was perhaps the strongest force in instigating the *modinha* craze that swept the metropolis in the late eighteenth century, but it was the Portuguese who reintroduced the genre in Brazil a few decades later, when the royal family, with an entourage of over 10,000 subjects, arrived in Rio in 1808 to flee from the Napoleonic threat. By the time the *modinha* made its way back to what was now the viceroyalty of Brazil, it had undergone considerable domestication. The shameful themes that had made António Ribeiro dos Santos blush with embarrassment had been suppressed in favour of more respectful forms of amorous expression, and the *viola* had been replaced by the piano. Repatriated, however, the same deeply embodied hybrid sensibilities that had guided Caldas Barbosa's musical orientations would once again act upon the *modinha*, reinjecting it with local flavour.

Pianos and Guitars in the Imperial Era

Just as the mass immigration of Portuguese during the mining era had a strong 'Europeanizing' impact upon the musical orientations of the elites in Brazil, the arrival of the court and its entourage reignited the Eurocentric focus of the colony's privileged classes. Gilberto Freyre (1968 [1936]) even portrayed this period as a turning point in Brazil's cultural history. He argued that the 'Lusitanian invasion' drove Brazilians to conceal the hybrid elements of their local culture, because they had now come to be viewed as the embodiment of colonial cultural inferiority.

This Eurocentric shift is epitomized in the place pianos came to acquire for Brazilian polite society. Pianos were one of the great novelties to be introduced by the Portuguese, and these modern, noble instruments rapidly became central status symbols amongst the Brazilian elites. Families of sufficient means scrambled to acquire one, and young ladies set about enhancing their profiles by learning to play it. The demand was so great that by 1834, pianos were being constructed in Brazil, and local publishers were supplying the market with scores of *modinhas* and other drawing-room styles popular in Europe at the time (Vasconcelos 1988a: 52–3). As the prestige of the piano increased, that of the guitar – which was rapidly replacing the *viola* in the urban context – went into decline, and it was progressively ousted from respectable spheres. The guitar came to be viewed as the instrument of street musicians of low station (*seresteiros* and *chorões*), and in opposition to the 'serious' tastes of the elites, their hybrid repertoire came to viewed as vulgar and 'popular'.

The emergence of a dichotomy between the piano and the guitar encapsulates a broader spectrum of civilising measures introduced by the monarch, Dom João VI. During the fourteen years the royal family was in the viceroyalty, Brazil was thrust onto the international scene, and it would emerge in 1822 as an independent nation. Since Rio de Janeiro had become the capital of the colony in 1763, it was chosen to house the court. Overnight Rio was transformed into an imperial capital, and by independence the sleepy town of 50,000 inhabitants had become a bustling cultural centre with a population of 100,000 (Skidmore 1999: 36). Following in the long-standing tradition of the Portuguese royal family, Dom João was a great patron of the arts and sciences, and during his stay he graced the city with the National Library (which by 1814 boasted a collection of 60,000 volumes, one of the largest in Latin America), the Medical School, the Botanical Gardens, the School of Fine Arts and many other institutions.

Music received special attention from the monarch. There were many musicians in the royal family's entourage, and many more were to follow, including Marcos Portugal (1762–1830), the most prominent Portuguese composer at the time. Indeed, the court actively recruited Portuguese musicians as well as Italian *castrati* to meet the demands of the new institutions (Mariz 1983: 49). Dom João launched his musical initiatives in the already established ecclesiastical sphere, with the founding of the Imperial Chapel. At its zenith, 300,000 francs were expended each a year on this establishment, which sustained fifty singers, a full orchestra and two chapel masters (Mariz 1983: 49). Of special note, though, was the introduction of secular public events into the musical life of upper-class *cariocas* (inhabitants of Rio de Janeiro). In 1813 the construction of the Royal Theatre of Saint John, modelled on the great Saint Charles Theatre in Lisbon, was completed, and it was inaugurated with the performance of the opera *O Juramento dos Nunes*, by Marcos Portugal (Appleby 1983: 44). Opera, especially the work of Rossini, was all the rage, and this highbrow form of entertainment would remain popular throughout the nineteenth century.

When Dom João VI returned to Portugal in 1821 with a much reduced entourage of 4,000 subjects, the musical orientations of the Brazilian elites had been altered dramatically. In the first decades of the new nation, however, *carioca* musical life lost much of its lustre. Although the prince-regent-turned-emperor, Dom Pedro I, was himself an accomplished musician, the debts incurred with independence forced him to drastically curtail state sponsorship of the music institutions founded by his father, leaving scores of musicians unemployed. The Imperial Chapel was particularly hard-hit; its orchestra had to be disbanded, and the number of musicians it supported fell to twenty-seven (Mariz 1983: 55).

With the growth of the coffee economy in the 1840s, however, the national deficit rapidly declined, allowing for greater imperial patronage. The new emperor, Dom Pedro II, was a willing supporter of the arts, but the funds he could make available were insufficient to match the demands of an emergent bourgeoisie in search of cultural spaces worthy of their station. Thus, the *carioca* elites took to founding exclusive 'clubs' and 'societies', some more well-endowed than others, which became the main organizations for the promotion of secular concerts of serious music from the 1830s to the late nineteenth century. Each society promoted regular soirées, with a staple diet of Italian and French arias as well as light instrumental pieces and selected movements from chamber and orchestral repertoires; often poetry reading and short theatrical productions featured alongside the vocal and instrumental performances. After the official programme, dinner or refreshments were served, and the evening typically closed with a ball. As Cristina Magaldi (1995: 2) has pointed out, these events were more social than artistic, but the performance of art music served to demarcate the discerning tastes of those in attendance.

Throughout the nineteenth century musical markers played a significant role in defining the social boundaries which distinguished privileged (white) *cariocas* from the masses of dark-skinned popular classes that surrounded them. Herman Vianna (1999 [1995]), however, has argued that, in actual practice, the boundaries were far more porous than they have been made out to be; however entrenched the discourses separating the musical spheres of the privileged and the underprivileged may have been, musical interactions across the divide were frequent, everyday occurrences. Despite the disdain with which it was treated, the guitar was a primary mediator of these interactions, and its mediatory role was closely linked to the comings-and-goings firstly of the *modinha* and later of the *choro*.

Soon after its repatriation, the *modinha* – in its domesticated form, of course – gained popularity in Rio's drawing-rooms, where it remained popular throughout the imperial era, its repertoire enhanced by many of Brazil's most eminent composers, including José Maurício Nunes Garcia (1767–1830), Francisco Manuel da Silva (1795–1865), Carlos Gomes (1836–96) and many others. Although the piano was the favoured instrument for accompanying the *modinha* in the parlour context, it did not remain confined for long to this setting, nor did it remain restricted to the piano. According to Carlos Maul, Dom Pedro I's mistress, the Marquesa de Santos, promoted soirées at her home during the 1820s, in which she 'sang melancholy *modinhas* and *lundus*, accompanying herself on the gently plucked strings of the plaintive [guitar]' (Maul quoted in Vianna 1999: 19) to a very distinguished audience of aristocrats and high-ranking civil servants. Popular musicians in Rio also took to the *modinha*, and guitar-playing street *modinheiros* (*modinha* performers) were quite prevalent in the imperial capital, some of them receiving acclaim from members of the *carioca* elites. The work of the informally trained guitarist Joaquim Manuel, for example, drew the attention of the Austrian composer Sigismund Neukomm (1778–1858), a student of Haydn, whose sojourn in Rio lasted from 1816–21; he edited a collection in Paris of *modinhas* by the popular musician, which he had harmonised for piano. Joaquim Manuel also attracted the attention of the Frenchman Louise de Freycinet, who had this to say of him:

> In terms of performance, nothing seems more surprising than the rare talent on the guitar of a . . . *mestiço* from Rio de Janeiro called Joaquim Manuel. On his fingers the instrument has an indescribable charm, which I have never encountered amongst our European guitarists, even the most notable. (Quoted in M. de Araújo 1969: 69)

As the decades went by, social boundaries hardened, becoming particularly entrenched during the reign of Dom Pedro II. Nonetheless, spaces for inter-class cultural interaction never disappeared completely. Perhaps the most documented of these spaces for the mid nineteenth century is Paula Brito's printing shop, a meeting place for eminent *carioca* artists and intellectuals. But their activities were not restricted to highbrow cultural debates: they also engaged in light entertainment, often to the sounds of popular *sereteiros*. Some of the intellectuals even engaged in the performance of popular styles, most notably the Gypsy poet Laurindo Rabelo (1826–64), who 'played sentimental *modinhas* and turbulent *lundus* on the guitar that made even the most sober and responsible attendants laugh uncontrollably' (Moraes Filho 1904: 171). Allegedly even the eminent Francisco Manuel da Silva found respite at the shop, as here he could present his lighter repertoire of *modinhas* and *lundus* (Vianna 1995: 20).

During the 1860s the guitarist Xisto Bahia (1841–94) began to gain acclaim as an actor and a popular *modinheiro*, and his professional activities spanned several decades. Through his association with Artur Azevedo, a north-eastern playwright of national prominence, Xisto Bahia gained access to respectable spheres, his looks perhaps being one of his main attractions to the ladies, but others were won over by his 'spirit of harmonious grace, unmatched for the special way in which he knew how to sing his own *modinhas* and those of other composers' (Vincenzo Cernic-chiaro quoted in Tinhorão 1986: 26). Xisto Bahia even received the applause of the emperor, Dom Pedro II (Marcondes 1977: 61), and several eminent poets provided him with lyrics, requesting that he put them to music (Tinhorão 1986: 27).

And there was also the renowned Catulo da Paixão Cearence (1866–1946), who was initiated on the guitar in Rio de Janeiro by a medical student, no less (Marcondes 1977: 182). Catulo began his musical career at a time in which the cultural discourses of the elites were at their most entrenched, and considerable energy was being expended to cleanse the country of its African heritage. It is perhaps for this reason that Brazilian musicologists have often argued that he was the primary figure in the 'rehabilitation of the guitar' (Marcondes 1977: 183). For Vianna (1999 [1995]), however, his acceptance into upper class circles might be better viewed as an indication of the degree to which the dominant discourses contradicted everyday practice. Indeed, alongside a disdain for all things popular, incipient nationalist sentiments were fuelling a vogue for the country's exoticisms, spawning some of the first major publications of local folklore by such eminent intellectuals as Amadeu Amaral, Arthur Azevedo, Mello Moraes Filho, Silvio Romero and others.

It is also worth noting that, although the piano repertoire was primarily European in origin, it was not restricted to serious music. The successive cycles of European dance crazes, such as the polka, the quadrille, the schottische and the waltz, also crossed the Atlantic, finding favour in Brazilian drawing-rooms. Just as the *modinha* had quickly seeped out into the streets to find its way to the guitar, these dance forms were also taken up by street musicians. Within these circles a popular instrumental style would develop which came to be known as the *choro*.

According to the standard narrative,[7] the *choro* emerged around 1870 less as a distinct musical genre and more as a local way of performing European dance tunes, especially the polka. In its early phase the style was performed by an instrumental ensemble called a *trio de pau e corda* (wood and string trio), consisting of an ebony flute, which played the melody line, a *cavaquinho* (small, four coursed, instrument similar to a ukulele), which provided a percussive harmonic accompaniment, and a guitar, which provided the bass. In time, the *choro* would become ever more virtuosic and improvizational, and around the turn of the twentieth century other melody instruments started to be used in place of the flute, such as the *bandolim*, the clarinet and the ophicleide. *Chorões* typically performed at the house parties of their social equals as well as in cafés, hotels and cabarets, often in exchange for nothing more than food and drink.

Soon after its development amongst street musicians, the *choro* began a return journey into more respectable spheres, as a number of musically trained composers, such as Chiquinha Gonzaga (1847–1935), Alexandre Levy (1864–92), Ernesto Nazaré (1863–1933) among others, started to write *choros* for the piano. It is worth noting, however, that these composers often called their pieces Brazilian tangos; by thus distancing them from the street form, they hoped to give them greater respectability. As this popular piano style developed, however, a new distinction was to emerge, that between *pianeiros* – a derogatory term that referred to popular pianists – and *pianistas* – 'real' pianists, thereby redrawing the boundaries to safeguard the sanctity of the piano.

Throughout the nineteenth century, discourse focused upon the demarcation and preservation of musical boundaries, against a backdrop in which they were being continuously transgressed, the guitar serving as a primary mediator of these transgressions. As the century came to a close, however, nationalist sentiments had become increasingly marked amongst influential sectors of the country's intellectuals, shifting the focus of debate onto the stances of the elites toward the cultural manifestations of the popular classes. These voices challenged Eurocentrism by highlighting the cultural dependence it had engendered in the nation. If the country was to free itself from this cultural bondage, stock would have to be taken of its hybridity, a move that threatened to break down the barriers that had been so studiously constructed throughout the century to preserve the segregation of the country's distinct cultural worlds.

The Tupi's Lute: The Guitar in the Modernist Movement

The tensions between syncretism and segregation came to a head in the early twentieth century, when an *avant-garde* intelligentsia linked to the nationalist-oriented modernist movement embarked upon the project of defining the symbols of national identity. As Santuza Cambraia Naves (1998: 25) has pointed out, the guitar played a prominent symbolic role in Brazilian modernism, for its potential to mediate between the local cultures of the nation's popular classes and the 'universal' aesthetics of high art. This mediatory role is cogently embodied in an image in Mário de Andrade's poem, 'O Trovador' (the troubadour), from the collection, *Paulicéia Desvairada* (deranged São Paulo) published in 1922: *Sou um Tupi tangendo um alaúde* (*I am a Tupi Indian Playing a Lute*). In a rather less poetic – but certainly more explicit – fashion, Manuel Bandeira (1886–1968), a leading modernist poet, presented his discourse on the guitar in 1924 in an article published in *Ariel – Revista de Cultura Musical*, a cultural periodical widely read in modernist circles at the time:

> For us Brazilians the guitar had to be the national, racial instrument. If the *modinha* is the expression of our people, the guitar is the instrumental timbre to which it is best suited . . .
> Unfortunately up to now the guitar has been cultivated among us in a careless manner . . .
> The guitar has also been resisted for its fame as an instrument of the low-minded, of intrigue and as an accomplice to roguery in seductive late-night revelries . . . It has been rehabilitated, however, with the visit of two foreign artists, who revealed its resources and the true school of the great Spanish virtuosi to our amateurs. I am referring to Agostinho Barrios and Josefina Robledo . . . Besides the repertoire of the guitar itself, it has all of the repertoire of the lute . . . Our guitarists have composed very interesting pieces with a Brazilian character. Yet we have only heard about them. This is the case of the *maxixes*[8] by Arthiodoro da Costa, João Pernambucano, Quincas Laranjeiras and others of equal merit. (Bandeira, quoted in Naves 1998: 26–7)

Not surprisingly Bandeira concluded his discussion with a reference to Heitor Villa-Lobos (1887–1959), an obvious candidate to the honourable role of the Tupi with a lute, even though the composer was rather reluctant to embrace the role, a fact not lost on the poet:

Villa-Lobos . . ., who is now in Paris . . . played the guitar when he was young. And he composed quite a bit which is tightly locked away . . . And I don't know if he has thrown them into the sea . . . He doesn't like to speak of this. This prejudice is not modern and it isn't the least bit national. (Bandeira, quoted in Naves 1998: 27)

Today, of course, Villa-Lobos may be best remembered for some of his guitar solos, such as the *Choro No. 1* (1921), the *Estudos* (1929) and the *Prelúdios* (1940), which have become standard repertoire for the instrument. Indeed, his relationship to the guitar was at best ambiguous, and this was already evident even at a time in which his skills as a guitarist were still at their height. His first wife, Lucília Guimarães, an outstanding pianist in her own right, perceived this, and in her diary she noted her impressions of the day they met, 1 November 1912. Villa-Lobos had been taken to her home by a family friend, where he was to play guitar to entertain the household. Her remarks on the soirée are as follows:

The evening of music went well, extremely pleasant, and for us the guitar in Villa-Lobos's hands was a success. When he finished his presentation, Villa-Lobos indicated his desire to hear the pianist, and I played a few pieces by Chopin, and it seemed to me that he was impressed by the technique and interpretation of the performance.

However, Villa-Lobos felt embarrassed, perhaps diminished even, because at that time the guitar was not a parlour instrument, for real music, but rather a vulgar instrument played by street musicians (*chorões*) and serenaders (*seresteiros*). Suddenly, as though overcoming a depression, he declared that his real instrument was the cello, and he insisted that we arrange a meeting at our house to hear him play it. (Quoted in Horta 1987: 24–5.)

Villa-Lobos was born in Rio to a fairly comfortable middle-class family.[9] His father, Raul Villa-Lobos, an employee of the National Library, had a keen interest in music, and he sponsored frequent soirées of chamber music in the family home. He had studied the cello at conservatory, and he took it upon himself to initiate his son on the instrument at the age of six, followed some years later by clarinet tuition. The young musician showed early signs of his musical aptitude, but his father's premature death when he was only twelve years old threatened his further musical development. Against his mother's wishes, who envisaged for him a secure career as a physician, the lad slipped away from home as often as he could to join the *chorões*, amongst whom he acquired his skills as a guitarist. At the age of sixteen he moved to the house of an aunt, which gave him greater liberty to pursue his interest in the popular styles of the era.

After his marriage Villa-Lobos did not only start neglecting the guitar, he also began to avoid any reference to his days amongst *chorões* until much later in life. By the time he met Andrés Segovia in Paris in 1924, he was so out of practice he was unable to play more than a few bars (Santos 1975: 12–15). But had he not met the Spaniard he may never have written the *Estudos*, the *Prelúdios* or any of the other pieces he dedicated to the master guitarist. Most of the extant guitar pieces he wrote during his bohemian days still remain unpublished.

The symbolic value of the guitar for the ideologues of Brazilian modernists hinged upon its potential to mediate between cultural spheres on both horizontal and vertical axes. Horizontally, it could mediate between the rural and the urban, the regional and the national, the national and the international; vertically, it provided a link for integrating popular culture and high art as well as the racially defined social classes related to these disparate spheres. But if Brazil was to participate as an equal in the 'concert of nations', the guitar would have to be cultivated in accordance with the universal aesthetic ideals of high art, while preserving its national character. According to Bandeira, this is precisely what the Spanish virtuosi had achieved for their country. Before the guitar could become the national instrument, the deeply rooted prejudices still held against it by many influential members of the art world, including some of those attached to the modernist movement itself, would have to be overcome. Despite their efforts, however, it would be several decades before the piano would finally lose its place of prominence in Brazilian parlours.

The Aftermath: Guitars in Twentieth-century Brazil

Although the guitar would remain relatively marginal to the world of Brazilian art music, the modernist movement pre-empted the nationalist fervour that would soon take the country by storm, shifting the national focus away from the aesthetic preferences of the elites to those of the popular classes. To be sure, this shift was boosted by the populist agenda of Getúlio Vargas, who came to power in 1930, where he remained until 1945.[10] The Vargas regime focussed upon industrialization, coupling this drive with a strong nationalist discourse, aimed at integrating the popular classes into the country's economic and political structures. The nationalist project centred on the image of the 'cordial *mestiço*', a dignified hybrid labourer proud to be contributing to the prosperity of the country. Emblems of hybridity were forcefully promoted as symbols of national identity by the Vargas propaganda machine, and with the advent of the radio, music played a leading role in defining what would be taken for national culture.

The onset of the Vargas regime coincided with the emergence of *samba*, a hybrid popular style which drew on musical elements from the *lundu*, the *maxixi* and the *choro*, providing the Vargas regime with a ready-made musical form well suited to its agenda. *Samba* was co-opted and fashioned through censorship to promote 'Brazilian-ness'. With its carnivalesque associations, *samba* could be heralded as the felicitous integration of diverse cultural and racial groups that had been achieved in the country, and through the radio, this image was propagated across the entire country.

In the early decades of the twentieth century *samba* began to take shape within a few circles of popular musicians of low income, who met informally for their own entertainment, just as *modinheiros* and *chorões* had done before them. The most influential of these enclaves were the *sambistas* (*samba* musicians) who met in the home of Tia 'Aunt' Ciata, in the wharf district of Saúde, and those of Estácio de Sá, who founded 'Deixa Falar' (Let Them Speak), the first *samba* school, in 1928. The new style attracted the attention of the nascent music industry, but its rusticity offended the aesthetic sensibilities of record producers, who also felt the style would displease their target audiences, namely those with sufficient income to afford radio receivers. In response, they took to contracting trained arrangers to polish the popular compositions, while also drafting in songwriters and singers from comfortable backgrounds to insure the standard of their recordings (Schreiner 1993: 111; Shaw 1999: 50). Thus, alongside the rustic *samba* of the *morros* (hills), a reference to the slums built on the hills of Rio, a more melodious high-brow *samba* emerged, which came to be known as 'city *samba*' or *samba-canção* (song-*samba*); it was the latter which dominated the airwaves, its stars becoming household names throughout the country. The golden age of *samba* was dominated by exuberant singers with powerful throats, often backed by big-band-type orchestras. *Samba* promoted an image of tropical flamboyance and *alegria* (joy, happiness) coherent with the Vargas agenda.

With *samba* declared the national music, the guitar, the favoured instrument of *samba* composers, began to take on the aura of a national instrument. Indeed, Donga (1891–1974), who – together with *pianeiro* Sinhô (1888–1930) – claimed authorship of the first ever *samba* to be recorded, *Pelo Telefone* (By Telephone), in 1917, was an accomplished guitarist and *cavaquinho* player. The great demand for a steady supply of new *sambas* gave rise to numerous meeting places for *sambistas*, ranging from studios to cafés and music stores, and these circles of musicians tended to congregate around master guitarists. The Café Nice was a well-known meeting place for popular musicians (Shaw 1999: 47), as was the music store 'O Cavaquinho de Ouro' (Máximo and Didier 1990: 65). It is said that guitarist Noel Rosa (1910–37), one of the most prolific and enduring *samba* composers, wrote many of his songs in the bar De Carvalho, located in his neighbourhood of Vila Isabel (Shaw 1999: 92).

Samba certainly fostered national interest in the guitar, but it was insufficient to overthrow the dominant view amongst the upper class that it was not a serious instrument. Indeed, resistance from parents could be heavy handed toward youths who showed excessive interest in taking up the instrument. For those who did, the guitar became a symbol of renunciation. Noel Rosa, for example, had been prepared by his family to attend medical school, but he rejected this profession in favour of the less respectable world of popular music (Bastos 1996: 160). Amongst the darker lower classes, however, *samba* was one of the few available means of social ascent

(Pereira 1967). It is due to their guitar skills that such musicians as Donga, Ataúlfo Alves (1909–69), Bide (1902–75) and countless others from underprivileged backgrounds were able to secure a livelihood that did not involve manual labour.

As central as guitarists were to the world of *samba*, the focus of popular attention was directed primarily toward the singers; they were the undisputed stars of the radio. Yet with the emergence of *bossa nova* in the late 1950s national – and inter-national – attention was drawn specifically to Brazilian guitar techniques. Epitomized in the figure of João Gilberto (b. 1931), *bossa nova* centred on the image of a crooner sitting alone on a bench in the far corner of an intimate night-club, picking out sophisticated chords in smooth, but disjointed, rhythmic patterns to the sound of a soft speech-like melodic line that invoked an utopian dream world of 'love, smiles and flowers'.[11] Sitting at the interface between popular music and art music, *bossa nova*, with its distinctly Brazilian character, would finally produce the lute-playing Tupi which the modernists had envisaged. Furthermore, *bossa nova* definitively established the legitimacy of the guitar amongst the country's middle and upper classes, consolidating its place as the quintessential national instrument. In urban centres across the country, middle-class youths rushed to take up the guitar, all attempting to imitate João Gilberto's unique guitar technique. Carlos Lyra (b. 1936) and Roberto Menescal (b. 1937) were amongst the first to capitalize upon this surge of interest, setting up a guitar academy in 1958, which initiated anxious youths into the secrets of their idol. From then on piano teachers would lose ground to the legions of guitar instructors responding to the new demand.

With the emergence of *bossa nova* the guitar became the instrument to cross-cut the social divisions of the country. It could be heard from the poorest and darkest quarters to the richest and whitest, in both rural and urban contexts. Yet *bossa nova* also laid bare the musical boundaries marked by style which samba had striven so forcefully to conceal. Although it drew on elements from samba, the elitism and gimmicky character of *bossa nova* distanced it from its popular roots (Reily 1996; Treece 1997). Its lyrics addressed the carefree existence of an affluent youth culture, downplaying the stereotypical carnivalesque image of Brazilians as over-emotive and exuberant people, typical of *samba*, to portray them as contemplative, sophisticated and cosmopolitan. Thus, despite the hegemonic status it achieved, the actual popularity of *bossa nova* was restricted. Even when MPB (Música Popular Brasileira [Brazilian Popular Music]), which succeeded *bossa nova*, attempted to create styles that consciously drew on regional musical referents, the mainstream remained the reserve of the middle and upper classes.

Meanwhile guitars and guitar-like instruments were being employed in countless localized styles, most of which were – and many continue to be – entirely ignored by the mainstream music industry. *Violas*, for example, are the most common instruments used in north-eastern *cantoria*, a musical duel between two performers;

many gaucho traditions of southern Brazil are accompanied by the guitar; and in the South-east a *viola* and a guitar are the main instruments used to accompany *música sertaneja*, something of a Brazilian counterpart to American country music, which is typically performed by a duo (*dupla*) singing in parallel thirds or sixth. Though highly popular within their restricted spheres, these sounds – like those of Arthiodoro da Costa, João Pernambucano, Quincas Laranjeiras and others of equal merit during Bandeira's time – have remained unheard by the vast majority of middle and upper class audiences. It is worth noting, however, that *música sertaneja* did manage to make a break-through into the mainstream toward the end of the 1980s, much to the dismay of those with discerning tastes. This was achieved by the shear numerical force of low-income fans with sufficient buying-power to set national trends.

The struggle, therefore, continues. Indeed, today it is the very legitimacy of the guitar as national instrument that is being challenged, with voices emerging in defence of other popular instruments. For Roberto Nunes Correa, for example, the 'real' Tupi's lute is the *viola*, and he has prepared a tutor for the instrument to make his point. The manual contains information about the *viola* in Brazil, followed by musical scores for eight pieces which exemplify its artistic potential in a manner reminiscent of the modernist discourse. In his own words:

> Besides not finding a place for their music, *violeiros* today also face the . . . depreciation of their art. It is common to find people using the terms *viola caipira* and *violeiro* in a belittling way, even pejoratively, as though the figure of the *violeiro* were old-fashioned, or, as the *violeiros* themselves say, an old useless rogue. This distorted mentality is gratuitous . . . ; besides being the most representative instrument of our folklore, it is not a limited instrument. On the contrary, it has great potential, and it is of an impressive timbral richness; the variety of its tuning systems provides extremely original harmonic fields. Our intention is to restore and promote what has been done in relation to the *viola*, and amplify its space, that is, to use it as a solo instrument as well as to integrate it in chamber orchestras. (Corrêa 1989: 18)

Other voices reject string instruments altogether in favour of the drum, the instrument which in Débret's time was exclusive to slaves. In fact, today Brazil's main contribution to global culture is its percussion-based traditions. Over the past decade, samba bands have emerged in many parts of the world, including Europe, America, Australia, Japan and other places. These groups draw their repertoire from the rhythms of the famous samba schools of Rio, but also – and perhaps more importantly – from the *blocos Afro* of the Northeast, which are alleged to be more 'authentic'. It may be difficult to image the drum ever to be taken for a serious instrument; but surely nineteenth century Brazilians would have found it difficult to conceive that the piano could ever be displaced by such a vulgar instrument as the guitar.

Notes

1. The *cavaquinho* is a four-coursed string instrument which looks like a ukulele.
2. All translations are my own unless otherwise stated.
3. The Portuguese *viola* was most commonly described as a six double-coursed string instrument shaped like the modern guitar, though it was somewhat smaller and had a wider 'waist'. This instrument was the forerunner of the Brazilian *viola*, but in its most common forms in Brazil today the *viola* is a five double-coursed instrument with a much narrower waist than the Portuguese prototype; tuning systems for the instrument vary considerably. In Brazil the lute left its mark on the *bandola* and the much smaller *bandolim*. Although *bandolas* have become virtually obsolete, the *bandolim*, a mandolin-type instrument with four double courses typically tuned in fifths (g-d-a-e), is still used as a melody instrument in several Brazilian musical styles. The *machete* is the antecedent of the *cavaquinho*, which, like its Portuguese counterpart, is shaped like a small guitar and has four single courses. In Brazil it is generally played with a plectrum to provide an harmonic percussive accompaniment to a number of styles, and its two most common tunings are d-g-b-d and d-g-b-e. The *guitarra*, a single-coursed instrument, was, of course, the forerunner of the guitar, which in Brazil came to be known as the *violão* (large *viola*). It was standardized in the mid nineteenth century, and today the Brazilian *violão* is virtually identical to the acoustic Spanish guitar.
4. The original dates of Pereira's manuscripts are not known, but he was born in 1652 in Bahia and died in Lisbon some time after 1733 (Tinhorão 1990: 68).
5. Because the *modinha* is seen to be central to the development of a Brazilian national musical culture, it has been the object of considerable research, including major studies by Mário de Andrade (1980 [1930]), Mozart de Araújo (1963) and João Batista Siqueira (1979) as well as numerous studies of lesser breadth. A survey of this vast literature has been conducted recently by Manuel Veiga (1998).
6. The lyrics to many of his songs were first published in two volumes, called *Viola de Leredo*, between 1798 and 1826; a few scores of his compositions were also made available after they were discovered several decades ago in the Ajuda Library in Lisbon (Béhague 1968).
7. On the *choro*, see: Appleby (1983: 70-3), Schreiner (1993: 85–101), Tinhorão (1986: 103–10; 1997: 107–25), Vasconcelos (1988b) among others.
8. A fast syncopated dance music form of the late nineteenth century commonly viewed as the forerunner of the samba.
9. On the life and work of Villa-Lobos, see: Appleby (1983: 116–38), Béhague (1979: 183–204), Horta (1987), Keifer (1986), Mariz (1977) among others.

10. Getúlio Vargas regained power from 1950 to his death in 1954.
11. The title of João Gilberto's second LP, released in 1960, was *O amor, o sorriso e a flor* (Love, Smile and Flower), epitomizing the thematic material of *bossa nova* lyrics.

References

Andrade, M. de (1922), *Paulicéia Desvairada*, São Paulo: Casa Mayença.
—— (1933), *Compêndio de História da Música*, 2nd edn, São Paulo: Miranda.
—— (1980 [1930]), *Modinha Iimperiais*, Belo Horizonte: Editora Itatiaia.
Appleby, D.P. (1983), *The Music of Brazil*, Austin: University of Texas Press.
Araújo, A.M. de (1964), *Folclore Nacional*, 3 vols, São Paulo: Melhoramentos.
Araújo, M. de (1963), *A Modinha e o Lundu no Século XVIII*, São Paulo: Ricordi Brasileira.
Azevedo, C. de and L. Heitor (1997), 'Portuguese Musicians in Brazil: An introduction to the study of the Portuguese contribution to the development of Brazilian Musical Culture', in S.E-S. Castelo-Branco (ed.), *Portugal and the World: The encounter of cultures in music*, Lisbon: Publicações Dom Quixote: 439–45.
Bastos, R.J. de Menezes (1996), 'A "Origem do Samba" Como Invenção do Brasil (por que as canções têm música?)', *Revista Brasileira de Ciências Sociais* 31: 156–77.
Béhahue, G. (1968), 'Biblioteca da Ajuda (Lisbon) MSS 1595/1596: Two Eighteenth-Century Anonymous Collections of Modinhas', *Yearbook of Inter-American Institute for Musical Research* 4: 44–81.
—— (1979), *Music in Latin America*, Englewood Cliffs NJ: Prentice-Hall.
Bourdieu, P. (1979), *La Distinction*, Paris: Éditions de Minuir.
Boxer, C.R (1969), *The Golden Age of Brazil: 1695–1750*, Berkeley: University of California Press.
Canclini, N.G. (1998 [1989]), *Culturas Híbridas:Eestratégias para entrar e sair da modernidade*, São Paulo: Editora da Universidade de São Paulo.
Cearense, C. da Paixão (1924), *Matta Iluminada*, Rio de Janeiro: Leite Ribeiro.
Corrêa, R.N. (1989), *Viola caipira*. Brasília: Viola Corrêa.
Débret, J.B. (1940 [1834–9]), *Viagem Pitoresca e História Através do Brasil*, São Paulo: Martins.
Freyre, G. (1968 [1936]), *Sobrados e Mucambos*, Rio de Janeiro: José Olympio.
Horta, L.P. (1987), *Villa-Lobos: Uma introdução*, Rio de Janeiro: Jorge Zahar.
Karasch, M. (1992), 'Catequese e Cativeiro: Política indigenista em Goiás', in M.C. da Cunha (ed.), *História dos Indios no Brasil*. São Paulo: Companhia das Letras/Secretaria Municipal da Cultura/FAPESP: 397–412.

Kiefer, B. (1977), *A Modinha e o Lundu*, Porto Alegre: Editora Movimento.

—— (1986), *Villa-Lobos e o Modernismo na Música Brasileira*, Porto Alegre: Editora Movimento.

La Rue, H. (1994), 'Music, Literature and Etiquette: Musical instruments and social identity from Castiglione to Austen', in M. Stokes (ed.), *Ethnicity, Identity and Music: The musical construction of place*. Oxford: Berg.

Lange, F.C. (1966), *A Organização Musical Durante o Período Colonial Brasileiro*, Coimbra: Separata do Volume IV das Actas do V Coloquio Internacional de Estudos Luso-brasileiros.

Leite, S. (1937–49), *História da Companhia de Jesus no Brasil*, Rio de Janeiro: Imprensa Nacional.

Lima, R.T. de (1964), 'Estudo Sôbre a Viola', *Revista Brasileira de folclore* 4: 29–38.

Magaldi, C. (1995), 'Music for the Elite: Musical societies in imperial Rio de Janeiro', *Latin American Music Review* 16(1): 1–41.

Marcondes, M.A. (ed.) (1977), *Enciclopédia da Música Brasileira – Erudita, Folclórica, Popular*, São Paulo: Art Editora.

Mariz, V. (1977), *Heitor Villa-Lobos: Compositor brasileiro*, Rio de Janeiro: Museu Villa-Lobos.

—— (1983), *História da Música no Brasil*, Rio de Janeiro: Civilização Brasileira.

Máximo, J. and C. Didier (1990), *Noel Rosa: Uma biografia*, Brasília: Editora UnB.

Montanaro, B.R. (1983), *Guitares Hispano-américaines*, La Calade, Aix-en-Provance: Édisud.

Moraes Filho, M. (1904), *Artistas do Meu Tempo*, Rio de Janeiro: H. Garnier.

Naves, S.C. (1998), *O Violão Azul: Modernismo e música popular*, Rio de Janeiro: Fundação Getúlio Vargas.

Oliveira, E.V. de (1966), *Instrumentos Musicais Populares Portugueses*, Lisbon: Fundação Calouste Gulbenkian.

Pereira, J.B.B. (1967), *Cor, Profissão e Mobilidade (O Negro e o Rádio de São Paulo)*, São Paulo: Pioneira.

Pereira, N.M. (1939), *Compêndio Narrativo do Peregrino da América*, Rio de Janeiro: Publicações da Academia Brasileira.

Reily, S.A. (1998), 'Central and Southern Brazil', *The Garland Encyclopedia of World Music*, vol IX: 300–22.

—— (1996), 'Tom Jobim and the Bossa Nova Era', *Popular Music* 15(1): 1–16.

Santos, T. (1975), *Heitor Villa-Lobos e o Violão*, Rio de Janeiro: Museu Villa-Lobos/MEC.

Schreiner, C. (1993), *Música Brasileira: A history of popular music and the people of Brazil*, New York: Marion Books.

Shaw, L. (1999), *The Social History of Brazilian Samba*, Aldershot: Ashgate.

Preface

Siqueira, J.B. (1979 [1956]), *Modinhas do Passado*, Rio de Janeiro: Folha Carioca.

Skidmore, T.E. (1999), *Brazil: Five centuries of change*, New York: Oxford University Press.

Staunton, Sir George (1797), *An Authentic Account of an Embassy from the King of Great Britain to the Emperor of China*, London: W. Bulmer Co.

Tinhorão, J.R. (1986), *Pequena História da Música Popular: Da modinha ao tropicalismo*, São Paulo: Art Editora.

—— (1990), *História Social da Música Popular Brasileira*, Lisbon: Caminho da Música.

—— (1997 [1966]), *Música Popular – Um Tema em Debate*, São Paulo: Editora 34.

Treece, D. (1997), 'Guns and Roses: Bossa Nova and Brazil's music of popular protest, 1958–68', *Popular Music* 16(1): 1–29.

Vasconcelos, A. (1988a), 'Aculturação e Ressonâncias', in T. de Souza, A. Vascocelos, R.M. Moura, J. Makimo, L.C. Mansur, T. Santos, A.R. de Sant'Anna, R. Cáurio (eds) *Brasil Musical*. Rio de Janeiro: Edições de Arte: 46–69.

—— (1988b), 'Choro: Um ritmo bem brasileiro', in T. de Souza, A. Vascocelos, R.M. Moura, J. Makimo, L.C. Mansur, T. Santos, A.R. de Sant'Anna, R. Cáurio (eds) *Brasil Musical*, Rio de Janeiro: Edições de Arte: 70–99.

Veiga, M. (1998), 'O Estudo da Modinha Brasileira', *Latin American Music Review* 19(1): 47–91.

Vianna, H. (1999 [1995]), *The Mystery of Samba: Popular music and national identity in Brazil*, Chapel Hill: The University of North Carolina Press.

Zemella, M.P. (1990), *O Abastecimento da Capitania das Minas Gerais no Século XVIII*, São Paulo: Hucitec/EDUSP.

–10–

Rock to Raga: The Many Lives of the Indian Guitar

Martin Clayton

Introduction

What roles does the guitar play, and what meanings does it convey in India?[1] These are not easy questions to answer, because the instrument has spread into many different musical genres, in various geographical regions of the subcontinent. This chapter is nonetheless an attempt, in response to those questions, to sketch out the main features of guitar culture in India. I see it as a kind of snapshot: partial, blurred and lacking fine definition perhaps, but offering a perspective that more focused and tightly framed studies could not.

My account is based on a few weeks' travel in India,[2] concentrating on the main metropolitan cities of Chennai, Mumbai, Calcutta and Delhi – although it also draws on the reports of many inhabitants of these cities who have migrated from other regions, particularly those rich in guitar culture such as Goa and the north-eastern states. In other respects it draws on as balanced a sample of accounts as could be achieved in a short time: those of players from professional virtuosi to rank amateurs, of repertoires from Indian classical to rock and jazz, as well as those of makers, retailers and repairers. Finally, this account draws on many years studying the music of India – albeit most of those years studiously ignoring the very genres to which, in the winter of 1998–99, I turned my attention.

What I knew of the Indian guitar before my research began included Brij Bhushan Kabra's excellent recordings of North Indian classical music on slide guitar, the first of which date from the 1960s [3] and those of his successors including Vishwa Mohan Bhatt, who had recently made an international name for himself by recording a well-received album with Ry Cooder. (That album, *A Meeting by the River*,[4] had won the pair a Grammy Award in 1994, a fact of which I was reminded in India on many occasions.) I also knew that the guitar was one of many instruments used in Indian film music, where the Hawaiian style of playing had once been prominent, and that imported recordings of guitar-based rock music are easily found in metropolitan record shops.

Figure 10.1 Mondal Brothers' guitar shop in Calcutta

That was the skeleton I wanted to flesh out. More importantly I wanted to gauge how the instrument was regarded – as a foreign import suitable mainly for foreign music? If so, how and why had it been adapted to Hindustani classical music?[5] In a society proud of its own musical heritage, how and why had a foreign instrument like the guitar made such an impact? How, in brief, had the dialectic between the guitar as a bringer of global (i.e. largely Euro-American) culture to the world, and its local adaptations and appropriations, panned out in India?

Figure 10.2 Gibtone, Calcutta with shopowner Enamul Haque standing in the doorway and a crate of guitars in the foreground

This chapter will emphasize the wide spread of the instrument – the guitar is extremely common and familiar throughout urban India, although rather less so in most rural areas by all accounts – and the wide range of repertoires performed. In short, the huge popularity of the guitar in contemporary India should be clear. The guitar, in its various guises, is also inevitably associated with a variety of other factors, such as the ethnic, linguistic and religious background of players – above all the instrument is associated with the West, with Christianity, and with

Goan and Anglo-Indian mixed-race communities. More widely, attitudes to the guitar in India are bound up with attitudes to 'Indianness' and 'the West', to conceptions of Indian cultural identity and to notions of 'tradition' and 'modernity', which give a particular local colour to responses to globalization.

Before discussing the current use and status of the guitar in India, it will be helpful to set the instrument's Indian presence in historical context, since the history of the guitar in India is inextricably bound up with the history of European colonialism and Christian proselytization.

Christians, Europeans and Western music in India: history, ethnicity and identity

A Brief History of the Indian Christians

One of the major themes of this chapter is ethnicity and identity, and in particular those of the groups described by the labels Christian, Anglo-Indian and Goan. The easiest way to begin an explanation of these categories is with a brief history of Christianity in India. The oldest Christian communities in India are those of the southern states of Kerala and Tamil Nadu, often referred to as Syriac (or Syrian) Christian, which were, local tradition has it, established by Saint Thomas the Apostle after his arrival in the year 52 CE. This community was joined by further converts following the conquest of Goa by Portugal in 1510 CE and the subsequent establishment of a string of European trading stations around the Indian coast.[6] The Portuguese always claimed proselytization to be at least as important an aim of their colonial expansion as trading profit. As a result, according to one estimate, by 1600 there were about 175,000 Christians in India, about 50,000 of whom were in Goa (Pearson 1987: 121).

The Portuguese authorities actively encouraged intermarriage, and there was in many respects little discrimination in Portuguese India between Indian Christians, settled Portuguese and *mestiços* (those of mixed parentage). In later centuries these 'Goans' were to be found not only in the latter-day Portuguese colonies of Goa, Daman and Diu, but further afield, particularly around the European trading posts and garrisons (see Abel 1988: 9–11), to which they soon began to migrate. According to one recent account, 'There are around 730,000 Portuguese Indians, commonly known as Goans or Goanese, about half of whom live in the state of Goa and the others elsewhere in India' (Library of Congress 1996: 211).

The term 'Anglo-Indian' has been used in a range of senses, but the usage assumed here (and by most of my informants) is that of the Government of India Act 1935, in which an Anglo-Indian is described as a person of European descent in the male line, born in India of parents who were habitually resident there.[7] 'Anglo-Indian' applied in this sense principally to the descendants of British men and their Indian wives – as with the Portuguese, in the early decades of British involvement in India few European women travelled to India, and intermarriage was officially encouraged from 1687 to around 1785, although attitudes changed thereafter. The British colonial authorities were not always so sanguine as the Portuguese about the benefits of missionary activity: nonetheless, both Protestant and Catholic missionaries were active in British India from the eighteenth century, and had some success in converting members of tribal, lower caste and *dalit* ('untouchable') groups.

In the British period and latterly in independent India, the status of Anglo-Indians has been famously marginal and problematic – at the risk of gross generalization, the classic picture describes them as looked down on by the British as 'half-breeds' and also mistrusted by Indians who perceived them to be loyal to British rule (Anglo-Indians did indeed play an important role in putting down the revolt or 'Mutiny' of 1857). Partly as a result of their rejection by both British and Indian populations, the Anglo-Indians effectively became an endogamous group some time in the nineteenth century, which they largely remain. They are the only group in India acknowledged as having English as their first language, are mostly Christian and tend to favour Western dress.

The Anglo-Indian population has dwindled since independence as many emigrated (to the UK, Australia and Canada in particular), although a contingent remained behind, largely in urban centres. Estimates for the size of the Anglo-Indian community range from 100,000 to 300,000.[8] It is difficult to be at all precise, but as the population of India soars over the billion mark it is unlikely that the combined Goan and Anglo-Indian communities number much more than a million, or 0.1 per cent of the total. The total Christian population was estimated as 20 million, around 2.3 per cent of the Indian population, in the 1991 census. Their significance to Indian guitar culture, however, far exceeds this numerical strength – besides the Goans and Anglo-Indians, the converted 'tribal' populations of the north-eastern states have also enthusiastically adopted the guitar.[9]

During my visit in the winter of 1998–99, Christians were in the news in India. Partly because of a strong showing by the Congress Party under Sonia Gandhi, Rajiv's Italian-born widow, the Hindu nationalist parties decided to turn their attentions from the Muslim minority to the even smaller Christian community. Reports started to reach the press of attacks on missionaries and the burning of churches. Some Hindu organizations stepped up reconversion programmes, and disseminated anti-Christian propaganda. The Nobel Prize awarded to the UK-based economist Amartya Sen was, we were told, part of a global Christian plot to destabilize Hindu India; Christianity and anti-national activity always went hand in hand.[10] While it would be an exaggeration to describe anti-Christian feeling as endemic in India, this effort to portray Christians as an 'enemy within' is significant, not least because it taps into wider concerns over India's national identity and destiny, and its relationship to the powers of the industrialised West.

Western Music in India

The history of Western music in India has hardly begun to be written, but it is known that various forms of Western musical culture were to be found on Indian soil soon after the arrival of the Europeans. Ian Woodfield reports that the 'guitar was the preferred instrument of Portuguese and Spanish sailors' in the sixteenth and seventeenth centuries (Woodfield 1995: 82), and the instrument was certainly imported into Goa: there is no reason to suppose that the presence of the instrument, in its various forms, in the territory has not been continuous since the early sixteenth century.[11]

The Portuguese banned many forms of indigenous music, while teaching their own repertoires in seminaries and parish schools; church music in particular thrived (Harrison 1975: 343–4). As Goans began to migrate to the factories and garrisons of other European powers in the seventeenth century, they took the guitar with them. Abbé Carré reported in sarcastic fashion from a Dutch factory near Golconda in 1673:

> The Dutch employ . . . among others a fine troop of musicians. These are poor Christians from Kanara, near Goa. They had passed their youth in slavery with some Portuguese nobles, where they had learned to strum a guitar and sing some airs, almost as melodious as penitential psalms. They have become so proud of their accomplishments that, finding nothing to attract them in their own country, they visit the oriental courts, as they think there is nothing more charming and melodious than their music. I had this diversion at all our meals. One tortured a harp, another strummed a guitar, a third scraped a violin, and two others, having no instruments but their voices, joined in with the rest in such a way that one could not listen to their harmonies without pity and compassion. (Abbé Carré, cited by Woodfield 1995: 245.)

By the late eighteenth century, as the British sought to cement and bureaucratize their rule and men began to bring wives over from home rather than marry locally, their households became the site of European-style domestic music making – as in Britain at that time, the harpsichord was a particularly favoured instrument – as well as public performance, at least in major centres such as Calcutta.[12] It is not clear just how widely used the guitar was in British India in the eighteenth and nineteenth centuries, although there is some evidence that it was used as a chamber instrument by Europeans.[13] Since the instrument was popular with women in Europe at the time, it seems probable that guitars were imported in greater numbers as the numbers of European women in India increased in the nineteenth century.

It is not clear from published accounts at what point Anglo-Indians assumed an important role in the musical history of India. Unlike the Goans, Anglo-Indians (at least those of British descent) do not have a particularly 'musical' image in India – which may mean simply that they were less inclined to take up music as a profession.

Anglo-Indians were prominent within the Army until the late eighteenth century, when the British authorities became nervous of their presence and drove them out; they may, however, have continued to make up the great majority of military bandsmen after that watershed.[14]

References to music in accounts of the Anglo-Indian community are generally brief, but tend to confirm the importance of dance and music in the community's social life. Gist and Wright, for instance, reported in 1973 that dance and singing were important forms of recreation for the Anglo-Indians:

> Group singing of popular and sentimental songs – invariably Western in theme and music – is a favorite form of informal recreation when Anglo-Indians gather together in a spirit of good fellowship. Teenagers and young adults usually prefer 'rock' and other forms of popular music to the familiar melodies which are favorites of the older adults. (Gist and Wright 1973: 147)

This picture is corroborated by the Calcuttan jazz guitarist Arthur Gracias:

> Basically the Anglo-Indians are very fun-loving people and very very musical. They have a lot of music, they love fun and frolic and there's music almost every day in most Anglo-Indian homes. They sing, they play guitar, piano . . . and they love to interact. (Arthur Gracias, pers. com.)

Where the services of professional performers of Western instruments were required, Goans (along with, perhaps, small numbers of Europeans and Anglo-Indians) answered the call. Pearson reports that as many Goans migrated, 'in the nineteenth century Goans in British India acquired a reputation as servants, cooks and musicians' (Pearson 1987: 155). By the 1950s, he continues, 'Of [the 80,000 Goans] in Bombay, the main occupations were seamen (37 per cent), cooks and waiters (18 percent), clerks, tailors and *ayahs* [maids or nurses] (each 8 per cent) and musicians (2 percent)' (Pearson 1987: 156). This would suggest a figure of roughly 1,600 professional Goan musicians resident in Bombay, most if not all Christians and performers on Western instruments, and many no doubt employed in the film industry.

The Guitar's Indian Origins

This history is not, however, universally accepted: in India, the suggestion of foreign origin is always likely to produce strong reactions. At the Archive and Research Center for Ethnomusicology (ARCE), the invaluable ethnomusicology archive in Delhi, a press cutting caught my eye: a piece from a Hindi newspaper, it suggested that the modern guitar is none other than the *kacchap vina*, an ancient Indian instrument long since forgotten at home but taken up abroad and popularized by the Americans:

... some Indians and many foreigners labour under the misapprehension that the guitar
is a foreign instrument and that its use in India began in this present era. But this is not
true. (Sinha 1998, my translation).

The author of this piece goes on to explain, with reference to musicologist
Swami Avanindranath Thakur, that the *kacchap* ('tortoise') *vina*, whose form is
'the same as' the modern guitar, is mentioned in the Samaveda, one of the most
ancient and sacred of Hindu texts.[15] His conjecture is that the instrument gradually
became more popular in the West whilst new instruments began to supersede it in
India; eventually it was lost together with the *prabandha* songs (precursors of the
modern *dhrupad*) which it had accompanied, while a new type emerged in America
under the name 'guitar'. How had this happened? The guitar must have been taken
to Hawaii from India by Anglo-Indians, and from there spread to the rest of the
world. A second type of *kacchap vina* meanwhile spread to Spain, where it became
known as the 'Spanish guitar'. Moreover, the name is actually not gi Œr (the usual
Hindi transliteration), but g′tŒr, a contraction of g′t (song) + tŒr (string or wire),
the name given because it was used to accompany songs.[16]

The attribution of Indian origins to anything of perceived cultural value is
often mocked and satirized by Indians themselves: a character on the BBC comedy
series *Goodness Gracious Me*, for instance, repeatedly tries to persuade his son
of the Indian origin of phenomena from Superman to the British Royal Family,
with hilarious effect. In some respects the argument cited here is indeed rather
far-fetched (to the point of absurdity when, for instance, the author claims that
'Hawaiian' is a contraction of 'Hawaii' plus '(Indi)an'). The idea is of interest
however, and not only as an instance of a perceived need to ascribe Indian origins
to the guitar before it can be fully accepted. What the author fails to discuss is the
more specific point that the technique of playing guitar (or other stringed instruments) with a slide may in fact have been disseminated from India.

The Hawaiian guitar's origins remain contested, but one story involves Indian
influence. Donald Mitchell and George Kanahele report a tale told by the Hawaiian
composer Charles E. King, in which he describes an occasion in 1884 when he
saw 'Gabriel Davion – a young man who was born in India, kidnapped by a sea
captain and finally brought to Honolulu', who had attracted attention for his 'new
way' of playing guitar with a slide (Kanahele 1979: 366–7).

The guitar itself had by this time been known in Hawaii for some decades,
having been introduced via north America in the early decades of the nineteenth
century:[17] the motivation for slide playing seems to have been, as elsewhere, a
desire to better imitate vocal nuances. This fact was noted by Mantle Hood, who
suggested that: 'The manner in which the text of a Hawaiian song is sung and the
manner in which the same song is played on the Hawaiian guitar are very similar.
It is difficult to say which influences the other, but since the singing voice was
present long before the steel guitar, it is probably safe to assume that the instrument

is imitating the voice' (1983: 142–3). As Hood suggests, this strong affinity between voice and stringed instrument is common at least to India and Java besides Hawaii.

The technique of playing slide guitar was popularised by a Hawaiian, Joseph Kekuku, around the turn of the century (Kekuku was the first to record on slide guitar, in 1909),[18] but Hood is convinced that he was inspired by Davion's intro-duction of a technique he had learned in India: 'Fairly stated, we should say Davion introduced the principle to the Islands and Kekuku developed a Hawaiian version of the guitar that became the steel guitar' (1983: 145). This technique is used on both the north Indian *vichitra vina* and the south Indian *gottuvadyam*, and was probably first used on the *ekatantri vina* (a single-stringed stick zither), certainly by the seventh century CE and possibly as early as 200 BCE (Hood 1983: 144-5, drawing on the work of B. C. Deva).

The international craze for Hawaiian music took in not only America and Europe but also many Asian countries.[19] In India, John Marsden and Charles Kohlhoff report, Hawaiian hit records and movies of the 1930s and 1940s enjoyed great popularity. Hawaiian touring groups began to visit India, and also, 'a number of Indian musicians began to take up Hawaiian music. (All of these performers were Anglo-Indians, Anglo-Burmese, Goans and Indonesians rather than full-blooded Indians)' (Kanahele 1979: 166). The best known of these musicians was Garney Nyss (1916–98), who formed his band the Aloha Boys in 1938 and continued to perform Hawaiian guitar for the next 60 years, recording with HMV India and broadcasting through All India Radio.[20]

The sound of the Hawaiian guitar was to remain an important part of the Indian soundscape for several decades, as it became part of the film-music sound-palette[21] and was also employed in other popular genres, particularly in Bengal. Before long, moreover, the potential of the instrument as a vehicle for Hindustani (North Indian) classical music was recognised. Slide guitar is now widely accepted as a suitable instrument for classical music, and I was fortunate to be able to interview the two leading performers, Vishwa Mohan Bhatt and Debashish Bhattacharya. My account of present-day Indian guitar culture begins with Bhattacharya.

Travelogue I: Calcutta

The Classicist

I found Debashish Bhattacharya's flat after criss-crossing south Calcutta's bewilder-ing residential colonies for what seemed an age. Street signs, let alone maps, are a rarity here, but this is a place governed by human geography – there is always someone around to ask. When I finally arrived Debashish was there at his balcony to welcome me, smartly dressed in blue silk *kurta* and waistcoat, sending his student down to carry my bags: he was ready for my video camera . . .

One of the new breed of brilliant classical guitar virtuosi, Debashish Bhatta-charya was brought up in a musical family: both his father and mother sang *khyal* and light-classical songs. The first instrument he touched, at the age of four, was a six-string acoustic Hawaiian guitar belonging to his mother. Surprising as this may sound, at the time (Debashish was born in 1963) the Hawaiian guitar would have been a common sight in middle-class Calcuttan households. Apparently the Hawaiian guitar craze was such – his comment was confirmed by other Bengali friends – that it became almost de riguer for a middle class Bengali girl to learn to play *Rabindrasangeet* (Tagore songs) on the Hawaiian guitar, a skill acquired largely to help her marriage prospects.

The guitar has been used in Bengal, in genres from theatre music to *adhunik gan* ('modern songs') for many years. One reason for its popularity in Calcutta, Bhattacharya explained, was that a Hawaiian master named Tau Moe (b. 1909) had visited India several times (the first time in 1930) and actually stayed in Calcutta from 1940 to 1947 where he performed regularly at the Grand Hotel, and took over responsibility the hotel's entertainment.[22] Tau Moe's influence was significant in the burgeoning popularity of the Hawaiian guitar in India. Moe's student, the Calcuttan Anglo-Indian Garney Nyss, had apparently won second prize in an international Hawaiian guitar competition some years back: Nyss had taught a Bengali Christian named Rajat Nandy, and Nandy had taught Bhattacharya. Thus, Bhattacharya is not only linked to the Hindustani vocal tradition through his guru Ajoy Chakraborty, and to the nascent Hindustani guitar tradition through Brij Bhushan Kabra, but also to a sixty-year-old Calcuttan Hawaiian guitar tradition.

The first attempts to play Indian music on the guitar may have been those of Van Shipley, a Methodist originally of Lucknow (latterly resident in Mumbai) who learned from Ustad Allauddin Khan and designed his own eight-string electric guitar back in the 1940s.[23] Bhattacharya credits the well-known musician and teacher Jnan Prakash Ghosh with playing Hindustani music on 'slide *tanpura*' on All India Radio broadcasts, and encouraging a Western-style guitarist named Sujit Nath to try to play a little Indian music. Mark Humphrey cites the 1953 film *Ladki* in which one song 'opens with a brief meditative slide guitar line reminiscent of a slow *alap* . . .'(1994: 110).[24]

To most Indian classical music lovers however, the guitar is associated most strongly with the name of Debashish Bhattacharya's teacher, Brij Bhushan Kabra. Kabra it was who in the 1960s made the first recordings on guitar as a classical soloist, playing an f-hole archtop with three of its six strings used as *chikari* – strings tuned to the system tonic Sa, found on Indian instruments such as the *bin* (*rudra vina*), *sarod* and *sitar*, which are plucked repeatedly to provide a high-pitched drone and rhythmic punctuation. Bhattacharya claims to have added extra *chikari* strings in 1978 (thereby freeing up more of the main strings for melodic work), and by the mid 1980s was playing an instrument with both the added *chikari* and *taraf*

Figure 10.3 Debashish Bhattacharya with student

(sympathetic strings). 'Chikari' or 'tarafdar' guitars (those with *chikari* strings only, or with both *chikari* and *taraf*) can now be bought as standard models from several Indian manufacturers.

The current instruments are by no means standardised however, either in design, tuning or playing technique. Vishwa Mohan Bhatt, for instance, currently plays a twenty-string guitar (with eight main machine heads, plus twelve for the *taraf* mounted on a special neck extension), while Debashish Bhattacharya plays a twenty-two-string instrument with just six main machine heads, plus fourteen on a neck extension and two more at the front (treble side) for *chikari*.[25] Bhatt favours a *vina*-like[26] layout and technique: *chikaris* are placed on the bass side (i.e. closer to the player's body) and played with a thumb pick, while the main strokes of Hindustani instrumental technique, represented by the spoken syllables (*bols*) da and ra, are produced with picks on the first two fingers of the right hand.[27] Debashish Bhattacharya has moved the *chikari* to the treble side of the instrument (closer to the audience) and produces da and ra strokes with thumb and first finger respectively, which he suggests facilitates greater speed and produces less stress on the player's body.

Bhattacharya explained to me that the guitar, in its adapted form, is actually an ideal instrument for Hindustani classical music, on account of its tone and impressive sustain – the latter being the main reason all the classical players give for taking up the instrument. The key is that these features, together with the possibility of producing subtle pitch inflections, make it possible to imitate Indian vocal style to an uncanny degree (which of course parallels the story that Blues players took up the bottleneck guitar in order to better imitate the human voice, and may also be the key to its appeal to Hawaiians). It is beyond dispute that in sustain and freedom of pitch modulation, a slide guitarist does indeed have a considerable advantage over, for instance, a sitarist.

The other advantage of the guitar is, according to Bhattacharya, that as a Western instrument it is more easily accepted abroad – and it is clear that he sees his innovations in terms of global appeal.

> It is always better to communicate [with] people of the world and of different culture with an instrument which is already popular . . . the language is already learned by the global people. So if I play Jaunpuri in sursringar, [28] maybe it [would be] a very interesting and very rare thing of acknowledgement, but if I play the same raga on *guitar* it will touch people's heart much faster and much deeper.
>
> [The] guitar has its maybe 20, 25 or 30 varieties around the world – who knows, maybe more than that. And it imitates the sound of different culture, all over the world. The world has changed a lot, at this point we are sitting within the globalisation era, the world is becoming smaller and smaller. We have different dialects, different moods, different fooding, different clothing, language everything. But thanks, guitar all over the world sounds the same, the language is the same. (Debashish Bhattacharya, personal communication.)

Bhattacharya's instrument, whose design he has copyrighted, goes under the name 'Hindustani Slide Guitar': the name is not his own, any more than 'Mohan Veena' is Vishwa Mohan Bhatt's own idea. In fact, Bhatt seemed almost uncomfortable with his instrument's new name: while the renaming might appear to be an overt sign of Indianization and distancing from the instrument's foreign origins, this motivation was not apparent in either musician's account. Both artists stressed the primacy of the music played on the instrument (as well as their own role in its popularization). According to Bhatt,

> This instrument is named as Mohan Veena – Mohan is my middle name. Some American recording company and magazine suggested this name . . . There was a magazine in which they wrote 'this is a Mohan Veena, not a guitar'. Now a lot of people are coming up after this, and they're following this style of mine and also the instrument I made. There is very good following now, and many young boys, musicians are coming up, they're taking up this instrument as their career.
>
> [The instrument is] a guitar, no doubt about it, the body, everything is of the guitar. It's a modified guitar, so I always write 'modified guitar' – 'Mohan Veena, A Modified Guitar'. I think the name is not important, it's the work and the music which I play. Guitar is a Western instrument, I know that, and what I play on it is Indian classical . . . (V. M. Bhatt, personal communication.)

Figure 10.4 Debashish Bhattacharya's guitar

Calcutta Jazzmen

Fascinating and impressive as the Hindustani guitar style of Debashish Bhattacharya, Vishwa Mohan Bhatt and others is, the number of such players is very
small and the number of adapted instruments sold likewise.[29] India is home to far
more players of Western genres such as jazz, rock and pop; in Calcutta I was lucky
to meet the city's two leading jazz players, Carlton Kitto and Arthur Gracias.

Arthur Gracias lives in the Anglo-Indian district of Calcutta, around the corner from Mother Teresa's headquarters. A slightly nervous, but utterly charming man, Gracias was rather embarrassed by the building work going on in his flat: he could only show me his guitar cases, and the corner which normally houses the PC work-station on which he composes film music. Gracias's grandfather was Spanish, his father born in India; his mother was Anglo-Indian. Brought up in a family full of musicians he soon took up guitar and piano, studying classical music through the Royal School of Music in London but above all developing a taste for jazz. After a period playing with Sonny Lobo's big band at the Grand Hotel, Gracias decided it was time to move on:

I thought I should branch out on my own, because I had to have my own identity, and I studied Indian classical music [with] some very good Indian classical musicians . . . And I thought it would be a very good idea to fuse Indian classical music with jazz, which are both very powerful improvisation forms. So I began researching that, and I was recorded by Humphrey Walden in the early seventies for BBC, and they broadcast some of my music. (Arthur Gracias, personal communication.)

Gracias is one of India's original Indo-jazz fusion musicians: he has performed with a variety of bands working with various combinations of Indian and Western instruments (Gracias himself playing both piano and arch-top acoustic-electric guitar) since the late 1960s. He was the only Anglo-Indian musician I met who expressed a desire to meld musics – far more commonly Anglo-Indian musicians to whom I spoke expressed disinterest in local musical forms.[30] When I asked him how much interest there was amongst Anglo-Indians in Indian music, in fact, Gracias could speak only of his own personal experience and motivation:

It depends. I thought it was very very impressive from the improvisational point of view, and also meditational values are there, and I thought I could bring about the mix of the two creative forms. Of course today things are moving so much faster, the introduction of computers, the world is much more smaller, you get to interact with other musicians all over the world and I think music doesn't belong to any one person. It's a very free thing, it's a global thing today, it's world music . . . It's music, it's either good music or bad music, that's it! (Arthur Gracias, personal communication.)

Gracias's neighbour Carlton Kitto, a Bangalore-born Anglo-Indian,[31] takes a rather different line: a jazz purist in stark contrast to Gracias's approach, he told me he argues with Gracias about it, but good-naturedly by the sound of it. Kitto plays at the Grand Hotel with his jazz quartet every Saturday, and teaches about forty students at the Calcutta School of Music and another thirty-five privately; he told me that all his students are Bengalis (not Anglo-Indian), since 'the Anglo-Indian youth all want to be Springsteen or Bryan Adams'. He cares only for 'pure jazz', and that means bebop in particular, although he played me a selection including cool jazz and *bossa nova*.

> I'm trying to spread the movement of Bebop, and get them to understand pure jazz, you see, rather than fusion and rock- and funk-jazz . . . I think [Bebop] is the greatest thing that has happened to jazz. (Carlton Kitto, personal communication.)

He had taught thousands of students in his time, and was proud that his proselytization had achieved some success;

> One of our jazz club members [is] Ajay Ray, he's an authority on jazz . . . Ajay had gone to one of these remote villages and found a fellow over there playing a solo of John Coltrane, He said 'Good God, where did he pick this up?' Fellow couldn't speak English also. He said 'My Sir taught me this', [Ray] said 'Who's your Sir?', and he said 'Carlton Kitto!'. (Carlton Kitto, personal communication.)

My unavoidable impression talking to Carlton Kitto was of a man out of place and out of time. Kitto spent years teaching himself to play by ear from American records, and avidly reading all he could of Charlie Christian and his peers at the American library. His relatives have mostly moved away to the UK and Australia, leaving him adrift in an ever-shrinking community: he expects to send his three daughters abroad too, but won't himself leave. Kitto complained at the difficulty in obtaining jazz recordings in Calcutta, and the general decline in the music scene in the city since he moved there in the 1960s to be at the centre of the music industry. Perhaps his biggest complaint was that so few people appreciated his music anymore – like many of my interviewees I sensed a barely contained excitement that someone was, at last, showing an interest. He dismissed any thought of interesting himself in Indian music – 'No, no I never heard, I never liked that part of it!' On the contrary, the highlights of his musical life were encounters with jazz greats on their rare visits to Indian shores.

> I played here with Charlie Byrd, I did a duet with him . . . that was about 75–76 . . . I played with a lot of greats. I played with Duke Ellington initially, that's where it all happened, you know! He was rehearsing when he came down to Madras, and some of my fans . . . pushed me on the stage with a guitar and said 'Go on, play. Here's your chance man!' So Duke turned around and said 'Hey, what have we got here . . . you wanna play son?', and I said 'Yeah, I'd love to!' So Billy Strayhorn went on the keyboard and they [said] 'What do you wanna play?' and I said 'Satin Doll'. He said 'Where did you get our tune from?' I said I knocked it off a record . . . 'Okay, play!' – they were curious. I played about five tunes with them, they were sort of impressed, they said 'How the hell did you do this on your own, you mean to say you didn't have any formal studies?', I said 'No, nothing, I'm just a self-taught guy'. (Carlton Kitto, personal communication.)

Travelogue II: Mumbai

Pepsi Powerblast

On the evening of 12 December I found myself waiting outside the gates of Rang Bhavan, an open-air venue in central Mumbai, for the promised 6.30 pm start of the 'Pepsi Powerblast' rock gig. The crowd, mostly of college-aged men, many in Iron Maiden or Metallica T-shirts, gathered and formed an orderly queue – across the street stood a small knot of middle-aged women in short hair and Western dress, whom I took to be Parsis. The scheduled start time came and went, the crowd became understandably annoyed and briefly threatened trouble – but without serious intent, and the early evening passed slowly. Once the long-awaited event was underway, the first of the local cover bands took to the stage, a technically able but lacklustre group. 'School's Out!' bellowed one fan, 'Play some grunge man!', 'Nirvana!': they were rewarded with some Led Zeppelin songs, which went down well enough.

My attention wandering to the banners at the back of the stage, I read that the event was 'A charity concert in aid of the World Zoroastrian Organization youth wing for the destitutes' – hence the visible Parsi presence. The Parsi community are descended from Persian Zoroastrian refugees who arrived in India some time between the eighth and tenth centuries CE. They retain their religion, but are nonetheless generally perceived to be one of India's more Westernized, as well as its wealthiest, community. Despite their tiny numbers (perhaps as low as 80,000 in total) Parsi patronage, as well as a number of talented musicians, have had an impact on both Indian and Western music: many Parsi musicians are employed in the film industry; Zubin Mehta is a Parsi, as is the noted *khyal* singer Firoz Dastur, as was rock star Freddie Mercury.[32] Locally made rock is often associated in India with communities perceived as Westernized – and this includes Parsis as well as the various Christian communities and some middle-class Hindus and Muslims.

Unfortunately I had another date elsewhere that evening and missed the headline act, a local band called Brahma.[33] Looking for their tapes in record shops the next day, I had no success: recordings of Indian rock bands are extremely hard to find. Sales for locally produced rock music have been negligible, save for a tiny handful of stars such as the Goan, Remo Fernandes: they are dwarfed by those of filmi and other Hindi (and to some extent Punjabi) language pop and *ghazals*.[34] The difficulty in establishing a market for local English-language rock is demonstrated by the fact that lately even Remo has abandoned English and started to sing in Hindi.[35] Rock music is not, however, difficult to find in India. It can be found in the form of recordings and occasional tours by foreign bands (Iron Maiden visited India during my research trip),[36] and also in the local rock scene, mainly on the college circuit.

Locally produced rock music in India is generally played by 'college bands': most play exclusively covers, few record and most disband shortly after leaving college. As one magazine feature put it:

> For years, the rock music scene in India has followed a predictable and most unexciting path. A rock band normally starts out playing the college circuit, soldiers on for a few years, becomes disillusioned by the lack of opportunities, ultimately leading to its members hunting for more 'standard' jobs. Meanwhile, the latest and the glitziest that the Europeans and the Americans have to offer is gobbled up by an avaricious public. (Sreenivasan 1991)

Pepsi- and Coca-Cola, in time-honoured fashion, fight over the Indian soft drinks market (in this case in a three-way battle with local pretender Thumbs-Up). In the best traditions of glocalization they must tread the fine line between offering the glamour and sex-appeal of American popular culture, and appearing to support *desi* (local) culture and local heroes. In the winter of 1998–9 Pepsi stole a march over their rivals by signing cricketer Sachin Tendulkar to endorse their product: all three Cola manufacturers feature prominently amongst advertisers on cable television pop music shows, and here in Mumbai Pepsi threw considerable pro-motional weight behind what was, effectively, a small-scale showpiece for a handful of local cover bands. If Indian-produced rock is ever to make a commercial impact, it will be surprising if the sponsorship of such multinational corporations does not figure prominently in the tale.

Guitars on Film

Also in Mumbai I managed to meet a very popular young music director[37] by the name of Vishal Bharadwaj. I asked Vishal about two of his recent soundtracks, which I'd been listening to in my hotel room: *Satya*, which featured a wide range of guitar styles, and *Maachis*, which largely avoided the instrument.[38] Why did he use it more in some movies than in others? The difference, he replied, was in the setting: the guitar is suitable for a modern, urban situation, which is the case for *Satya* (Truth); *Maachis* (Matches) is set in rural Punjab, where a *rabab* would be more suitable.[39] *Satya* is a story set in the modern Mumbai underworld, a romance between a young gangster and a girl from whom he must keep his criminal life secret. The opening number *Badalon se* ('From the clouds . . .') features the greatest variety of guitar styles, acoustic and electric: Vishal explained that piece is from the hero's perspective – the boy is saying he can't believe he's falling in love. 'It was a Bombay, modern character, so . . .' 'So it's modern music?' 'It's modern music . . . and I love guitars!'

The player on that song, Tushar Parte, is a professional session player whose father used to be a music arranger and director in the films. In fact, the family tradition in music goes back a little further: Tushar's grandmother Kamala Devi was a sitarist employed as companion to the Queen of Kolhapur in the 1930s and 1940s;[40] her husband Anantrao Parte, besides being a music lover and patron was personal doctor to the famous stage and film actor Prithviraj Kapoor. Through the Kapoors, Anantrao was able to introduce his son Jaykumar into the Bombay film industry in the 1940s: Jaykumar Parte became a successful music director and arranger, working extensively with the famous music directors Kalyanji-Anandji. Jaykumar had studied both Hindustani music and piano, on which instrument he took Trinity College examinations.

Jaykumar's son Tushar, then, was brought up in the Bombay film music scene. He has seen the shift from the days of big studios and the big sound – orchestras of seventy-five to one hundred musicians were common – to modern studios based on digital hard-disc recording systems where, thanks to click-tracks, there is no need for musicians to actually play together. Tushar, a consummate session man, is at home in this world, moulding his sound to the dictates of his music director. He also, nevertheless, avows a deep love of his family farm in Kolhapur, and of the local *lavani* songs – his musical diet included such local forms alongside film music and Western styles.

T.P.: I am from Kolhapur, which has got a tradition of *lavani*,[41] a different style of Indian music . . .

M.C.: They're Marathi songs?

T.P.: Yes, Marathi songs; there's a *dholki* [42] and a woman dancing . . . ethnic clothes, *sari* she's wearing, ornaments, and the tunes are very exciting, they're very beautiful, it's got a different colour.

M.C.: So you grew up listening to this?

T.P.: Yeah, I'm quite familiar with the *lavanis*, because this is what we heard. At the same time, I also did a lot of listening, listening to the Voice of America, to the BBC jazz hour or whatever . . . (Tushar Parte, personal communication.)

Tushar now has a project, called Mythological Wine Music, which involves him playing guitar and emulator,[43] with his wife Suchita singing Sanskrit *shlokas*,[44] and had been making demos for a Western record company shortly before my visit. Parte was fairly relaxed about the project: since he can make a good living playing for the films, he has time to indulge himself doing something he wants to do. That also includes, as he demonstrated to me, developing a new style of playing which incorporates – alongside riffs borrowed from the late Texas bluesman Stevie Ray Vaughan – the rhythms of the *lavani* songs of his native Maharashtra.

Figure 10.5 Tushar and Suchita Parte, aka Mythological Wine Music publicity shot

Conclusions: Interpreting the Indian Guitar

Although guitars have been played in India since the sixteenth century – well before the modern six-string standard was developed in the late eighteenth century[45] – the instrument seems to have had little impact, at least outside Goa, until the early twentieth-century Hawaiian guitar craze. The fashion for Hawaiian guitar having declined, the instrument is now found in many genres: in Hindustani music,

Figure 10.6 Music and Dance Teacher – a Hindi textbook cover

where modified forms of the Hawaiian guitar have been developed; in Western genres such as rock and jazz and in Indian popular music including film songs and *ghazals*. Professional guitarists have been drawn largely from the Goan, Anglo-Indian and north-eastern Christian communities, although in recent years increasing numbers of Hindus have taken up the instrument.[46]

The guitar is at present amongst the most popular instruments in India, in all senses of the word; if the shops I selected at random are representative, it is probable that more are sold – at least in the metropolitan cities – than any other instrument bar the harmonium. It is used for an incredible variety of repertoires and played in many different styles. But, since it is identified as foreign, Western, 'modern' and largely Christian, its place in Indian culture is bound to be problematic – especially in times when secularism is in retreat and the politics of religious nationalism have taken root.

The sometimes bewildering array of positions taken up with respect to 'The West' is of course not surprising in view of India's colonial history, and its enduring weakness in economic and strategic terms *vis-à-vis* the US and other Western powers. Political, media and not least academic discourse is peppered with refer-ences to India's pride in its ancient cultural heritage and expressions of resentment at the former colonial powers; meanwhile the country rushes headlong towards industrialization and urbanization, and the distant goal of 'catching up' with the West. For all the protestations of India's greatness, the excitement with which any international recognition of India or an individual Indian's achievement is met – whether the world's discomfiture at India's 1998 nuclear tests, Amartya Sen's Nobel Prize or indeed V. M. Bhatt's Grammy – is telling. Advertising takes up similar themes: a Calcutta tram proclaims the Bank of Baroda slogan, 'Indian roots, Inter-national spread', while a huge hand-painted hoarding in Chennai proclaims 'Indian biscuits, International quality'.

Notions of tradition and modernity are of crucial importance to current debates on Indian national identity. For many people in India, 'tradition' is assimilated to Indianness and 'modernity' to the West: after all, the idea of an ancient cultural heritage is central to most constructions of Indian cultural identity, while techno-logical innovation has largely been seen as imported by Europeans. Set against this simplistic dichotomy are those who would claim the existence, or at least the possibility, of a distinctively Indian take on modernity – described in terms of an integration of the best of India's 'cultural heritage' with an outward-looking, tech-nologically advanced national consciousness – an idea that resurfaces continually in various forms of discourse. Contestations of the guitar's status and meaning can usefully be interpreted against this background.

The guitar obviously has the potential to act as a symbol of the West: a foreign instrument which, perhaps, presents a challenge to India's great musical heritage. The fact that it is largely associated within India with the Christian community, and with a Westernized anglophone elite, makes this all the more likely. And yet this very status makes the appropriation of the guitar a powerfully symbolic gesture, and the Grammy Award to Vishwa Mohan Bhatt unsurprisingly made a huge impact. As Bhatt himself explained to me, since the Grammy, 'Now a layman also knows me – not only the musician – but a layman also [will think] "Oh, he's the one who has brought honour to our country".'

Moreover, the appropriation can work on many different levels. Not only can the instrument itself be adapted; as the guitar spreads from Westernized, Christian communities to the rest of Indian society, musicians begin to conceive of socio-musical relationships in terms of the bond between *guru* and *shishya* (master and disciple): in this respect it is telling that Tushar Parte speaks of a Mumbai-resident American, D Wood as his 'guru'. Taking this theme even further, Debashish Bhatta-charya explained the lineage behind his Hawaiian guitar knowledge; 'So I'm the fourth generation. If you want to know more you should go to Bob Brozman: he learned from Tau Moe directly so he is only the second generation.' [47] The Hindu tradition that musical knowledge (like other forms of knowledge) was handed down from the Gods to mortal men in the distant past, and that this knowledge has been gradually corrupted and forgotten since that time, still has some currency. To be closer to the source, to have fewer links in the chain and thus have allowed less opportunity for the corruption of knowledge – this is important even where the source is a Samoan-born master of the Hawaiian slide guitar.

Mainstream popular culture maintains and thrives upon a dialectic between the local and the global. Hindi songs outsell English songs by some distance on the Indian market, yet their musical accompaniment incorporates the latest sounds and techniques of the (US- and UK-dominated) global pop music industry. India's musical production is not about to abandon its distinctive sounds, but it will continue to absorb and adapt what it can from abroad. Professional rock and pop musicians in India are always conscious of the West – not least because they have to obtain imported equipment,[48] but also because they understand the paradox that in order to develop an international market they must localize their style. The Indian classical players are doing to the guitar what their predecessors did to Central Asian instruments to produce the modern *sitar* and *sarod* – in some respects quite literally, as in the additions of *chikari* and *taraf* strings. By doing so they prove the same point, that the guardians of Indian culture will only feel totally comfortable with foreign artefacts once they have been fully assimilated to the local mainstream.

The *kacchap vina* argument shows how important it is, for some, to demonstrate the Indian lineage of the guitar in order that it can be fully accepted. This story is not widely accepted however, even in India – much more commonly expressed is the view that the guitar is an imported instrument which can be and is being appropriated. For the classical players, the adaptation is justified by the successful results (according to the aesthetic criteria of Hindustani classical music), and moreover since the ploy may be expanding the global audience for Indian music. Indian musicians see themselves as players in every sense, not merely as pawns, in the game of globalization.

Those players who have mastered Western styles but who do not (unlike most Anglo-Indians and Goans) identify overwhelmingly with the West, face a slightly more subtle challenge – one can see a response to that in Tushar Parte's Mythological Wine Music and his experiments with *lavani* rhythms, the impulse to bring together guitar technique and a distinctively Hindu, Maharashtrian consciousness. The sense I picked up from many Christian musicians, on the other hand, was of the guitar acting as a link into global networks which hold more appeal than those on offer closer to home. The love of British and American guitar magazines, the devotion to the great jazz masters, the years spent learning by ear from difficult-to-find recordings with no support structure to speak of, all tell the story of the guitar linking its Indian players to the wider world.

When Indians wanted guitars and guitarists, as with other forms of Western music, it was largely Goans and Anglo-Indians who filled that need; the Christian domination of Indian guitar culture is only now being significantly challenged as Hindu Indian boys take up the instrument in large numbers. It is in no way coincidental that this marginal group should be crucially involved in the Indian appropriation of the guitar, an 'intermediate' group acting as intermediaries in the absorption of a foreign musical instrument, a marginal group articulating the conflicts and tensions, but also (albeit often reluctantly) the creative and artistic potential of the meeting of Indian and Western musical cultures.

The story of the guitar also dramatizes many of the conflicts and dilemmas facing post-colonial India. The guitar is the instrument that most easily links one to the wealth and modernity of the West, its consumerism and individualism. And yet it is a foreign infiltrator, a Trojan horse promising glamour and yet bringing with it anti-national, decadent culture. To be made safe it has to be appropriated, adapted, Indianized – and, if at all possible, sold back to the outside world as a proclamation of India's musical genius on the global marketplace. The dazzling virtuosity of Bhattacharya and Bhatt are a testament to the benefits of this approach, yet it is ironic that to the outside world this brilliant Indianization, the music of a mere handful of virtuosi, becomes the only visible part of the Indian guitar scene – the remaining and far greater part remains unseen and unheard, since that part which wants to identify with the West is of no interest to the West. The far greater numbers of aspiring Methenys and Springsteens are, to all intents and purposes, invisible. This is perhaps the most telling paradox of all – that while the globally mediated impinges on each locality, only the locally rooted stands a chance of success in the global market.

Resources

For more information and web links on Indian guitars and guitarists visit: http://www.open.ac.uk/Arts/music/mclayton/indian-guitars

Acknowledgements

It would be impossible to exaggerate the importance of the help and support I received in preparing this chapter, or the debt I owe to those who have assisted me. First and foremost I must thank those who generously gave up their time to be interviewed and recorded: Kumar, Ananda Kumar, Isaac Joe, Patrick Fernandes, Vishal Bharadwaj, Tushar Parte, D Wood, Clifford Pereira, Laurie Lopez, Hannibal Castro, Hitesh Sonik, Debashish Bhattacharya, Arthur Gracias, Carlton Kitto, Peter Remedios, Enamul Haque, Sumith Ramachandran, Pradeep Mukherjee, Vishwa Mohan Bhatt, Kennedy Hlyccho, Jamyang Dolma, and Chimme Dorje. My only regret is that space did not allow me to give proper accounts of all the wonderful musicians who spoke and played for me, and time did not allow me to meet more of the fine guitarists I would like to have spoken to.

I would also like to thank the following people and institutions for help, advice, contacts and personal accounts of guitars, guitarists and guitar music, or for comments on an earlier draft of this paper: Sonjuhi Priyadarshini, Musee Musical, Pro-Music, Manohar Lal of Shruthi Musicals, Park Sheraton Hotel (Chennai), Music Academy Madras, Kenny Vassou, the waiters at the Four Seasons Hotel (Mumbai), K. J. Singh, Rekha Bharadwaj, Suchita Parte, Anna Morcom, Lopa, Bhargava's Musik, Anil, Veena and Hari Sahasrabuddhe, Danny the STD/cassette man, Deepak Choudhury, Ashim Malik, Sudha Kaur, Rila O'Brien, Reynolds, Gibtone, Mondal Bros, Calcutta School of Music, Maya Ghose, Barunkumar Pal, Shubha Choudhury and ARCE, Kai Friese, Rahul Ram and his colleagues in Indian Ocean, Dinesh Nigam of Adarsh Sangeet Karyalaya (Delhi), Sadhana at Bina Musical Stores, New Bharat Music House, Lhadup Tsering, Thinle Richen, Katherine Brown, Gerry Farrell, Gregory Booth, Edward Henry, Gordon Thompson, Peter Manuel, Daniel Neuman, Alison Arnold, Mark Trewin, Matt Allen, Scott Marcus, Amanda Weidman, Zoe Sherinian, Gayathri Kassebaum, Mark Humphrey, Nicola Dibben, Kevin Dawe and Andy Bennett.

This research was generously supported by The Open University's Arts Faculty Research Committee.

Notes

1. By India I refer here to the subcontinent as a whole before independence, and to the Indian state thereafter: the instrument's later history in Pakistan and Bangladesh, for instance, is not covered here.

2. From 4 December 1998 to 14 January 1999, my research was conducted in the four metropolitan cities. A list of interviewees and others who have assisted in this project will be found under 'Acknowledgments'.
3. See in particular *The Call of the Valley*, with Shiv Kumar Sharma, Hariprasad Chaurasia and Manikrao Popatkar. HMV ECSD 2382 (1968), re-released on EMI/Hemisphere 7243-8-32867-2-0.
4. Water Lily Acoustics, WLA-CS-29-CD (1993).
5. The guitar has been used rather differently in Carnatic (South Indian) classical music: here, R Prasanna has made a name for himself performing both classical and fusion styles on a six-string electric guitar.
6. The Portuguese had first landed at Calicut as early as 1498. For a survey of the history of Christianity in south India as it relates to musical performance, see Sherinian 1998: 55ff.
7. Abel 1988: 8; India 2001: D24. The term includes some but not all 'Goans', as well as so-called 'Domiciled Europeans', those of entirely European descent who nevertheless had settled in India for several generations.
8. The discrepancy may be due to some estimates including only those of British descent, and others including also Indo-Portuguese and others. See Gist and Wright 1973: 2–3.
9. The north-eastern states are those to the north and east of Bangladesh: Assam, Manipur, Nagaland, Meghalaya, Tripura, Mizoram and Arunachal Pradesh. Most of this area was only integrated politically with the rest of the subcontinent as a result of British expansion in the nineteenth and early twentieth centuries.
10. Sonia and her Congress Party were indeed defeated in the elections of the following autumn, although it is debatable what part this outburst of anti-Christian agitation played.
11. For an accessible survey of music in Goa, see Sardo 2000.
12. See Head 1985, Leppert 1987.
13. William Hamilton Bird's *The Oriental Miscellany*, for instance, published in Calcutta in 1789, includes arrangements of keyboard pieces for guitar, flute and violin, and a solo guitar arrangement of all the pieces (Gerry Farrell, personal communication.) Head notes an advertisement in the *Calcutta Gazette* of 15 July 1784, offering for sale 'Harpsichord, Forte-Pianos, Organs, Guitars, French and Spanish Violins, Violincello, Flutes, Florios, and common Aeolian Harps, Horns and Bassoons, Haut-Boys and Clarinets and all the new music . . .' (1985: 551). The place of the guitar in this list may indicate a prominence in European domestic music-making second only to keyboard instruments.
14. Gregory Booth, personal communication.
15. For more on the *kacchap* or *kacchapi vina* – which appears to refer most commonly, at least from the tenth century, to a fretless short-necked lute – see Deva 1977: 93–4, Miner 1993: 27.

16. I think the transliteration is best here, although the two 't's sound quite different; the one transliterated with a subscript dot is retroflex, and generally used for an English 't', while that without the dot is dental (like an Italian 't' but more so).

17. Hugh Davies writes, 'Around 1830 Mexican cattle traders introduced the guitar into Hawaii' (1984: 207). Other reports speak of Spanish-American or Portuguese cowboys as the agents. Kealoha Life suggests that 'the Spanish gut-strung guitar was introduced to Hawai'i from Spain and Mexico in 1830, and the steel-strung guitar imported from the Portuguese Azores Islands in 1865' (Ruymar 1996: 18).

18. Spottswood 1996: 68–9. For a fuller account of the version of the story which holds Kekuku to be the originator, see Roberts (1926: 10–11), who notes the existence of similar techniques in Japan and Africa. see also Ruymar 1996. The first recordings of slide guitar in the Blues was made in 1923, and that in country music in 1927 (Evans 1977: 319).

19. And, perhaps later, African: Gerhard Kubik notes that 'In the 1940s and 1950s the Hawaiian guitar attained popularity in southern Africa. This led to a revitalisation of an old instrumental technique: playing on one string by means of a "slider" ... The term Hawaiian has been adapted into the local Bantu languages, hence "hauyani"' (1984: 207). Similar phonetic adjustments have occurred in India: although there is no standard spelling, that favoured by a Delhi music school – 'havion' – is not atypical.

20. Zachariah 1998.

21. Miner reports: 'Film-music directors have included Western instruments in their orchestras since the early years of sound film in the 1930s. In the first few decades [of sound film], film orchestras included the accordion, mandolin, Hawaiian guitar, clarinet and conga drums" (2000: 347).

22. Arthur Gracias (personal communication.). See also Moe's own account in Ruymar, 1996: 33–8. Moe is actually Samoan-born, but moved to Hawaii at the age of 11 and married a fellow Hawaiian musician (Rose) with whom he established a family troupe.

23. Dale, personal communication.

24. *Alap* is an unmeasured introductory movement in Indian art music.

25. Five of the six main strings are used for melody, twelve of the fourteen are *taraf*: between these two sets, the other three strings are called 'supporting strings', in imitation of Ali Akbar's *sarod* layout.

26. That is, based on the north Indian *rudra* and *vichitra vinas*, both plucked stick zithers.

27. On the *sitar* these are produced with inward and outward strokes respectively, on the *sarod* downward and upward plectrum strokes.

28. *Rag Jaunpuri* on the archaic plucked lute *sursringar*.

29. One of Calcutta's (and therefore India's) biggest guitar manufacturers, Gibtone, estimated that the proportion of such instruments sold was less than 1 per cent of the total (Enamul Haque, personal communication.).

30. This perception is echoed in Sardo's report of music in Goa: 'Catholics neither learn nor perform Indian classical music' (2000: 737). Sherinian (1998), however, mentions a Christian performer of Carnatic music on guitar, named M. J. Ravindran. The general picture seems to be one of very little interest shown by Christian communities in Indian classical music, but of a handful of notable exceptions such as Gracias and Ravindran.

31. Kitto's mother was English, and his father Philippino. Due to the war, both were stationed in Bangalore where Carlton was born in 1942. He does not meet the official criteria for definition as 'Anglo-Indian', although this is his unequivocal self-identification.

32. The late Freddie Mercury was born Farokh Bulsara in Zanzibar, in 1946, the son of Indian Parsi parents. He was schooled in Bombay between the ages of five and fourteen, where he began his music study on the piano (Sky 1992: 8–13). Mercury, lead singer of the British rock group Queen, was in most respects a mainstream figure – Western media attention rarely focused on his ethnicity. Nor did I encounter evidence of his being regarded in India as an 'Indian' rock star, or indeed evidence of his band being disproportionately popular, for that or any other reason. *Khyal* is the most widely performed genre of North Indian classical vocal music.

33. Interestingly, Indian rock bands are often named in a distinctively Hindu fashion.

34. The *ghazal* is a poetic form, originating in the Farsi (Persian) language but adapted to South Asian languages, particularly Urdu. *Ghazals*, sung in a variety of styles, are extremely popular on the subcontinent.

35. Like most Goans, Remo Fernandes speaks English more fluently than Hindi: since he began singing in Hindi, Indian media coverage has often drawn attention to his (allegedly poor) pronunciation of the language.

36. It is difficult to be sure which varieties of Western pop and rock music attract the greatest interest in India. During my visit the three major Western attractions were Iron Maiden, Sting and Ricky Martin.

37. That is, composer of film music.

38. *Maachis*, Pan Music MPX 5416 (1996); *Satya*, Venus VCDD 753 (circa 1997).

39. The *rabab* referred to is the plucked short-necked lute played in Afghanistan, Pakistan and north-west India.

40. Kolhapur now lies in Maharashtra state, south of Mumbai and north of Goa.

41. *Lavani* is a distinctively Maharashtrian variety of song sung mainly by professional female entertainers.

42. The *dholki* or *dholak* is a small barrel drum, popular in a wide range of folk and popular music contexts throughout north and central India and Pakistan.
43. Keyboard-based sampler.
44. A *shloka* is a Sanskrit couplet, usually comprising sixteen-syllable lines and generally addressing religious (Hindu) themes.
45. See, for example, Turnbull and Tyler 1984: 99f.
46. Enamul Haque, joint owner of Gibtone, told me that interest in the guitar amongst the Muslim community was 'almost zero'. Muslim guitarists are how-ever to be found in some rock bands, and in the performance of specifically Muslim genres in some areas (see Booth 2000: 428, Groesbeck and Palackal 2000: 948).

    The guitar appears currently to be very much identified as a male instrument in India, notwithstanding the post-war Bengali fashion for girls to play *Rabin-drasangeet* (the songs of Nobel laureate Rabindranath Tagore) on the instrument, or indeed the earlier feminine connotations of the instrument in European culture. Instrumental performance of Indian music remains largely male-dominated, although this is gradually being challenged by a number of female virtuosi.
47. Bob Brozman (b. 1954), a leading American slide guitar player and authority on early Hawaiian music, has collaborated with Tau Moe since the late 1980s.
48. Although Indian manufacturers (most of them based in Calcutta) produce thou-sands of guitars each year, even the makers themselves admit their instruments' quality is poor – they claim that their main concern is to keep prices very low. Peter Remedios, boss of one of India's leading guitar-makers Reynolds, sug-gested to me that the local market will not stand the higher prices that improved standards would bring. Professional guitarists all use imported gear (in past years equipment has been brought back from abroad by players on foreign trips; now imported Fenders are available in shops such as Reynolds), and they have no interest in slightly improved Indian models: most amateurs have a very limited budget, and it is to these players that the local makers cater (Peter Remedios, personal communication).

References

Abel, E. (1988), *The Anglo-Indian Community. Survival in India*, Delhi: Chanakya Publications.

Booth, G. (2000), 'Popular Artists and their Audiences' in A. Arnold (ed.), *South Asia: The Indian subcontinent. The Garland encyclopedia of world music*, Volume 5: 418–30, New York: Garland Publishing.

Davies, H. (1984), 'Hawaiian Guitar', in *Grove Instruments*, II: 207, London: Macmillan Ltd.

Deva, B.C. (1977), *Musical Instruments*, New Delhi: National Book Trust.

Evans, T. and Evans, M.A. (1977), *Guitars: Music, history, construction and players from the Renaissance to rock*, New York: Paddington Press.

Gist, N.P. and Wright, R.D. (1973), *Marginality and Identity: Anglo-Indians as a racially-mixed minority of India*, Leiden: E. J. Brill.

Groesbeck, R. and Palackal, J.J. (2000), 'Kerala' in A. Arnold (ed.), *South Asia: The Indian Subcontinent. The Garland encyclopedia of world music*, Volume 5: 929–52, New York: Garland Publishing.

Harrison, J.B. (1975), 'The Portuguese' in A.L. Basham (ed.), *A Cultural History of India*, Oxford: Clarendon Press.

Head, R. (1985), 'Corelli in Calcutta: Colonial music-making in India during the 17th and 18th Centuries' *Early Music*, 13: 548–53.

Hood, M. (1983), 'Musical Ornamentation as History: The Hawaiian Steel Guitar', *Yearbook for Traditional Music*, 15: 141.

Humphrey, M. (1994), 'Hindustani Slide. The Guitar finds its voice in India', *Guitar Player*, (December): 109–14.

—— (1995), Sleeve notes for *Hindustani Slide: Indian Classical Guitar/ Debashish Bhattacharya*, Vestapol Video OV 11322.

India 2001 (1995), *India 2001: Reference encyclopedia*, London: Jaya Books.

Kanahele, G. (1979), *Hawaiian Music and Musicians: An illustrated history*, Honolulu: University Press of Hawaii.

Kubik, G. (1984), 'Hauyani' in *Grove Instruments*, II: 206–7, London: Macmillan Ltd.

Leppert, R. (1987), 'Music, Domestic Life and Cultural Chauvinism: Images of British subjects at home in India', in R. Leppert and S. McClary (eds), *Music and Society: The politics of composition, performance and reception*, Cambridge: Cambridge University Press.

Library of Congress (1996), *India: A country study.* (eds J. Heitzman and R.L. Worden) Washington DC: Federal Research Division, Library of Congress.

Miner, A. (1993), *Sitar and Sarod in the 18th and 19th Centuries.* Wilhelmshaven: F. Noetzel.

—— (2000), 'Musical Instruments: Northern Area' in A. Arnold (ed.), *South Asia: The Indian subcontinent. The Garland encyclopedia of world music*, Volume 5: 331–49, New York: Garland Publishing.

Pearson, M.N. (1987), *The New Cambridge History of India, 1/1 The Portuguese in India.* Cambridge: Cambridge University Press.

Roberts, H.H. (1967/1926), *Ancient Hawaiian Music*, Honolulu: The Museum (repr.) New York: Dover Publications.

Ruymar, L., (ed.) (1996), *The Hawaiian Steel Guitar and its Great Hawaiian Musicians*, Anaheim Hills CA: Centerstream Publishing.

Sardo, S. (2000), 'Goa' in A. Arnold (ed.), *South Asia: The Indian Subcontinent. The Garland encyclopedia of world music*, Volume 5: 735–41, New York: Garland Publishing Inc.

Sherinian, Z.C. (1998), *The Indigenization of Tamil Christain Music: Folk music as a liberative transmission system.* Unpublished PhD thesis, Wesleyan University: UMI Microform 9828052.

Sinha, T.C. (1998), 'The modern guitar is actually the *kacchap vina*!', *Dainik Hindustan*, 13 July.

Sky, R. (1992), *The Show Must Go On: The life of Freddie Mercury*, London: Fontana.

Spottswood, D. (1996), 'Guitarcheology: The first guitars on cylinders and 78s', *Guitar Player* 30/313/5 (May): 65–70.

Sreenivasan, S. (1991), 'Any Takers for Indian Rock?', *New Generation*, 2.

Turnbull, H. and Tyler, J (1984), 'Guitar', *Grove Instruments*, II: 87–109, London: Macmillan Ltd.

Woodfield, I. (1995), *English Musicians in the Age of Exploration.* Stuyvesant, New York: Pendragon Press.

Zachariah, I. (1998), 'Aloha to a Fine Musician', *Asian Age* (25 June).

Index

Index

Index

Index